Research in Criminology

Series Editors
Alfred Blumstein
David P. Farrington

Research in Criminology

Martha A. Myers
Susette M. Talarico

The Social Contexts of Criminal Sentencing

With 12 Illustrations

Springer-Verlag
New York Berlin Heidelberg
London Paris Tokyo

Martha A. Myers
Department of Sociology, University of Georgia, Athens, Georgia 30602, USA

Susette M. Talarico
Department of Political Science, University of Georgia, Athens, Georgia 30602, USA

Series Editors
Alfred Blumstein
School of Urban and Public Affairs, Carnegie-Mellon University, Pittsburgh,
Pennsylvania 15213, USA

David P. Farrington
Institute of Criminology, University of Cambridge, Cambridge, CB3 9DT, England

Library of Congress Cataloging in Publication Data
Myers, Martha A.
   The social contexts of criminal sentencing.
   (Research in criminology)
   Bibliography: p.
   Includes indexes.
   1. Sentences (Criminal procedure) – United States –
Case studies.   2. Prison sentences – United States –
Case studies.   3. Discrimination in criminal justice
administration – United States – Case studies.
I. Talarico, Susette M.   II. Title.   III. Series.
HV8708.M94   1987   364.6'0973   87-4771

Typeset by Publishers Service, Bozeman, Montana.
Printed and bound by R.R. Donnelley & Sons, Harrisonburg, Virginia.
Printed in the United States of America.

9 8 7 6 5 4 3 2 1

ISBN 0-387-96483-5 Springer-Verlag New York Berlin Heidelberg
ISBN 3-540-96483-5 Springer-Verlag Berlin Heidelberg New York

Preface

Historically, the announcement and invocation of criminal penalties were public spectacles. Today, fear of crime and disaffection with the criminal justice system guarantee that this public fascination with punishment continues. In the past decade, virtually every legislature in the country has undertaken sentencing reform, in the hope that public concern with crime would be allayed and disparities in criminal sentences would be reduced if not eliminated. Scholars have intensified their longstanding preoccupation with discrimination and the sources of disparate treatment during sentencing—issues that continue to fuel contemporary reform efforts. As documented in Chapter 1, empirical research on sentencing has concentrated much of its attention on the offender. Only recently have attempts been made to imbed sentencing in its broader organizational and social contexts.

Our study extends these attempts by quantitatively analyzing the relationship between the offender and the social contexts in which he or she is sentenced. We use data on felony sentencing in Georgia between 1976 and 1985 to ask three questions. The first addresses an issue of perennial concern: during sentencing, how important are offender attributes, both those of explicit legal relevance and traits whose legal relevance is questionable or nonexistent? The second question directs attention to the social contexts of sentencing and asks whether they directly affect sentencing outcomes. Of particular interest to us are attributes of the surrounding community such as urbanization and economic inequality, judicial background and court characteristics such as caseload, and the element of time. The final and most central question we ask is whether, and precisely how, these three contexts condition the relevance of offender attributes. Put differently, to what extent do the county, the court, and time shape the magnitude and direction of differential treatment during sentencing? To answer this question, we focus particular attention on the relationship between selected dimensions of these contexts and two quite different offender attributes: the legally relevant variable of offense and the socially critical, but legally irrelevant, characteristic of race.

Chapter 1 lays the groundwork for the present research and is followed in Chapter 2 by a presentation of the methods used to answer the three questions of central interest. Chapters 3 through 5 report and discuss the results of analyses that focus on the county, the court, and sentencing over time. For each context, we find that its direct impact on sentences is usually limited. Instead, attributes of the county and court, as well as time, profoundly and in varying degrees shape the role race and offense play during sentencing. In documenting the contextually specific nature of differential treatment, the analyses reported in these chapters underscore the complexity of the sentencing process. At the same time, the analyses highlight the limitations of current theorizing and empirical work.

The final chapter is addressed to two audiences: scholars who study criminal justice processes, and policy-makers, whose decisions are based (at best) on empirical evidence or (at worst) on unexamined assumptions about the sentencing process. In this chapter, we summarize the empirical and theoretical implications of the study and suggest that claims of sentencing disparities in general and of racial discrimination in particular must be informed by research, such as ours, that is explicitly designed to capture both system-wide and context-specific patterns in sentencing.

In the course of conducting this research, we have incurred many debts, some financial in nature, others less tangible but nonetheless consequential. The National Institute of Justice provided support for early work (Grant #80-IJ-CX-0094), and a technical report based on 1976–1982 data deals in a preliminary way with some of the issues addressed in the book. The Georgia Department of Corrections generously provided us with the primary data. Neither agency bears any responsibility for the analysis and interpretations presented herein.

For release time from instructional obligations as well as for the extensive computer funds analysis required, we are greatly indebted to the Institute for Behavioral Research and to the Departments of Sociology and Political Science at the University of Georgia.

The course of data collection and analyses was a protracted and often arduous one, and sometimes it seemed as if we were constructing an elaborate but fragile house of cards. Several colleagues acted as both demolition experts and master builders. For their help in ensuring that our house had a solid foundation, we owe a debt of gratitude to Greg Lewis, E.M. Beck, and Stewart Tolnay. Through their ingenuity as programmers, William A. Furlow, Jr. and Doug MacLeod spared us the tedium and inexactness of hand calculations. None of these colleagues is responsible for any defects in design or construction that may remain.

As to the substance of this work, our greatest debt is to the series editors, Al Blumstein and David Farrington, who read several drafts of the manuscript and never failed to provide constructive criticism.

For their patience and fortitude when faced with yet another draft of the manuscript, we thank Lori Stapleton, Dori Porter, Linda Kundell, and Silvia Mapp. Finally, Rodger Carroll and William A. Furlow, Jr. demonstrated remarkable forbearance and words can only begin to express our feelings of gratitude.

Athens, Georgia   Martha A. Myers
January 1987   Susette M. Talarico

Contents

1
Criminal Punishment and Society

Criminal sentencing has always evoked considerable passion on the part of the judicial system and society. Judges frequently complain that it is one of their least favorite responsibilities, and the general public and many politicians think it exacerbates the problem of crime. Efforts to reform sentencing laws and practices have been introduced in virtually every state and the federal government (Shane-DuBow et al., 1985). As the National Academy of Sciences report emphasized, "the decade of the 1970's was characterized by a variety of efforts to modify sentencing practices, to establish more detailed criteria for sentencing, and to establish new sentencing institutions and procedures" (Blumstein et al., 1983:1).

In spite of this long-standing concern with criminal sentencing, our knowledge about related processes and outcomes is limited. James Gibson has observed that "research on criminal court decision making is currently characterized by a significant degree of balkanization" (1979:83). Similarly, the aforementioned report of the National Academy of Sciences concluded that existing research has provided information on the importance of some sentencing factors, but is largely inconclusive (Blumstein et al., 1983). Contributing to the limited explanatory power of previous research on sentencing are imprecise measures of critical variables, inadequate controls for potentially important factors, and the general failure to integrate different theoretical perspectives.

In this book we seek to help fill this research vacuum. As the title illustrates, we cast the sentencing decision in a broader context, and build on the premise that law reflects the social organization of the society in which it is embedded and must operate. In the process we extend the social scientific study of criminal sentencing in three important ways. First, we draw on a variety of pertinent theoretical currents and the historical scholarship that documents the relationship between criminal punishment and society. Second, we integrate earlier research strategies in our use of case, court, and county variables. Third, we offer an expansive contextual study of sentencing. Focusing on the county, court, and temporal contexts, we systematically explore the linkages between the social order and criminal sentencing. In the process we ask two central questions. First, how do county, court, and temporal contexts affect sentencing outcomes?

Second, do these contexts affect the role played by particular individual-level attributes in sentencing?

Before we set out to answer these two questions, we posed several background queries. Three in number, they focused on the degree to which individual attributes, role orientations, and organizational/social contexts affect criminal punishment.[1] This chapter provides summary responses to each query and, in the process, outlines the state of current knowledge of criminal sentencing. In the section "What Do Judges Prefer to Do?", we look at the literature on judicial sentencing philosophies. Assuming that individual attributes serve as surrogate measures of attitudinal perspectives, we also look at the relationship between judge and defendant characteristics and criminal sentencing. In the second section, "What Should Judges Do?", we examine research on judicial roles, and consider studies of both appellate and trial processes. In the last section, "What Are Judges Able to Do?", we focus on three topics: (1) research on court organizations, (2) broader theoretical and historical scholarship documenting the social character of criminal punishment, and (3) scientific studies that have enlarged our understanding of criminal sentencing.

What Do Judges Prefer to Do?

Observers have long since recognized that judges impose disparate sentences even in the face of identical facts and circumstances (e.g., Partridge and Eldridge, 1974). One would assume, quite naturally, that at least some of these differences could be attributed to contrasting preferences on the purpose of criminal law. Certainly, the demands of retribution, deterrence, incapacitation, and rehabilitation are not entirely compatible (Talarico, 1979a). Judges with retributivist leanings, for example, might be expected to pay particular attention to the severity of the offense, whereas those concerned with incapacitation might focus on an offender's risk of recidivism.

There is little research that directly explores the connection between judicial preferences and sentencing, and two very good reasons why this is so. First, individual sanction preferences do not automatically predict particular forms of punishment. For example, judges with rehabilitative inclinations have been known to impose particularly harsh terms of incarceration in the hope that the offender will eventually reform. This punitiveness belies the liberal characterization frequently associated with the treatment ethic. Second, it is extraordinarily difficult, perhaps impossible, to identify a judge's actual sanction preference. Leslie Wilkins once observed that the worst way to find out what someone was doing was to ask them. This caveat applies here because judges may not necessarily have thought about their sanction preferences, may not be honest about those actually operating, and/or may in fact be trying to accommodate different and even contrasting goals. As one defense attorney remarked of a Georgia Superior Court judge, "he didn't know what his [the judge's] philosophy was, but . . . he tries to be consistent in his sentences. He thinks it out real well."

John Hogarth (1971) and D. Thomas (1979) expanded on some of these themes in their respective studies of Canadian and British jurists. Although Hogarth demonstrated that penal philosophy conditioned criminal sentencing, he was cautious in drawing far-reaching conclusions about the association. Concluding that Canadian magistrates displayed a range of frequently conflicting penal philosophies and sentencing practices, he emphasized that individual jurists were "consistent within themselves." This internal consistency, however, was evident in the criteria that individual magistrates applied in sentencing and not in an explicit espousal of complex philosophical systems. In fact, Hogarth emphasized that "penal philosophy ha[d] very little meaning to a busy magistrate" (1971:68). Rather, magistrates sought more or less explicit, working guidelines to direct their sentencing decisions.

Somewhat less cautiously, Thomas argued that members of the British Court of Appeals were directed by one of two sanction goals, general deterrence or supervision. Thomas hypothesized that the tariff or deterrence penalty was selected when the judge wanted to focus on the seriousness of the offense and draw a general lesson for society. In contrast, more individualized sanctions were selected when the judge was inclined to try to shape the future behavior of the defendant. In either instance, it was clear that Thomas thought that attitudinal preferences forced judges to emphasize particular aspects of the case, much in the same way that Hogarth demonstrated that working "guidelines" compelled magistrates to look at specific criteria.

Both Hogarth's and Thomas's studies illustrate that judicial preferences are often exercised indirectly. In other words, researchers rarely have direct evidence on preferences. Rather, they must look at the criteria, variables, or facts that judges regularly use and emphasize in decision making. In this sense, it is obvious that there can be no doubt, as Gibson has emphasized, that "what judges prefer to do . . . influences their decision making behavior" (1983:9).

Because of this emphasis on indirect evidence and the simple fact that trial court records are inherently limited, most sentencing research has approached the question of judicial preferences in surrogate fashion. Typically, researchers have looked at those characteristics of the offender and the judge that they assume associate with attitudinal preferences. Indeed, much of the early literature on sentencing focused on this individual-level analysis, and concentrated on the extralegal or socioeconomic characteristics of the defendant.

Sellin introduced this line of inquiry with his study of the relationship between sentencing and race in 1928. Since Sellin, increasing numbers of studies have considered the effect of offender social background characteristics, either alone (e.g., Martin, 1934; Bedau, 1964, 1965; Forslund, 1969) or after controlling for legally relevant variables such as offense and prior record (e.g., Sellin, 1928; Lemert and Rosberg, 1948; Johnson, 1957; Green, 1961, 1964; Wolfgang et al., 1962; Nagel, 1969). Most of this research has implicitly or explicitly tested hypotheses drawn from conflict theory. As we shall see later in this chapter, this theory holds that judges and all political authorities seek primarily to reinforce the existing social, political, and economic orders. The aforementioned researchers, in the process, have assumed that legal variables were either irrelevant or would be outweighed by extralegal characteristics.

As Hagan and Bumiller (1983) and others (Hindelang, 1965; Hagan, 1974) have noted, this earlier sentencing research was seriously limited by the simplicity of the decision model, narrow jurisdictional foci, and methodological shortcomings. More recent research on the impact of extralegal defendant characteristics, however, has refined this work in several important ways. For example, more current analyses are based on broader and more carefully drawn samples (e.g., Pruitt and Wilson, 1983); include more extensive efforts to control for legally relevant variables (e.g., Petersilia, 1983; Welch et al., 1984); focus on more rigorously defined dependent variables (e.g., Bernstein et al., 1977; Lizotte, 1978); and use more sophisticated multivariate statistical techniques (e.g., Spohn et al., 1981–82). Even with these methodological refinements, however, contemporary studies often offer inconclusive evidence on the impact of extralegal or social background characteristics.

The race of the offender is an excellent case in point, for no other attribute has been the subject of such sustained empirical examination and controversy. Several summaries of the empirical literature are available, so we need not undertake a review here.[2] Of particular interest for our purposes is the absence of consistent evidence of systemic race discrimination. For example, race affects some but not all sentencing decisions (e.g., Spohn et al., 1981–1982), and may be an important consideration only for certain kinds of cases (e.g., Kleck, 1981; Radelet, 1981; Petersilia, 1983), in selected county or court contexts (e.g., Hagan, 1977; Austin, 1981; Pruitt and Wilson, 1983; Myers and Talarico, 1986a, 1986b; Phillips, 1986; Myers, 1987), or for certain kinds of offenders (e.g., Horan et al., 1982; Welch et al., 1984). The most recent research, then, underscores the need to change our focus of attention, and move away from an assessment of the relative importance of race and legally relevant factors toward an examination of the structural contexts where discrimination is likely to occur. In short, the question to pursue is not whether race affects treatment, but under what social and economic conditions and for which types of offenders and outcomes race makes a significant difference.

In addition to examining the characteristics of offenders, research has also focused on attributes of the sentencing judge. Once again, this line of inquiry has assumed that these characteristics serve as surrogate measures of actual preferences. Although it is debatable if judicial characteristics actually stand for ideological or preferential positions, Gibson has pointed out that "there can be little doubt that the behavior of judges is in fact predictable from their backgrounds" (1983:23). Research has demonstrated the importance of party affiliation, age, and prior experience as prosecutor. For example, Tate (1981) and Nagel (1961) indicated that Democrats were more inclined to take a liberal posture in decision making, whereas Republican judges were more conservative; Cook (1973) found that older judges were more punitive in draft resistance cases than younger colleagues; and Tate (1981) argued that prosecutorial experience contributed to specific decision patterns. Perhaps because of insignificant representation on the bench and, consequently, insufficient variation, other judicial attributes (e.g., sex and race) have not consistently emerged as important predictors of decision patterns.

When we ask the question, "What do judges prefer to do?", and look at criminal sentencing, our answer is, indeed, limited. As explained, few researchers have directly examined the degree to which sentencing differentials can be attributed to individual identification with retributive, deterrent, incapacitative, or rehabilitative norms. Most studies have addressed the question in indirect fashion by looking at the relationship between sentencing patterns and selected characteristics of the sentencing judge and defendant. As emphasized, this research is largely inconclusive. To be sure, there is some evidence that demonstrates the predictive power of some judicial characteristics (e.g., party affiliation). Even in those instances, however, it is difficult to identify the underlying causal agent. Take, for example, prosecutorial experience. Does such experience simply represent a fundamental preference that an individual harbored independent of work experience? Or, were preferences shaped and refined in the course of office? Similarly, it is difficult to draw far-reaching conclusions on the power of offender characteristics, even one as important as race. As we shall see in later sections of this chapter, our limited answer to the question of judicial preferences and criminal sentencing has more to do with the way we have conceptualized the sentencing decision than with the demonstrated impotence of individual, surrogate measures.

What Should Judges Do?

All positions of public authority carry role prescriptions. Although these prescriptions may not be unquestionably delineated, they do affect the exercise of authority. Judges have, perhaps, operated under the most severe role constraints as debate has raged for years on judicial review and the scope of related power. Currently this debate is quite pronounced. Commentators have reviewed the decisions and policy of a variety of federal and even some state tribunals, and argued the respective merits of activism and restraint (e.g., Horowitz, 1977; Choper, 1980; Ely, 1980; Miller, 1982; Perry, 1982).

Judicial activism is frequently described as noninterpretativist (Ely, 1980), whereas restraint is categorized as interpretativist or strict constructionist. Whatever the label, the two role prescriptions are clearly defined, at least in theory. Judicial activism suggests that judges should take substantial liberty in exercising the power of judicial review. This means that judges are not unduly confined by precedent, the intentions of either the founding fathers or a given Congress, or the strict application of the law. In short, judges are not confined by their role when faced with problems that have been left unattended by other branches of government or are so egregious that the judiciary must intervene.

Interpretativists emphasize that judges should be confined by their roles, especially federal judges who are not electorally accountable and who enjoy life tenure with little threat of removal. Under this scheme judges set their personal and policy preferences aside and stay within the confines of the law (e.g., Horowitz, 1977). This includes careful adherence to precedent and the intention of the founding fathers or legislative framers. Although there is, to be sure, a range of opinion on the desirability and feasibility of both options, suffice it to say that current debate is rather spirited (see, e.g., Halpern and Lamb, 1982; McDowell, 1982; Carter, 1985).

Some of the popular debate on the role of judges suggests that activist judges are liberal, whereas those who advocate a posture of restraint are conservative. However, "there is no reason to expect a relationship between role orientation and liberal policymaking" (Gibson, 1986:89). Historically, some of the U.S. Supreme Court judges regarded as most liberal (e.g., Holmes) have been the most staunch advocates of restraint and have argued, as Holmes did again and again, for judicial deference to the legislature.

In spite of the long-standing and currently spirited exchange on the role of judges in American politics, most of the related research is either prescriptive or descriptive in character. Normative arguments for judicial activism or restraint characterize the current controversy with many empirical assumptions left unsaid, untested, or anecdotally defended. Furthermore, descriptive assessments focus almost exclusively on appellate courts, although some recent studies draw attention to selected federal trial decisions (e.g., Chilton, 1986; Cooper, 1987).

It is not surprising that research has focused on appellate processes. Appellate tribunals feature most prominently in the judicial hierarchy and are frequently, although perhaps erroneously, thought to carry the greatest influence in the judicial system. This "upper court myth" contributed to much of what might be called the "mythology of law" that reflected the Blackstonian, apolitical conceptions that were attacked with considerable passion earlier in this century (e.g., Frank, 1949).

Related research on trial judge roles has largely been confined to the development of typologies (e.g., Galanter et al., 1979). There are, however, notable exceptions where social scientists have tested the effect of role constraints on decision processes and outcomes. Gibson's work deserves particular mention here because he not only offered an analysis of the relationship between role constructs and decision making, but also analyzed that association in conjunction with other kinds of variables (e.g., attitudes). In his study of Iowa trial court judges, for example, he demonstrated that attitudes were related to decision making behavior in certain circumstances (1978a:919). When Gibson analyzed the relationship of liberalism, crime, and criminal justice to attitudes on political decision making, he found little evidence of association. Once he introduced the construct of role, however, he found that attitudes played an important part in the decision making process (1978a:919) because "considered separately, neither attitudes nor role orientations adequately explain sentencing behavior; it is only when they are placed in a multivariate model that a significant amount of variance is explained" (1978a:922).

Role constructs, however, rarely are observed directly. Rather, they guide judges in the selection and application of decision criteria. For example, activist trial judges might more easily focus on extralegal offender attributes (e.g., family stability, employment history) in the determination of criminal penalties than judges with a more restrained outlook. The latter might be more inclined to focus exclusively on those criteria that the law specifically emphasizes, namely the nature and severity of the offense and the defendant's prior record.

Similar patterns were observed in conversations with judges in Georgia's Superior Court. In one circuit, the presiding judges and court personnel prided themselves on focusing on the offense. Operating on the assumption that the public was considerably concerned with residential burglaries, these authorities emphasized that all convicted burglary offenders, regardless of any potentially redeeming personal qualities, were sentenced to 3-year prison terms. In contrast, many other judges emphasized that individual circumstances and "character" entered into the sentencing process. Describing one Superior Court judge, a public defender commented that offenders were helped if they had "parents or relatives who [were] willing to help ... having a job [was] also a plus factor." Similarly, a judge explicitly detailed the factors he considered in evaluating an offender's character:

I don't know how you judge character except on information. And the information you have to go on is always skimpy, never as much or exactly as you would like to have. A great deal of it has to come from the offender himself and it is always ... you look for things such as roots ... patterns of stability ... a person who has lived in one place, held a job for a good period of time, has family, extended family, resources and support—that sort of thing—that person is more likely to be favorably considered for probation than someone who is a transient through town, staying at the alcohol treatment hotel, and apt to get involved in some type of criminal thing ...

When we ask the question, then, "What should judges do?", we must consider the application of role theory to the study of judicial decision making. As summarized in this section, that literature is rather limited, being largely confined to normative and descriptive assessments of appellate court processes. However, recent applications to the study of trial courts provide useful direction to the study of sentencing and suggest two strategies. First, that indirect explorations of judicial role focus on the criteria and variables that judges use in decision making, and second, that this indirect analysis be conducted in conjunction with other research strategies and approaches. Recognizing this last point, we turn now to our third background question, the issue of feasibility. Here we look at a more comprehensive approach to the study of criminal sentencing and lay the groundwork for the contribution reported in this book.

What Are Judges Able to Do?

Judges do not function in isolation. Their preferences and expectations are substantially conditioned by the environment in which they work. The limits imposed by the immediate environment and society in which judges function relate to feasibility in obvious ways. First, judges function in organizations with real operational pressures in caseload management, interpersonal relations, and group dynamics. Second, courts function within the broader political system and are dependent on it in a variety of ways. The allocation of budgets, the selection of court personnel, and support from other branches of government in the definition and enforcement of the law are the most obvious. Furthermore, the social system exerts pressures on courts. Although the judicial branch is not required to "follow the election returns," court decisions have been known to correspond to patterns in public opinion (e.g., Kuklinski and Stanga, 1979); to correlate with community characteristics (e.g., Hagan 1977; Miethe and Moore, 1986; Myers and Talarico, 1986a, 1986b); and to reflect popular sentiment about particular policy issues (e.g., Cook, 1977).

In the study of criminal sentencing, contextual analysis has been largely confined to studies of court organization. Organizational theories provide the theoretical framework for this line of inquiry, although the use of case characteristic controls (e.g., legal and extralegal defendant attributes) obviously speaks to the concerns of other conceptual frameworks (e.g., conflict theory).

Eisenstein and Jacob's *Felony Justice* (1977) was the path-breaking study of this genre. Critical of the focus of most criminal court studies, Eisenstein and Jacob argued for a broader conceptualization of sentencing and other case processing variables:

Public understanding of felony disposition and how felony courts make decisions remains murky despite numerous explanations. Some explanations focus on the characteristics of the defendants; others emphasize the characteristics of the decision maker. Still others focus on the operation of legal procedures. The trouble is that none adequately explains the variety of outcomes that we observe in felony courtrooms. Moreover, they conflict with one another. (1977:5)

For Eisenstein and Jacob, court work groups played pivotal roles in judicial decisions in general and criminal sentences in particular. Composed of judge, prosecutor, defense attorney, and support personnel (e.g., police, probation officer), these work groups varied in structure, cohesiveness, and style. Eisenstein and Jacob demonstrated the effect of work group variation on criminal case processing in three cities and argued that organizational analyses of criminal courts had considerable potential.

Prior to and after *Felony Justice*, social scientists examined the relationship between selected dimensions of court organizations and criminal sentencing. Most of these assumed the impact of court structure and organization by including individual-level variables that reflected the defendant's status in the court system. These include Hagan and Bumiller's study of the effect of case processing variables on sentencing (1983); Uhlman and Walker's analysis of guilty pleas and sentencing (1979); Lieberman et al.'s examination of the relationship between bail status, type of counsel, among other explanatory variables, and sentencing (1972); Bernstein et al.'s scrutiny of the relationship between sentencing and specific pretrial decisions (1977); and Hagan (1975), Myers (1979), and Talarico's (1979b) studies that included tests for the effect of presentence recommendations.

Two more recent studies that have expanded the *Felony Justice* model are Pruitt and Wilson's (1983) longitudinal analysis of sentencing in Milwaukee, and Nardulli et al.'s (1984) study of criminal court processes in nine counties. Pruitt and Wilson focused on the effect of race on criminal sentencing, and analyzed the explanatory power of offender characteristics, legally relevant variables, case processing factors, defense system, and judicial ideology over a 10-year period. Finding that the explanatory power of race declined in the later periods under scrutiny, they attributed the change to three organizational characteristics: composition of the judiciary, bureaucratization in the prosecutorial and defense bar, and decision rules that reduce the effect of individual ideology on outcomes (1983:613). Their study is important because they are among the few social scientists who have examined criminal sentences over time and because they have concerned themselves with the organization and structure of the court itself.

Nardulli et al. (1984) offered an even more comprehensive organizational study of criminal sentencing. They studied felony courts in nine counties, and examined plea-bargained sentences. Arguing that such sentences can best be understood in the context of face-to-face group decision making, Nardulli and colleagues examined the relationship between selected sociopolitical characteristics of decision makers and sentence severity. Finding that contextual factors such as kind of case, prosecutorial policy, and configurations of individual attributes affected the impact of the sociopolitical characteristics of the decision makers, they concluded that individual-level attributes cannot be analyzed apart from some appreciation of contextual factors.

As we shall see later in this chapter, few social scientific analyses have focused on the broader (i.e., social) context of criminal sentencing. This is quite ironic since jurisprudential and sociological theories provide a firm, albeit not mutually consistent, framework for such analysis. Although traditional schools of jurisprudence (most notably variants of natural law) have not always recognized the social character of law, contemporary theories explicitly advance a contextual theme. Legal realists, for example, have argued that judges and courts are products of the broader social and political systems in which they exist. As Oliver Wendell Holmes stated years ago:

The life of the law has not been logic; it has been experience. The felt necessities of the time, the prevalent moral and political theories, intuitions of public policy, avowed or unconscious, even the prejudices which judges share with their fellow men, have had a good deal more to do than syllogism in determining the rules by which men should be governed. The law embodies the story of a nation's development through many centuries . . . in order to know what it is, we must know what it has been and what it tends to become. (1963:5)

Similarly, social theorists have emphasized the intrinsic relationship between law and society. Writing in the 19th century, Durkheim, Weber, and Marx all reacted to the utilitarian calculus that defined social values and institutions as the simple sum of individual preferences and offered broader perspectives for the study of social phenomena. Although Durkheim, Weber, and Marx gave uneven attention to the specific relationship between law and society and came to contrasting conclusions on the character of that connection, they laid the theoretical foundation for a systematic study of the social context of court processes.

Two contemporary theories, in fact, can be traced to their work. The consensus school is grounded in the work of Durkheim and assumes that the fundamental relationship between law and society is a salutary one. Although Durkheim was primarily concerned with crime and society, he argued that criminal law reflected the concerns, values, and preferences common to the culture. The application of criminal penalties, then, reflected normative consensus and was necessary for social stability. For Marx and those conflict theorists who built on his work (e.g., Chambliss and Seidman, 1971; Quinney, 1974, 1977), historical, social, and political structures are determined by the clash of two different groups: those in control of property and production and those who labor under that authority. In a capitalist society, for example, there is no functional cooperation between the haves and have nots. Therefore, there is no salutary benefit from the application of criminal law because those penalties constitute another mechanism of class oppression.

Several historical studies touch on consensus and conflict themes, thereby providing additional support for a contextual study of criminal sentencing. These works take one of two forms: general studies of the history of punishment or more detailed analyses of crime and society in specific communities. Whether general or specific in scope, these works demonstrate that criminal punishment is directly related to the society in which courts function. This argument can be highlighted by looking at two particular issues: the development of the penitentiary and the relationship between criminal punishment and race.

The prison as an isolated institution removed from the communities of most offenders and victims is a rather recent invention. Historians agree that the change from more local, physical, and informal forms of punishment to institutionalized prison systems occurred in a variety of Western democratic societies. Furthermore, they agree that this change constituted a fairly sweeping departure in the administration of criminal law. Historians disagree, however, on two critical points: the character of related social movements and the actual benefit derived from the change. Critical commentators have argued that the development of the penitentiary did not represent a humane advancement in penology because it simply constituted another effort to control and oppress the lower class (e.g., Rusche and Kirchheimer, 1939; Foucault, 1977; Melossi and Pavarini, 1981). This position obviously represents a Marxian or conflict analysis of the relationship between criminal punishment and society.

On the other hand, consensual historians (e.g., Rothman, 1971, 1980) have argued that the advent of the penitentiary and other social institutions signaled a revolution in social practice, a revolution that was, by nature, benevolent as well as inevitable.

The response in the Jacksonian period to the deviant and the dependent was first and foremost a vigorous attempt to promote the stability of the society at a moment when traditional ideas and practices appeared outmoded, constricted, and ineffective. The almshouse and the orphan asylum all represented an effort to insure the cohesion of the community in new and changing circumstances. Legislators, philanthropists, and local officials, as well as students of poverty, crime and insanity were convinced that the nation faced unprecedented dangers and could restore a necessary social balance to the new republic, and at the same time eliminate long-standing problems. (Rothman, 1971:xviii)

Whether one agrees with the conflict historians that the penitentiary served simply to exacerbate already intolerable working and social conditions for the lower class, or one sides with the consensus school and emphasizes that change in criminal punishment was both egalitarian and humanistic, it is obvious that criminal punishment and society are inextricably related. More focused studies of crime and punishment in individual communities provide additional support for this argument. An unusually clear illustration is the evidence on criminal punishment and race. As Michael Hindus (1980) pointed out in his study of crime and justice in Massachusetts and South Carolina in the 18th and early 19th centuries, race affected criminal punishment in all parts of the country. In Massachusetts in 1826, for example, "the Boston Prison Discipline Society called attention to the high proportion of blacks in the Massachusetts State Prison" (1980:236). As Hindus explained, the Society did not think this represented an unsalutary association because the disproportional punishment was attributed to "the degraded character of the colored population" (quoted in Hindus, 1980:236).

Race, however, was a particularly important variable in criminal punishment in the southeastern states. Ample illustrations can be found in the criminal prohibitions applied to slaves before the Civil War and in the convict lease system of the postwar period. When slavery was legally in force, landowners supported state and local associations that functioned as vigilantes. Operating ostensibly under a salutary civic purpose, these groups prosecuted runaway slaves and set up a bounty system for their capture and punishment (Hindus, 1980:40). As Hindus and other historians have pointed out, even innocent free blacks were executed in lynchings that, if not formally sanctioned by the legal system, were allowed to exist or ignored. In fact, Hindus explained that such mob violence, although not tolerated by the Massachusetts civil authority, was actually encouraged by South Carolina officials.

The convict lease system developed in the wake of penitentiary and the Industrial Revolution. Prison systems contracted with private employers for the labor of inmates. As Edward Ayers pointed out in his study of crime and punishment in the 19th-century American South, "the lease system was tailor-made for capitalists concerned only with making money fast" (1984:193). With the rise of organized labor, the lease system was especially attractive to entrepreneurs anxious to have access to a steady and cheap supply of workers. In many respects, the lease system substituted for the slavery institutionalized and legalized in an earlier period. In fact, the office holder and entrepreneur were frequently one and the same person in a prison system that was characterized by abject conditions. High rates of disease and death, for example, were not unusual. Little public concern was aroused, however, because the bulk, if not all, of the affected inmates were black.

Whatever his ethnicity, any Southern white man of wealth stood little danger of finding himself in a convict camp. As an Alabama prison official aptly noted, middle-aged and upper-class white men either "do not commit crime, or else they are safely insulated from the penitentiary by greenbacks or other penal nonconductors." (Ayers, 1984:198)

Ayers explained that relatively few whites were sentenced to prison. Those who were incarcerated were segregated from black prisoner/laborers and were considered, as Ayers emphasized, "the lowest of their race" (1984:198). The discriminatory design and impact of the convict labor system has been noted by other scholars (e.g., Adamson, 1983, 1984), while other researchers have explored the relationship between general rates of imprisonment and unemployment (e.g., Rusche and Kirchheimer, 1939; Jankovic, 1977).

These historical works clearly lay the groundwork for a contextual study of criminal sentencing. Ironically, few researchers have systematically explored the relationship between criminal courts and social structures. There are, however, notable exceptions in political science research on criminal court processes and political culture, in sociological studies exploring the impact of urbanization on penal sanctions, and in the aggregate analyses of criminal justice policies and specific features of the economic system.

Pertinent political science research usually concentrates on the relationship between geographic variation in sentencing and political culture (e.g., Harries, 1974; Kritzer, 1979; Neubauer, 1979; Ryan, 1980). Of this research, Levin's (1977) study of criminal court processes in Pittsburgh and Minneapolis is the leading example. Examining the relationship between courts and the broader political order, Levin hypothesized that criminal sentences would be more severe in the partisan, traditional, machine government of Pittsburgh. Correspondingly, he argued that sentences would be more moderate, if not lenient, in Minneapolis with its rational, reformist political system. Interestingly, he marshalled empirical evidence that contradicted his original expectation. Levin persisted, and quite correctly, in arguing that trial courts are embedded in and sensitive to political culture and concluded that "the behavior of the Minneapolis and Pittsburgh judges seems to be the indirect product of the political system of their respective cities" (1977:6).

Other research has expanded on Levin's analysis. In misdemeanor courts, Ragona and Ryan, for example, demonstrated that "sentencing variations are responsive to extralegal environmental conditions" (1983:35). Kuklinski and Stanga (1979) studied California's superior courts, and found that sentencing in marijuana cases corresponded to public opinion about the use of marijuana.

Sociological studies on the relationship between urbanization and penal sanctions are particularly germane to the present research. Following Thomson and Zingraff's (1981) exhortation to move beyond the individual and court contexts of earlier studies, social scientists examined the impact of urbanization on court processes. Drawing on traditional (e.g., Durkheim, 1933, 1973; Weber, 1954) and contemporary (e.g., Black, 1976) theoretical frameworks, this scholarship built on broader studies of social structure and crime itself (e.g., Krohn, 1978). Some of this research (e.g., Pope, 1976; Hagan, 1977; Clayton,

1983) demonstrated that rural courts are more likely to discriminate against minorities in sentencing than urban courts. Other studies documented the punitive character of urban courts (e.g., Kempf and Austin, 1986; Miethe and Moore, 1986; Myers and Talarico, 1986a). Whatever their specific content, the findings of this line of inquiry graphically illustrate the need to study criminal sentencing in its social content.

A related line of research has analyzed the relationship between selected criminal justice policies and the broader economic system. Discussed in greater detail in the next chapter, these studies have linked police and correctional policies with economic inequality (e.g., Jacobs, 1978, 1979; Williams and Drake, 1980), unemployment (e.g., Jankovic, 1977; Wallace, 1981), and community racial composition (e.g., Jacobs and Britt, 1979; Jackson and Carroll, 1981).

These three research strategies—the study of political culture and court processes, of urbanization and penal sanctions, and of criminal justice policy and economic indicators—demonstrate the potential of a contextual analysis of criminal sentencing. Built, albeit indirectly, on theoretical and historical scholarship that demonstrates that courts do not function in isolation, they remind us that society exerts powerful if not obvious constraints on judicial authority.

Conclusion

As the preceding sections demonstrate, available answers to the three questions on judicial preferences, role orientation, and decision feasibility indicate that our knowledge of court processes and criminal sentencing is limited. The research cited, however, offers important and useful direction to our study of criminal sentencing. First and most important, it compels us to situate the sentencing process and decision in a variety of contexts. Second, it directs our scrutiny of the legal and extralegal offender attributes that feature in the analysis of judicial role. Finally, it guides our selection of surrogate measures of defendant and judge background characteristics.

As mentioned in the beginning of this chapter, we examine sentencing in three contexts. First, we look at the relationship between the broader social order and criminal sentencing, focusing particular attention on the direct and indirect effects of urbanization, economic inequality, unemployment, minority population, and crime rates. Next, we examine the more proximate context of criminal sentencing, and analyze the impact of court and judicial characteristics. Finally, we focus on the element of time, a context that has been largely ignored in the literature.

In all three respects, we build on and extend relevant research by focusing on individual cases, and incorporating the influences that stem from other levels and theories (Gibson, 1983). We do not, however, directly test the two major social theories (conflict and consensus) of criminal justice and society. Although these theories have been emphasized in historical studies and help justify our contextual focus, we think direct tests are inappropriate for theoretical reasons.

In his comment on the theoretical and practical limitations of functionalist, Marxist, and structuralist histories of crime and punishment, Michael Ignatieff (1983) emphasized that criminologists must acknowledge the consensual *and* coercive characteristics of criminal punishment and recognize the complexity in any use of penal sanctions. It strikes us, then, as theoretically unsound to test the utility of either a conflict or consensual perspective because any such attempt is tantamount to setting up straw men for inevitable rejection. In our study, then, we try to analyze the social contexts of criminal sentencing in a way that acknowledges the complexity of the process.

The remaining chapters of the book provide an outline of our analytic strategy, the results of our three separate studies of criminal sentencing, and a discussion of the general results. Chapter 2 includes a detailed explanation of the study site, data sources, sampling, and qualitative as well as quantitative analytic strategies. Chapter 3 reports our findings on the study of the broadest context of criminal sentencing, the county. In this chapter, we ask five central questions: Does urbanization reduce race differences in sentencing? Do economic inequality and large subordinate populations foster disproportionate harshness toward property offenders? Can the argument linking inequality with the punishment of property offenders be extended to black offenders as well? Do economic conditions have any effect on the sentences of violent offenders? Do high crime rates foster a climate of punitiveness toward offenders whose criminality may be perceived as particularly threatening? As we address these five questions we systematically analyze the direct and indirect effects of urbanization, economic conditions, and crime on criminal sentencing.

Chapter 4 focuses on the more proximate context of the court. Here we examine the direct and indirect effects of two kinds of court variables: (1) characteristics of the organization and (2) attributes of the sentencing judge. Our basic question, however, remains the same: To what extent do these contextual variables condition the intensity and direction of the effects of offender attributes in sentencing? Chapter 5 studies sentencing patterns over time. This part of the analysis explicitly draws on site visit information in which judges and other court authorities consistently emphasized two points: the increasing problems of prison overcrowding and public clamor for more punitive criminal sentences. Although we do not explicitly test the weight of prison population or public opinion, we scrutinize sentencing patterns over time in a surrogate analysis of longitudinal patterns. Chapter 6 summarizes the results from the three analyses of criminal sentencing, considers the theoretical and practical ramifications of our findings, and comments on the broader relationship between science and law.

Notes

1. These background questions reflect our interpretation of Gibson's argument that judges' decisions are "a function of what they prefer to do, tempered by what they think they ought to do, but constrained by what they perceive is feasible to do" (1983:9).

2. For reviews of race differences in treatment, see Hagan and Bumiller (1983), Hardy (1983), Wilbanks (1987), and Zatz (1987). For studies that review the effect of gender, see Nagel and Hagan (1983) and Kruttschnitt and Green (1984). The impact of offender socioeconomic status has been examined by Chiricos and Waldo (1975), Farrell and Swigert (1978), and Lizotte (1978).

2
Methods

As noted in Chapter 1, the analysis reported in this book addresses two key questions: first, do county, court, and temporal contexts affect sentencing outcomes, and second, do these contexts affect the role offender characteristics play during sentencing? In this chapter, we describe the research site and the sources of data we use to answer these questions. We also present our measures of sentencing outcomes and social contexts. The chapter concludes with a discussion of analytic procedures and strategy.

Study Site

We consider it appropriate, if not essential, to focus on the sentencing process within a single state. Although the Federal criminal code prohibits a range of behaviors and is in force nationally, the bulk of criminal law is defined and applied at the state level (Koppel, 1984). Recent proposals for sentencing reform, most of which are designed to reduce or eliminate jurisdictional differences in sentencing, have also been developed at the state level (Shane-DuBow et al., 1985). Although our research is not designed to evaluate these reform proposals, it nonetheless empirically addresses the issues that have fueled contemporary concern with fairness in sentencing. By considering all jurisdictions within a single state, then, this study can shed light on the desirability and feasibility of reforms currently under consideration.

For a variety of reasons, the state of Georgia is a particularly advantageous research site. These include historical research documenting the social role of criminal law in the South, the existence of considerable sentencing discretion, the social diversity of the state, and the pronounced social, political, and legal importance of counties in Georgia.

As described earlier, several historical studies of criminal punishment (e.g., Hindus, 1980; Chapin, 1983; Ayers, 1984) have concentrated on Southern cities or states and have emphasized the distinct forms punishment has taken in the region. In addition, historical studies have documented the relationship between law and the broader social structure, as well as the political, economic, and legal significance of race. Since the issue of race discrimination, both in the South and elsewhere, continues to concern researchers (e.g., Kleck, 1981; Georges-Abeyie, 1984; Peterson and Hagan, 1984; Wilbanks, 1987), the choice of Georgia is particularly strategic. Moreover, the presence of historical research on the South provides a strong empirical foundation for studying contemporary punishment in Georgia.

Unlike judges in states with sentencing guidelines (e.g., Minnesota), Superior Court judges in Georgia have considerable discretion. Later in the chapter, we will consider recent legislative restrictions on the sentencing of specific offenders (e.g., armed robbers). For the most part, however, judges can continue to determine the type and duration of punishment. They may impose probation rather than prison; set prison terms from within a wide range of imprisonment (e.g., 1 to 20 years for statutory rape); and combine probation and prison terms in any way they deem appropriate.

Exacerbating the discretion inherent in statutory penalties is the absence of any legislative consensus or prescriptions on sanction philosophy. In a variety of laws and resolutions, the legislature has endorsed retribution, deterrence, incapacitation, and other sanction objectives. For example, legislatively created institutions concerned with rehabilitation (e.g., probation, parole, juvenile court) persist. So, too, does the death penalty, which, along with lengthy prison terms, reflects retributivist concerns. Recently, the Georgia legislature passed a bill (GA Code 27-3001) indicating that "restitution by those found guilty of crimes to their victims is a primary concern of the criminal justice system." In short, the state gives judges considerable discretion in sentencing with virtually no direction in sanction philosophy.

The social and cultural diversity of Georgia adds to its value as a research site. The state has three regions, each with a widely acknowledged distinctive character. The northern sector includes counties that did not join the majority of the state in the Confederacy (Bryan, 1953). The climate, rough terrain, and affinity with the Appalachian heritage of Tennessee foster independence, reticence, and a sense of vigor. The agrarian central and southern plains hold most of the state's land mass and farmlands. The pace in this part of the state is slower, and the politics traditionally conservative and populist. The coastal region includes Savannah, the major port city. It is the home of the state's oldest and most distinctive ethnic groups. Resort areas dot the coastline and adjacent islands, where industry centers on trade and tourism.

Finally, Georgia is a particularly appropriate research location because of the structure of its Superior Court system. Although courts are administratively organized into circuits, the basic and most important unit is the county (Coulter, 1947; Coleman et al., 1977). Circuits respect county boundaries (encompassing between one and eight counties), and appropriations for Superior Courts are largely drawn from county governments. More relevant for our purposes, courts do not function in central locations. As has traditionally been the case, prosecution and sentencing occur in the county where the offense was committed. Site visits to several circuits further confirm the importance of the county. Court officials expressed sensitivity to county preferences and opinions, and often observed that county peculiarities affect criminal court processes.

The county-based character of the Superior Court system reflects the long-standing political and social dominance of county government in Georgia (Hughes, 1944; Saye, 1950; Bartley, 1983). Although the demise of county-unit rule and subsequent reapportionment have diminished their political power (Dixon, 1972), counties continue to overshadow their inclusive cities. Their continued vitality is well illustrated by stiff opposition to recent (1985) legislative efforts designed to facilitate county consolidation. According to Representative G. D. Adams (D–Fulton County), chair of the State Planning and Community Affairs Committee,

Nobody wants to do anything to offend their local people. . . . We've got some very poor counties in Georgia and we've got some small counties. Still, they're proud of their status, and the local politicians just don't want to give up their county rights. (Toner and Galloway, 1985:1A,12A)

Coupled with the loss of identity and political prerogatives, consolidation has been opposed on economic grounds as well. Particularly in rural counties without a manufacturing base, the local government employs a significant number of county residents. For example, in Georgia's 10 smallest counties, local government (including schools) accounted for 24.7% of all jobs in 1983. The comparable figure in Georgia's 10 largest counties was 8.9% (Toner and Galloway, 1985). In short, then, Georgia's 159 counties continue to be socially, politically, and economically meaningful units, whose continued vitality offers particularly fertile ground for a contextual analysis of criminal sentencing.

Sample

Information about sentencing in Georgia is based on a sample of felons convicted between January 1976 and June 1985. We relied on two diagnostic and administrative files compiled and made available by the Department of Corrections. The first includes all felons sentenced to prison or to a combination of prison and probation (split sentence); the second consists of the population of felons sentenced only to probation. We combined these data sets and drew a stratified random sample ($N = 26,223$). To ensure that all counties were adequately represented, sampling proportions (.01, .05, .10, .25, .50, and 1.00) varied inversely with the number of offenders sentenced in the county. To prevent rural counties from dominating the analysis, cases were subsequently weighted during analysis by the reciprocal of their sampling proportion.

Before July 1983, the probationer file lacked entries from Fulton and DeKalb counties, which had maintained their own records until that time. Since these counties are part of the important metropolitan area of Atlanta, we drew comparable samples of convicted felons from files maintained by the clerk of the Superior Court in Fulton County ($N = 382$) and by the prosecutor of DeKalb

County ($N = 1,115$).[1] When added to the stratified random sample, these supplemental cases produced a total of 27,720 offenders.

Although quantitative data represent our primary source of information about sentencing, we obtained qualitative data from visits to 11 of the state's 45 judicial circuits. We chose circuits that maximized representation of geographical region (e.g., coastal, piedmont, mountain), rural-urban differences, and court and circuit size (e.g., single-judge vs. multiple-judge circuits; single-county vs. multiple-county circuits).

For 2 to 3 days, we observed court processes and interviewed a variety of court and community officials (e.g., judges, district attorneys, public defenders, private attorneys, probation officers, city and county leaders). We sought information about the punishment philosophy of judges, perceptions of the court and the sentencing process, and court and community idiosyncracies that could affect sentencing. We used this information to put the results of quantitative analysis into perspective.

Sentencing Outcomes

Researchers have considered a variety of sentencing decisions. Many have focused on the decision to incarcerate the offender (e.g., Pope, 1976; Hagan, 1977; Myers, 1979; Uhlman and Walker, 1979; Farnworth and Horan, 1980; Unnever et al., 1980; Austin, 1981; Unnever, 1982; Pruitt and Wilson, 1983), whereas others have focused on the length of prison sentences (e.g., Lizotte, 1978; Thomson and Zingraff, 1981; Peterson and Hagan, 1984; Zatz, 1984). The complexity of the sentencing process has led some researchers to develop a single ordinal scale that encompasses several different sentencing options (e.g., Bernstein et al., 1977; Gibson, 1983). The most commonly used scale was developed in the early 1970s by the Administrative Office of the U.S. Courts. It includes sanctions that range in seriousness from a suspended sentence (assigned a score of 1) to life imprisonment (assigned a score of 93). This scale has been used to measure the sentences imposed in both Federal (Cook, 1973) and state courts (e.g., Tiffany et al., 1975; Uhlman, 1977, 1978; Gibson, 1978a, 1980; Uhlman and Walker, 1979; Gruhl et al., 1981).

Rather than combine sentencing decisions into a single ordinal scale, however, we chose to distinguish among three outcomes. We based this choice on strong evidence that decisions about the type and the duration of punishment are conceptually and empirically distinct phenomena (e.g., Sutton, 1978; Spohn et al., 1981–82; Wheeler et al., 1982). In a sense, sentencing decisions are themselves contexts (Thomson and Zingraff, 1981) and, as such, they condition the role offense and offender characteristics play during the decision-making process. Put differently, the effect that case attributes have on outcomes may depend strongly on the decision being made. An offender attribute such as race may not affect the decision to incarcerate in the same way that it affects subsequent decisions about sentence length (for evidence this is the case, see Myers, 1979;

Horan et al., 1982; Miethe and Moore, 1986). Furthermore, there is recent evidence (Spohn et al., 1981–82) that the 93-point ordinal scale discussed above masks important race differences in punishment. For these reasons, we differentiate the initial decision to imprison from subsequent decisions about the duration of imprisonment.

The first sentencing outcome represents the critical decision to incarcerate the offender. In this sample, 35.2% of all offenders received some form of incarceration. They were assigned a score of 1. The remaining offenders received probation, and were assigned a value of 0. Once the initial decision to imprison the offender has been made, judges must decide whether to impose a split or a straight prison sentence. Split sentences involve a specified term of prison, followed by a specified term of probationary supervision. Straight prison terms entail only imprisonment. In this sample, 45.7% of all prisoners, or 16.1% of the total sample, received a split sentence ($N = 4,465$). Slightly over 54% of all prisoners, 19.1% of the total sample, received a straight prison term ($N = 5,302$).

Split sentences are difficult to measure, in large part because they combine two very different sanctions, prison and probation. When considered separately in preliminary analysis, neither probation nor prison sentence length was well predicted by the case, county, and court variables included in the model. These preliminary results corroborate the evidence we obtained during interviews that judges consider the two elements as a single unit.[2]

A simple sum of probation and prison sentences would successfully capture the sense that the split sentence is a unitary phenomenon. Yet this sum would be misleading, because it ignores differences in the seriousness of the two sanctions. Confinement is obviously a more severe sanction than probationary supervision. We can capture this difference in seriousness by constructing a variable that measures the percentage of the total split sentence for which the judge mandates confinement. This variable is also problematic. Consider two offenders, both of whom received a split sentence. The first offender received 5 years in prison and 5 years on probation, and the second offender received 10 years in prison, with 10 additional years on probation. Were we to rely exclusively on the percentage of split sentence mandating confinement, both offenders would receive the same score (50%).

To capture differences both in split sentence severity and in the length of prison terms, we added prison sentence length to the percentage of split sentence for which the judge ordered prison ($\overline{X} = 50.3$, $SD = 19.7$). Alternatively represented, split sentence severity is

$$[(a/(a + b)) * 100] + a,$$

where $a =$ prison sentence length and $b =$ probation sentence length.

The final sentencing outcome, length of straight prison terms, is straightforwardly measured in years, for felons sentenced only to prison ($\overline{X} = 10.5$; $SD = 12$). Offenders sentenced to life imprisonment were coded 42 years, and those sentenced to death were coded 60 years.

Case Characteristics

The nature and quality of the data limited the range of offender and offense attributes we could consider during the analysis. The probationer file was less than ideal in this respect because it lacked prior record and social class information. On the basis of separate preliminary analysis of Fulton and DeKalb cases, where prior record was available, we can be somewhat confident of our findings. For these offenders, social background characteristics continue to affect the probability of imprisonment, even after prior record is controlled. Both Fulton and DeKalb are urban counties, however, so we have no way of knowing whether the situation would be the same in rural counties. In general, then, data limitations inject a note of caution when interpreting findings for the first sentencing outcome.

Factors of Explicit Legal Relevance

Table 2.1 presents the distribution of case variables for the total sample, split prisoners, and straight prisoners. For the sample as a whole, we considered two factors of legal relevance: type of crime and gravity of the most serious conviction charge. Because of space and resource constraints, offenses were categorized instead of analyzed separately. Although categorization may obscure some crime-specific differences, it succeeds in capturing the basic distinctions court and county personnel draw. To some extent, offense seriousness, described below, controls for within-category differences.

Offenses are categorized as common-law violent, robbery, burglary, property theft and damage, and drug crimes. Admittedly, the property theft and damage category is broad, and later, when considering county contexts, we will have reason to suspect differences in treatment within this category. Where this is the case, we focus more specifically on four subcategories of property offenders: larceny, white-collar (i.e., forgery, fraud, and embezzlement), vehicle theft, and property damage/possession of stolen goods.

Table 2.2 presents the distribution of offenses within the five major categories. During the analysis, type of offense is effect-coded, with drug crimes being designated the −1 category. This coding permits us to compare each crime category with the unweighted mean, rather than with an arbitrarily excluded category of offenses (e.g., common-law violent).

The second variable of explicit legal relevance is the seriousness of the offense. An ordinal variable, it is operationalized as the midpoint of the range of imprisonment stipulated by law for the offense. The remaining legally relevant factors measure prior record, and are available only for prisoners. Unfortunately, the preferred indicator, prior felony convictions, was not reliably coded in the Department of Corrections data set. Based on recent work (Welch et al., 1984), omission of this variable may be less problematic than it appears. After comparing several measures of prior record, Welch and her colleagues (1984) found that prior incarceration had the strongest and most uniform effect on sentences. We

TABLE 2.1. Descriptive statistics for case characteristics

Variable	Total sample (N = 27,720)		Split prisoners (N = 4,465)		Straight prisoners (N = 5,302)	
	$\bar{X}$	SD	$\bar{X}$	SD	$\bar{X}$	SD
Legally relevant factors						
Type of crime^a						
Common-law violent	.19	(.39)	.21	(.41)	.32	(.47)*
Robbery	.04	(.21)	.09	(.29)	.11	(.32)*
Burglary	.26	(.44)	.33	(.47)	.30	(.46)*
Property theft/damage	.31	(.46)	.20	(.40)	.19	(.39)
Drug	.18	(.39)	.17	(.38)	.08	(.27)*
Offense seriousness	8.57	(5.77)	9.82	(4.86)	12.93	(9.53)*
Prior arrests (>25 = 25)			2.27	(3.90)	2.63	(4.30)*
Prior incarceration in Georgia (no = 0; yes = 1)			.18	(.37)	.22	(.40)*
Social background factors						
Sex (female = 0; male = 1)	.88	(.32)	.93	(.25)	.95	(.23)
Race (black = 0; white = 1)	.57	(.49)	.52	(.50)	.46	(.50)*
Age (in years)	26.56	(7.97)	26.65	(8.58)	26.79	(9.16)
Marital status (unmarried = 0; married = 1)			.29	(.45)	.28	(.44)
Employment status (unemployed = 0; employed = 1)			.69	(.45)	.68	(.46)

^a For presentation purposes only, type of crime is dichotomized, with the category of interest being coded 1 and the remaining offenses coded 0. The variable is effect-coded during analysis, with drug offenses designated as the excluded category and assigned a value of −1.
*Split prisoners differ significantly from offenders receiving only prison ($p \leq .05$).

therefore relied on a dichotomous measure of whether the offender had been previously incarcerated in Georgia. We also included the number of prior arrests. An additional variable of legal relevance, the number of conviction charges, was also available for prisoners. In preliminary analysis, it had no significant effect on sentences, and to conserve degrees of freedom we did not include the measure in the analysis.

Offender Social Background

The data to which we had access provided important, although limited, information about the social background of offenders. As noted earlier, the probation file was particularly problematic. For the sample as a whole, we are therefore limited to the attributes of sex, race, and age. On the surface, the prisoner file was a richer source of data. Yet here we encountered insufficient variation (e.g., nearly all report being Baptist) and excessive amounts of missing data (e.g., for

TABLE 2.2. Distribution of offenses within crime categories

Offense	N	Category total	Percent of total
Common law violent		4,001	14.5
Homicide			
First-degree murder	365		
Manslaughter	613		
Other (e.g., attempts)	80		
Aggravated assault	2,260		
Sexual assault			
Rape	430		
Sodomy	247		
Other	6		
Robbery		1,341	4.8
Armed	736		
Unarmed	571		
Other (e.g., attempts)	34		
Burglary		7,597	27.4
Property theft and damage		9,333	33:7
Larceny	3,346		
Vehicle theft	920		
Forgery	2,123		
Fraud	803		
Embezzlement	199		
Criminal damage	702		
Arson	262		
Possession of stolen goods	965		
Other	13		
Drug crimes		5,448	19.6
Possession of opiates depressants, stimulants, LSD	986		
Possession of marijuana	1,948		
Possession of other drugs	944		
Sale/distribution of opiates, depressants, stimulants, LSD	359		
Sale/distribution of marijuana	1,163		
Trafficking in cocaine or narcotics	28		
Trafficking in marijuana	20		
		27,720	100.0

education, living arrangements, and number of children). In addition, other background information (e.g., rural vs. urban background, state of birth) was consistently available, but in preliminary analysis had no significant effect on sentences. To conserve degrees of freedom, we did not consider these characteristics.

Two important attributes, employment and marital status, were reliably and consistently available, however. Together with sex, race, and age, they give some indication of the offender's social position and, by implication, access to and control of resources.

The Community Context

We focus on dimensions of the community that have received attention in theoretical works on punishment or in empirical research on sentencing. They are urbanization, economic conditions, and the amount of crime. In the sections that follow, we summarize and critique the relevant literature, and describe the measures used in the analysis. Table 2.3 presents the descriptive statistics for the county variables used to analyze the community context.

Urbanization

Although the relationship between urbanization and crime is clearly established (Krohn, 1978; Shelley, 1981; Federal Bureau of Investigation, 1985; Bureau of Justice Statistics, 1986), the implications of urbanization for social control responses to crime are less well understood. Several theorists (e.g., Durkheim, 1933, 1973; Weber, 1954; Black, 1976) have defined a role for urbanization in social control, but empirical examinations have only recently been undertaken.

As noted in Chapter 1, these examinations document the presence of significant rural-urban differences in sentencing. Hagan (1977) among others (Pope, 1976; Austin, 1981) found that differential treatment of racial minorities is more pronounced in rural courts. More generally, Austin (1981) discovered that social background factors are typically more important in rural courts, whereas legally relevant factors (e.g., prior record) play more prominent roles in urban courts.

Yet the issue is far from settled. Blacks appear to be at a particular disadvantage if sentenced in the urban areas of Minnesota, where their prison sentences are longer than those imposed on rural blacks and on white urban offenders (Miethe and Moore, 1986). Similarly, urban courts in Pennsylvania showed the greatest bias toward blacks in the initial decision to incarcerate, while suburban courts were noted for racial discrimination in sentence length (Kempf and Austin, 1986). Our own earlier work (Myers and Talarico, 1986a), based on felons

TABLE 2.3. Descriptive statistics for county variables

Variable	Mean	Standard deviation	Range
Urbanization[a]	24,068.4	47,405.9	675–230,210
Income standard deviation	13,543.3	2,148.5	9,280–23,960
Racial income inequality	7,493.5	3,492.8	−1,828–18,082
Lagged unemployment rate	6.9	2.1	2.6–22.5
Percent black[b]	27.5	16.5	0–78.2
Lagged crime rate	2,185.6	1,774.3	0–10,871

[a] Urbanization is a weighted linear composite of percent urban, population per square mile, and population size. Weights were derived from principal component factor analysis.
[b] Percent black is dummy-coded during the analysis to compare counties having few blacks (less than 25%) with counties that contain a substantial minority (25–49%) or a majority (50% and over) black population.

convicted in Georgia between 1976 and 1982, indicated that urbanization intensi-fies differential treatment by race. Yet only for the initial decision to imprison are urban blacks more harshly treated. Among offenders sentenced to prison, the terms imposed on blacks in urban courts tend to be significantly *shorter* than those imposed on white offenders.

Although laudable for focusing attention on urbanization, prior research has typically failed to consider aspects of the community that are confounded with urbanization (e.g., inequality, crime rate). Without controls for correlates of urbanization, we have no way of knowing whether urbanization itself, or some other related aspect of the community, is responsible for changes in differential treatment. To isolate more clearly its unique effect on sentencing, we examine urbanization in conjunction with other attributes of counties.

To be consistent with previous theorizing and research, we focus on the ecolog-ical meaning of urbanization. It is operationalized as the weighted linear compo-site of three intercorrelated ($r \geq .85$) measures of population size and density. These measures are percent urban (1980 Census figures), population per square mile (1980 Census figures), and population size (Census figures and annual county estimates). The weights in the composite are the standardized scoring co-efficients obtained from principal component factor analysis (eigenvalue = 2.6, accounting for 85% of the variation). Although we examine the ecological dimen-sion of urbanization, we depart from prior research in one major respect. Instead of using a dichotomy (rural, urban) or trichotomy (rural, suburban, urban), we examine the *degree* of urbanization and its implications for sentencing.

Economic Conditions

The second set of county factors taps several dimensions of economic life: income inequality, unemployment, and racial composition. Although the issue is far from settled empirically, these attributes have been conceptualized as struc-tural conditions that increase the amount of crime in the community as well as the perceived magnitude and fear of crime (Turk, 1969; Lizotte and Bordua, 1980; Liska et al. 1981).[3] Apart from their effect on crime, however, economic condi-tions are thought to affect social control responses directly. Greater inequality, for example, implies the presence of elites who are motivated and able to use legal mechanisms of social control to maintain their privileged position (Jacobs, 1978, 1979). Large economically subordinate populations (e.g., black, unem-ployed) are potentially troublesome, and can be contained in part by repressive forms of social control (Jankovic, 1977; Liska et al., 1981).

With some exceptions, the findings of empirical research are consistent with such conceptualizations. Greater inequality and larger black populations tend to foster stronger police forces (Jacobs, 1979; Huff and Stahura, 1980; Liska et al., 1981), greater use of deadly force (Jacobs and Britt, 1979), larger police expenditures (Jackson and Carroll, 1981; Lizotte et al., 1982), higher arrest rates (Williams and Drake, 1980; Liska and Chamlin, 1984), and higher imprison-ment rates (Jacobs, 1978; Joubert et al., 1981; but cf. Bailey, 1981; Carroll and Doubet, 1983). Similarly, high unemployment appears to increase the use of, and expenditures for, imprisonment (Greenberg, 1977; Jankovic, 1977; Yeager, 1979; Wallace, 1981; Box and Hale, 1982, 1985, 1986; but cf. Marenin et al., 1983; Parker and Horwitz, 1986), particularly in the South (Galster and Scaturo, 1985).

In addition to producing a general climate of coerciveness, these contexts may foster *selective* punitiveness as well (Williams and Drake, 1980). Jacobs (1978), for example, contended that property offenders are treated with disproportionate harshness in contexts where economic inequality is pronounced. This occurs because they pose a particularly salient threat to monied elite interests. Violent offenders, in contrast, pose less serious threats to the property interests of elites, largely because they tend to victimize the lower class. As a result, inequality may have little effect on the punishment of these offenders.

These theoretical arguments may apply as well to race differences in punishment. Blacks are culturally and racially dissimilar to whites, and historically have been economically disenfranchised. Furthermore, they are typically associated with criminal stereotypes (Swigert and Farrell, 1976) and serious crime problems (Lizotte and Bordua, 1980). For these reasons alone, black offenders may appear more threatening than comparable white offenders. However, their criminality may pose a threat that is *particularly* salient in certain contexts, namely, those where elites are in a defensive posture and are able to mobilize the legal system to defend their interests. That is, black offenders may appear particularly threatening where income inequality and racial inequities are pronounced, and where economically subordinate populations (e.g., black, unemployed) are large. This greater threat could provide the stimulus for disproportionately harsher treatment of blacks in these counties. Conversely, where there is less inequality and smaller subordinate populations, black and white offenders may appear to pose similar threats. Correspondingly, race differences in punishment may be less pronounced.

As measures of inequality, we use income standard deviation and black income inequality. Income standard deviation, based on 1979 Census data, is preferable to the more commonly used Gini coefficient for theoretical reasons. Much work on inequality is based on the conflict perspective, which is interpretable as differentiating strongly between the upper and all other classes (Jacobs, 1981a; Carroll and Jackson, 1982; Williams and Timberlake, 1984). A measure of inequality that is sensitive to income extremes is therefore more appropriate than less sensitive alternatives. That the Gini coefficient fared less well in preliminary analysis lends credence to this interpretation.

Although it is more appropriate than the Gini coefficient, income standard deviation does not capture race differences in inequality. These differences affect the amount of violent crime (Blau and Blau, 1982:121–2; Blau and Golden, 1986), and police force size and expenditures (Jackson and Carroll, 1981; Carroll and Jackson, 1982), as well as imprisonment rates (Bridges and Crutchfield, 1985). As a result, we considered it important to explore their relevance during sentencing. Based on 1979 Census data, racial income inequality is operationalized as the difference between white and black mean income.

The size of economically subordinate populations is indicated by two measures: the unemployment rate and percent of blacks in the county. Obtained from Georgia's Department of Labor, the annual unemployment rate is the percent of the total civilian labor force that is unemployed. Since there is aggregate-level evidence that changes in imprisonment occur after changes in unemployment (Greenberg, 1977; Yeager, 1979), we lagged the unemployment rate by 1 year. As expected, the use of the unlagged unemployment rate in preliminary models yielded similar, but much weaker, results.

Blalock (1967) and others (e.g., Jackson and Carroll, 1981) have suggested that the size of the black population has a curvilinear effect on the way blacks are treated in the community. Presumably, the threat an economically subordinate black population poses is greatest when the blacks are a substantial minority of the population. Once blacks become a numerical majority, they may achieve enough political power to ensure more evenhanded treatment. To test for curvilinearity, we dummy-coded percent black to compare counties having small black populations (less than 25%) with two other groups of counties. The first group consists of counties that contain a sizeable black minority (25–49%), and the second group consists of counties with a black majority (50% and over). Preliminary analysis supported this coding choice. The two-vector measure predicted sentences and differential treatment better than did an interval measure.

The Crime Problem in the Community

The final county factor measures the seriousness of the crime problem in the community. In previous work, the amount of crime has usually been considered either a dependent or a control variable. Researchers have attempted to predict crime from structural characteristics of the community, such as urbanization, racial composition, inequality, and unemployment.[4] In research of more direct relevance to this study, the crime rate is typically considered a control variable that permits researchers to accurately estimate the effects of theoretically important factors (e.g., urbanization, unemployment) on social control responses (see, e.g., Jacobs, 1979; Williams and Drake, 1980; Bailey, 1981; Liska et al., 1981).

Unlike previous research, we place greater emphasis on crime as an independent variable that may affect sentencing outcomes as well as differential treatment during sentencing. In the absence of specific guidance from previous research, we formulate the simple expectation that differential treatment will be more pronounced in counties that experience serious crime problems. In addition, we expect high crime rates to foster disproportionate harshness toward offenders whose criminality may appear particularly threatening to the community (e.g., black, violent, robbers).

As a measure of crime, we chose the Index crime rate because it provides a global indication of the amount of serious crime. We lagged the crime rate by a minimum of 1 year to eliminate the confounding influence of imprisonment on later crime rates. More importantly, we matched violent offenders with the lagged Index violent crime rate. Property and drug offenders were matched with the lagged Index property crime rate (drug crime rates were unavailable).[5]

The Court

As noted in Chapter 1, the structure of the court and attributes of its personnel have received considerable attention, particularly in qualitative and appellate court research. On the basis of the literature, we focus on court bureaucratization and selected characteristics of sentencing judges. Table 2.4 presents these dimensions.

Court Bureaucratization

As noted earlier, Weberian and conflict theories offer quite different expectations about the role bureaucratization plays during sentencing. To date, however, we lack strong empirical evidence that would permit us to evaluate either argument. Research on differential treatment (e.g., Hagan, 1977) has seldom measured bureaucratization directly. Nor has it differentiated bureaucratization from the urbanization of the surrounding community. Tepperman (1973), in contrast, measured both phenomena by focusing on community population and court size. Consistent with the Weberian perspective, he found that bureaucratization fostered more evenhanded treatment of male and female juveniles. Here, we examine whether bureaucratization fosters more evenhanded treatment of adult felons and instead of gender differences, we focus on differences based on race and offense.

For guidance in measuring bureaucratization, we relied on Blau's (1974) operationalization of the concept. Because of insufficient variation or information, we could not consider several dimensions such as the complexity of responsibilities, elaborateness of administrative apparatus, hierarchical organization, impersonal

TABLE 2.4. Descriptive statistics for court variables

Variable	Mean	Standard deviation	Range
Court bureaucratization			
Felony filings/judge	261.10	88.61	88–672
Lower court assistance	84.95	14.28	15.3–100
Judicial characteristics			
Sex (female = 0; male = 1)	.99	.07	.5–1
Age	54.10	6.25	34–78
Religion (non-Baptist = 0; Baptist = 1)	.35	.33	0–1
Years as prosecutor	2.94	4.24	0–21
Circuit of origin (Born outside circuit = 0; in circuit = 1)	.61	.41	0–1
Membership in community organizations	1.57	1.27	0–8
Years in local government	2.90	5.37	0–34
Opponents in primary	.13	.26	0–2
Election history (0–2 = 0; 3+ = 1)	.54	.50	0–1

detachment, and systems of rules and regulations. Furthermore, because court size was virtually redundant with county urbanization ($r = .8$), we could not disentangle its unique effect. Instead, we chose two dimensions along which courts in Georgia vary. Together, they offer a preliminary indication of the degree to which courts are bureaucratized.

The first is workload, operationalized as felony filings per judge. Although not identified by Blau as an indicator of bureaucratization, we include it here because previous research has often linked heavy workloads with bureaucratization (e.g., Hagan, 1977; Pruitt and Wilson, 1983). The second measure is court specialization, and is indicated by the amount of assistance judges receive from supporting courts. Assistance takes the form of hearing a certain percentage of misdemeanor and traffic cases. Courts that receive a large amount of assistance from lower state courts focus primarily, if not exclusively, on felonies and are highly specialized. Information on caseload and specialization was available from the Administrative Office of the Courts on a fiscal-year basis. It was matched with the sample by circuit and year.

Judicial Characteristics

In many respects, Georgia's Superior Court judges are a socially homogenous group of elected officials. During the period of this study, all were white, and the vast majority were male (96.7%), Protestant (93.8%), married (96%), and born in Georgia (84.2%). Nearly all judges were lawyers (98.7%), who had received their degrees in Georgia (88.8%), and virtually all (94.5%) were affiliated with the Democratic party. As a result of this homogeneity, we could not reliably estimate the effects of several attributes of concern to other researchers such as race (Engle, 1971; Uhlman, 1978), party affiliation (e.g., Vines, 1964; Ulmer, 1973; Goldman, 1975; Gibson, 1978b; Tate, 1981), or affiliation with Protestant religions (e.g., Tate, 1981). Nevertheless, we could consider several other characteristics of perennial concern in the literature.

At the most general level, Gibson's (1983) conceptualization of judicial decision making guided our choice of judicial variables. As noted earlier, Gibson (1983:9) contended that judges' decisions are a function of "what they prefer to do, tempered by what they think they ought to do, but constrained by what they perceive is feasible to do." In concrete terms, judicial decisions are affected by attitudes, values, role orientations, and environmental constraints. These factors are important in two respects, because they affect sentences directly and, more important for our purposes, they affect the weight judges assign to characteristics of the case (Gibson, 1983).

We have no direct measures of judicial attitudes, role orientations, and responsiveness to community pressures. Instead, we have information about the demographic characteristics and background experiences of judges. We presume, but cannot show, that these attributes and experiences affect socialization processes and, by extension, attitudes and role orientations. With the information that is available, we are able to focus on judicial conservatism and responsiveness to public pressure.

JUDICIAL CONSERVATISM

The first set of judicial characteristics has been linked with the placement of judicial attitudes and behaviors along the liberal-conservative continuum. It consists of sex, age, religion, and prior experience as a prosecutor. Despite the skew in gender, we chose to consider this characteristic because the previous literature has linked sex with both gender and offense differences in sentencing (Kritzer and Uhlman, 1977; Gruhl et al., 1981). Here, we are able to examine whether gender affects the weight attached to offense and race. Since female elites appear to be more liberal than male elites (Gibson, 1983), we expect female judges to be more lenient in general and more lenient toward blacks in particular.

Age has also been linked with conservatism (Cook, 1973; Ulmer, 1973; Goldman, 1975; Kritzer, 1978) and with more punitive sentencing decisions (Pruitt and Wilson, 1983). We measured judicial age at the time the judge sentenced the offender.

In examining the effect of religion on judicial decision making, the previous literature has distinguished between Protestants and non-Protestants (e.g., Vines, 1964; Ulmer, 1973; Goldman, 1975; Tate, 1981) or, in the South, between Fundamentalists and non-Fundamentalists (Gibson, 1978b). The underlying assumption has been that non-Protestants and Fundamentalists are more conservative than their counterparts. As a result, their decisions and the criteria on which they base their decisions will differ. For example, Gibson (1978b) has found that judges affiliated with Fundamentalist religions tend to discriminate more against black offenders than judges not so affiliated.

Neither of the traditional religious distinctions could be drawn here. As noted above, nearly 94% of all judges were Protestant, and only 2.3% were affiliated with Fundamentalist sects (e.g., Church of God, Disciples of Christ). Instead, we distinguished Southern Baptists from non-Baptists, and presumed that Southern Baptists are more conservative than judges affiliated with other religions.

Our final indicator of conservatism is the number of years judges served as county or circuit prosecutor. Based on appellate court research (e.g., Johnston, 1976; Tate, 1981), we expect former prosecutors to be harsher than their counterparts without such experience.

RESPONSIVENESS TO THE COMMUNITY

Several measures indicate judicial responsiveness to the surrounding community. The first determines whether the judge was born in the circuit (coded 1) or outside the circuit (coded 0). Two other variables measure the degree of judicial involvement in the community. They are the number of years experience in local government (e.g., mayor, Board of Commissioners) and the number of community organizations (e.g., Elk, Lions, Boy Scouts) to which judges report belonging.

The final measures provide an indication of electoral vulnerability. Since judges in Georgia are more likely to be opposed in primaries rather than elections, we considered whether judges had faced opposition in their most recent primary. We assumed that those who were opposed in the primary are electorally more vulnerable than their unopposed counterparts.

The second indicator of electoral vulnerability measures the judge's election history. Rather than use an interval scale, we dichotomized the number of times elected. Judges who had been elected fewer than three times were coded 0, and those who had been elected three or more times were coded 1. We based this decision on evidence of distinct stages in judicial careers (Alpert et al., 1979). After several years on the bench, judges become established and committed to a career as a Superior Court judge. At this point, they become isolated from, and less sensitive to, public needs and demands. Based on what we know of judicial careers in Georgia, judges are more likely to become established and committed after they have served two terms on the bench. Hence, three terms is the dividing point in our measure. In preliminary analysis, an interval measure proved to be a less successful predictor of sentences, and seldom conditioned the role played by race and offense during sentencing. These results provide additional justification for our coding decision.

In sum, we expect judges who were born in the circuit, have been active in the community politically and socially, and are electorally vulnerable to be more responsive to community pressures and demands. Although some judges reported being isolated from, and indifferent to, public opinion, many others conveyed a quite different impression of direct influence:

People want to talk business with judges all the time. (Judge, Eastern Circuit)

You get letters from the editor, people, and idle conversation. I know a lot of people and I talk to a lot. (Judge, Chattahoochee Circuit)

If you make a speech, most always there is going to be somebody who will want an opportunity to know why it is they can't do something about such and such. (Judge, Atlanta Circuit)

For other judges, public sentiments are transmitted indirectly, through the county sheriff:

They [judges] have to be sensitive to it [county differences], but the greatest indication that we have in most counties are the sheriffs. . . . Sometimes they request that the court give an automatic sentence . . . I go along with that. (Judge, Chattahoochee Circuit)

Regardless of the mechanisms through which public opinion is transmitted, its content is quite clear and remarkably uniform. In each circuit we visited, whether rural or urban, county and court officials thought the public was critical of the courts because sentences were too lenient:

. . . and [judges] have got a terrible problem on their hands of people being critical of the courts, turning people loose . . . (Mayor, Augusta)

They [the public] feel, for example, that judges are lenient. (Judge, Eastern Circuit)

I would say that the public thinks it [the court] should be more severe than what it is. (Sheriff, Mountain Circuit)

I think in general some people may think that he doesn't give enough jail time, that he is a little light on people. (Defense attorney, Houston Circuit)

I've had some criticism about mainly too lenient. Would you believe? (Judge, Piedmont Circuit)

They [the public] have a pretty tough law and order attitude. (Probation supervisor, Chattahoochee Circuit)

. . . there has been . . . a real feeling of people, that we need to give some stiff sentences. (Judge, Tift Circuit)

Interview data, then, provide unmistakable evidence of public pressures for a more punitive stance toward offenders. As a result, we expect that judges who are responsive to community pressures (i.e., socially and politically involved or electorally vulnerable) will generally sentence more harshly. Moreover, we expect them to single out for particularly harsh punishment those types of offenders (e.g., black, violent, burglars) that they believe may appear especially threatening to the community.

Judicial information was obtained from the most complete published source available, the Georgia Official and Statistical Register. Where published data were lacking, we relied on mailed questionnaires designed to obtain the same kinds of information contained in the Register.

Aggregating Judge Information

For 24% of the sample ($N = 6,618$), it was possible to identify the sentencing judge, and match judicial information with data about the offender and the offense. This was the case in circuits with only one judge, in the supplemental samples drawn from Fulton and DeKalb counties, and in selected counties where we specifically requested information about sentencing in 1984 and 1985. For the remaining cases, we aggregated information, and judicial characteristics are means (e.g., mean number of community organizations) or proportions (e.g., proportion male), based on all judges presiding in the court the year the offender was convicted.

To explore the implications of aggregation for our analysis, we compared cases for which the sentencing judge was known with those containing only aggregated information. The two groups did not differ significantly in sentencing outcomes or in most offense and offender characteristics. However, offenders whose sentencing judge had been identified were significantly more likely to be sentenced in counties that are urban, are racially unequal, and have higher crime rates. The sentencing judges themselves were more likely to face heavy caseloads and to sentence common-law violent offenders. These differences are attributable to the heavy representation of metropolitan Atlanta (Fulton and DeKalb counties) among cases where the sentencing judge was known.

In addition, we explored three possible consequences of aggregation. First, we determined whether the presence or absence of sentencing judge information directly affected sentencing outcomes. To do so we created a dichotomous variable, type of judge information. Offenders with sentencing judge information were coded 1 and offenders with aggregated judge data were coded 0. After entering this variable into preliminary models that included case, county, and court variables, we found that imprisonment was used more often and split sentences were more severe among cases where judicial information had been aggregated. These differences, although significant, were slight. The standardized regression coefficient for probability of imprisonment was $-.03$, and for split sentence severity, the effect was $-.04$. We also compared models that controlled for type of judicial information with models that did not include the variable. There were virtually no differences in the effects the remaining case, county, and court variables had on sentences. In short, then, not only does type of judge information have slight direct effects on sentences, but it also does not change the effects the remaining variables have on sentences.

The second consequence of aggregation was the unavoidable amount of imprecision it introduced into measures of judicial characteristics. We thought this imprecision could weaken or otherwise alter the effects judicial characteristics have on sentences. To examine this possibility, we again differentiated cases with aggregated judge information from those where the sentencing judge was known, and then compared the effects judicial characteristics had on sentences for each group of cases. Appendix A discusses the results of this comparison in greater detail. In general, however, there was no strong or consistent evidence that judicial characteristics have different effects if judicial information is aggregated.

Finally, we were concerned that the aggregation procedure might affect sentences more indirectly. As is the case for the variables of central interest, type of judge information could be a context that conditions the relevance of race and offense during sentencing. Put differently, the weight judges attach to offender race and offense may differ, depending on whether judicial information is aggregated or exact. We found little evidence that this is the case. Using the procedure described below, we estimated the interaction between type of judge information, race, and offense. For two of the three sentencing outcomes (probability of imprisonment and split sentence severity), the increases in explained variance were statistically significant. However, few interactions were significant and in comparison with many of the interactions discussed throughout the book, differences were slight.[6] More importantly, we need not control for them to estimate accurately the interactions of central interest to our study. We compared models that controlled for interactions involving type of judge information with models lacking such controls, and found no significant differences.

In sum, then, the aggregation of judicial information introduced some unavoidable imprecision in the measurement of judicial variables. As a result, a small number of judicial characteristics have weaker or different effects among cases where judge information is aggregated (see Appendix A). Most important, however, the aggregation procedure does not appear to bias systematically the additive and interactive effects that case, county, and court variables have on sentencing outcomes.

The Context of Time

Unlike many other states, Georgia has not undertaken extensive sentencing reform. Instead, the legislature has added statutes and modified penalties in a piecemeal fashion. Laws prohibiting racketeering were passed in 1980 (Georgia L., p. 405), as were statutes prohibiting and providing mandatory minimums for trafficking in opiates, cocaine, and marijuana (Georgia L., p. 432). Trafficking in methaqualone was made a criminal offense in 1982 (Georgia L., p. 2215).

Changes in penalties occurred more often and usually involved the imposition of mandatory minimums for certain offenders. Most changes applied to property offenders with prior convictions: robbery in 1976 (Georgia L., p. 1359), burglary in 1978 (Georgia L., p. 236), and motor vehicle theft in 1981 (Georgia L., p. 1577). The legislature has translated growing public concern about victimization into stiffer penalties for offenders who inflict injury during a robbery (1976 Georgia L., p. 1359); assault, defraud, or rob persons 65 years and older (1984 Georgia L., p. 900); or assault correctional officers (1985 Georgia L., p. 628).

Most recently, the legislature has turned its attention to penalties for violating drug laws. Persons who in the course of an armed robbery take controlled substances from a pharmacy or wholesale druggist now face a minimum of 10 years in prison and a maximum of life imprisonment. Should the offender also inflict serious injury, he must be sentenced to a minimum of 15 years in prison (1985 Georgia L., p. 1036). In March of 1985, the legislature created a Special Cocaine Task Force and doubled the mandatory minimum terms for cocaine trafficking. Traffickers in 400 or more grams of cocaine now face a mandatory minimum of 25 years in prison.

Taken together, these legislative changes reflect an increasingly punitive stance toward certain offenders. To some extent, they also restrict the exercise of judicial discretion. However, although legislative action leads us to expect more punitive sentences, appellate litigation in Federal courts may have the opposite effect. In 1972, the well-known Guthrie case was filed by Arthur S. Guthrie, Joseph Coggins II, and 50 other inmates at Reidsville, a large maximum security institution. The plaintiffs, who were black, charged that the prison facilities were unconstitutional. Federal Judge Anthony Alaimo of the U.S. District Court for the Southern District of Georgia agreed, and condemned conditions at Reidsville as constituting cruel and unusual punishment. In particular, he focused on segregation, overcrowding, poor medical care, miserable conditions, and unfair treatment of black and white inmates.

Desegregation was ordered on April 10, 1974. Litigation on medical care and living conditions continued, and consent orders (remedial decrees) were issued from Alaimo's office in 1978. In 1979, Alaimo appointed Vincent Nathan special monitor. Although state authority was not absent, Nathan virtually served as *de facto* if not official warden for several years. By July of 1982, Alaimo believed that enough progress had been made to return administration of the facility back to state officials. However, on the basis of monitor reports in 1982 and 1983,

Alaimo indicated the required improvements had *not* occurred and court supervision would continue. A final order relinquishing court jurisdiction was not issued until 1985, 13 years after the litigation began.

Throughout the period of this study, the Guthrie case intensified concern with prison overcrowding. Indeed, both the Department of Corrections and the Administrative Office of the Courts have taken great pains to inform Superior Court judges about the magnitude of the overcrowding problem. For example, the Commissioner of Corrections has recently sent letters to all Superior Court judges documenting the existence of overcrowding and specifically asking judges to consider it during sentencing.

Thus, despite the "get tough" stance of the legislature, judges have become more aware of the costs of prison, both financial and in terms of Federal court intervention. Not surprisingly, Table 2.5 indicates that judicial reliance on probation has increased, the use of straight prison terms has declined, and split sentences have become less severe. But while judges rely more often on probation, they have also lengthened the period of supervision for both probationers and split sentencers. Furthermore, they use straight imprisonment less often, but tend to impose longer terms, a result either of statutorily imposed minimums or of a tendency to reserve prison for the most dangerous or hardened offenders.

In addition to the Guthrie case, the more recent McCleskey suit (1984, 1985) has intensified awareness of racial disparities in punishment. This suit alleged discrimination by race of victim in the imposition of the death penalty. The defendant based his contention, in part, on a well-known empirical study of capital sentencing in Georgia, originally begun in 1980 (Baldus, Pulaski, and Woodworth, 1983; Baldus, Woodworth, and Pulaski, 1983). Although appellate

TABLE 2.5. Sentencing outcomes, by year

Year	N	Probation		Split sentence				Straight prison	
		%	Mean length	%	Severity $\bar{X}$	Probation $\bar{X}$	Prison $\bar{X}$	%	Mean length
1974*	119	71.4	2.64	7.6	57.54	2.78	4.11	21.0	8.36
1975*	226	63.7	2.73	11.1	54.09	3.18	3.86	25.2	6.88
1976	2,048	52.3	3.00	15.7	50.09	3.90	3.60	32.0	9.65
1977	2,288	55.9	3.25	15.6	49.78	4.17	3.80	28.5	10.08
1978	2,302	59.9	3.59	14.8	49.42	4.00	3.75	25.3	9.52
1979	3,437	69.0	4.23	13.0	49.54	4.24	3.85	18.0	10.05
1980	3,538	66.7	4.38	16.4	48.99	4.41	3.92	16.9	10.14
1981	2,911	62.3	4.83	18.8	50.87	4.94	4.53	18.8	11.88
1982	3,230	61.0	4.85	20.1	51.33	4.86	4.62	18.9	11.55
1983	3,294	69.9	5.08	15.9	49.38	4.98	4.50	14.2	11.38
1984	3,249	72.3	5.19	15.6	48.12	5.31	4.62	12.1	11.85
1985*	1,078	76.4	5.19	14.3	45.23	5.36	4.13	9.3	6.72
	27,720	64.8	4.45	16.1	50.31	4.63	4.20	19.1	10.46

*1974 and 1975 figures for Fulton and DeKalb counties only; 1985 figures through the month of May.

courts have rejected the discrimination claim, the McClesky case has received considerable publicity and undoubtedly contributed to judicial sensitivity to the potential importance of race during sentencing.

In short, then, judges throughout the state are well aware that punishment in general and sentencing in particular have been under intense legal and empirical scrutiny. Has this awareness led to a corresponding decline over time in the significance of race and greater uniformity of treatment? The analytic strategy described below will address this issue.

Analytic Procedures

Our choice of appropriate analytic techniques hinged on their ability to deal with three problems the data posed: collinearity, heteroskedasticity, and sample selection bias.

Intercorrelations among contextual variables posed problems when estimating their unique effects on sentencing decisions (see Appendix Table A). The statistical procedure we used provides a diagnostic that identifies collinear variables and indicates collinearity's effect on estimates and their variances (Belsley et al., 1980). Where collinearity appeared harmful,[7] we relaxed the statistical criterion and examined the finding for substantive significance.

A second problematic feature of the data was the violation of the homoskedasticity assumption by the first sentencing outcome, type of sentence. The use of ordinary regression in this instance would produce inefficient parameter estimates, so a weighted least squares procedure (Hanushek and Jackson, 1977:150–53) was preferred.[8] It computes estimates by weighting each observation of the dependent and independent variable, and then performs ordinary least squares regression on the transformed values. The resulting estimates are linear, unbiased, and best among a set of unbiased linear estimators.

Sample selection bias, the final issue of concern, occurs when analyzing a subsample of the population from which some observations have been excluded in a systematic manner (e.g., prisoners). Its extent varies by sample (cf. Berk, 1983, and Peterson and Hagan, 1984), and can be completely corrected only by modeling accurately all previous selection decisions. We could correct bias partially by using the two-stage estimation procedure recommended by Berk (1983) and used with success elsewhere (see Peterson and Hagan, 1984; Hagan and Parker, 1985). For this sample, partial correction proved to be a prerequisite for detecting many interactions and for accurately estimating the effects of sex and age.

The two-stage procedure involved estimating a selection equation and an equation of substantive interest. The selection equation estimated a logit model[9] for the total sample of convicted felons. The dependent variable was coded 0 if the obserservation was included in the second-stage substantive estimation and 1 if the observation was excluded. For example, where we were substantively interested in predicting prison terms, the dependent variable in the selection equation was 0 for felons who received a straight prison sentence and 1 for those who received either probation or a split sentence. For substantive equations predicting split sentence severity, the selection equation predicted the probability of receiving a split sentence (0) rather than probation or a straight prison term (1).

The logit model produced for each case its predicted probability of being excluded from the sample of substantive interest (e.g., the sample of straight prisoners). This predicted probability of exclusion, the hazard rate, was included in all substantive equations as a control for the effects of nonrandom selection. The substantive equations themselves used ordinary least squares regression procedures.

Analytic Strategy

The analysis first estimated the additive effects of contexts on sentencing. Since it was not technically possible to consider county, court, and temporal contexts together, we examined each separately. After estimating additive effects, we considered the possibility of interaction between contexts and offender attributes. Since we are interested in illustrating the contextual embeddedness of sentencing, we selected two key offender characteristics, race and offense. While gender, age, and employment status may sometimes be construed as legitimate considerations during sentencing, race is clearly an impermissible criterion on which to base punishment. In light of the continuing controversy about its role in Georgia and elsewhere, its examination here is particularly timely.

Unlike race, the offense is clearly an appropriate consideration during sentencing. Given its obvious legal relevance, and the considerable social homogeneity among sentencing judges, we might expect somewhat greater uniformity in the role it plays across counties, courts, and time. Hence, its inclusion here offers a more stringent test of contextual effects on sentencing.

To examine interactions, we constructed product terms between each context and the case variables of race and offense (see Allison, 1977, for a discussion of the appropriateness of this procedure). For example, the seven county variables were multiplied with race and the four offense vectors to produce a total of 35 interaction terms. The 11 court variables were multiplied with race and offense to produce 55 interaction terms.

To test for the significance of interaction, we compared the proportions of variance explained by two models. The first was an additive model that included all variables, and the second was an interactive model that included all variables and the product terms. The test for the significance of the increment in explained variance is

$$F = \frac{(R_i^2 - R_a^2) / (k_i - k_a)}{(1 - R_i^2) / (N - k_i - 1)} \, ,$$

where R_i^2 = the proportion of variance explained by the interactive model; R_a^2 = the proportion of variance explained by the additive model; k_i = number of regressors in the interactive model; k_a = number of regressors in the additive model; and N = total number of cases (Pedhazur, 1982:62).

Because sample sizes were large, we set the statistical criterion at a fairly rigorous level of significance. If the addition of product terms failed to increase the proportion of explained variance at the .005 level of significance, we concluded that the contexts in question do *not* condition the effect race and offense have on sentences. In contrast, if the increase in explained variance was significant (i.e., $p \le .005$), we concluded that the effects of race and offense are not uniform, but rather vary as a function of the specific context where sentencing occurs.

Where this was the case, we intensively examined significant interactions, that is, variables whose product term was significant. To offset the collinearity present in interactive models we chose a less stringent, although still acceptable, statistical criterion ($p \le .05$) for discussing interactions. The method used to estimate the conditioning effect of county, court, and temporal contexts will be described in greater detail in the next chapter. Briefly put, it involved deriving and comparing predicted outcomes for each group of offenders (e.g., black, white) whose sentences are affected by a specific context (e.g., urbanization).

Conclusion

In the following chapter, we report the results of analysis that determines whether the county factors of urbanization, economic conditions, and crime affect sentencing outcomes and differential treatment during sentencing. Chapter 4 focuses on court bureaucratization and judicial characteristics. In Chapter 5, we consider changes over time in the punitiveness of sentencing and in the significance judges attach to race and offense.

Notes

1. The data compiled by the Clerk of the Superior Court were not in a form amenable to quantitative analysis, because crucial variables such as the offense and sentence were alphabetically recorded. We could not therefore examine the population of over 60,000 cases and recode all information in machine-readable form. Initially, we drew a random sample of 1,500 cases, but incomplete records and resource constraints dictated we choose the most complete 400 of the original 1,500, of which 382 were used in this analysis (the remainder involved crimes not analyzed, such as incest and statutory rape). For DeKalb County, we devised a codesheet and, together with law students, transferred information obtained from a random sample of 1,115 prosecutor files. Reliability was enhanced by random checks on coder accuracy.

   Supplemental data from Fulton and DeKalb counties cover the period 1974–80. They had already been collected when the Department of Corrections offered us sentencing data from July 1980 through May 1985 and informed us that data collected prior to 1976 were unreliable. The updated file we received in 1985 included all persons sentenced in Fulton and DeKalb counties after July 1983 and an unspecified proportion of all cases sentenced before then who were currently in prison or on probation. Hence, probationers from Fulton and DeKalb counties are likely to be greatly overrepresented in 1974 and 1975, and slightly underrepresented between 1981 and 1983.

2. As Table 2.1 indicates, offenders who receive split sentences differ significantly from those receiving only prison. They are less likely to have been convicted of common-law violence and robbery, but more likely to have been convicted of burglary and drug offenses. Their offenses are much less serious than those committed by offenders sentenced only to prison, as are their prior records (i.e., fewer arrests and less likelihood of having been previously incarcerated in Georgia). In one respect, the social background of split sentence prisoners differs from that of offenders sentenced only to prison: they are more likely to be black. Based on these differences, we considered it inappropriate to analyze split and straight prisoners together.

3. The relationship between inequality and crime has recently been examined by Krahn et al. (1986) and Messner and Tardiff (1986), among others (e.g., Danziger and Wheeler, 1975; Braithwaite, 1979; Messner, 1980, 1982; Jacobs, 1981b; Blau and Blau, 1982; Balkwell, 1983; Bailey, 1984; Sampson, 1985b). Several works have focused particular attention on racial inequality (Blau and Blau, 1982; Balkwell, 1983; Blau and Golden, 1986; Golden and Messner, 1986; Messner and South, 1986), while others have examined the role of unemployment (for reviews, see Long and Witte, 1981; Parker and Horwitz, 1986; Cantor and Land, 1985; Chiricos, 1987). Though usually not the center of empirical attention, percent black is included in most models and typically is associated with higher crime rates (see, e.g., Blau and Blau, 1982; Messner, 1982, 1983; Balkwell, 1983; Bailey, 1984; Williams, 1984; Loftin and Parker, 1985; Sampson, 1985a; Messner and South, 1986; Messner and Tardiff, 1986).

4. Research that links crime with inequality, unemployment, and the racial composition of the community is noted in Footnote 3. For the relationship between crime and urbanization, see Krohn (1978) and Shelley (1981).

5. Index property and violent crime rates were available only for 1975, 1980, and 1984. As a result, offenders sentenced before 1980 were matched with 1975 data. Offenders sentenced between 1980 and 1984 were matched with 1980 data, while offenders sentenced in 1985 received 1984 crime data. In exploratory analysis, several other measures of crime produced estimates that were identical in direction but weaker in magnitude.

The first alternative measure of crime was an unlagged Index crime rate, matched by the exact or closest year of conviction. The second alternative was a weighted linear composite, whose weights were the standardized scoring coefficients obtained from principal component factor analysis. The composite consisted of the Index crime rate (matched by closest year of conviction) and two qualitative dimensions of crime: The percent of Index crime involving weapons (1979 figures) and the percent of black Index crime arrestees (1979 figures). The third alternative crime measure was a lagged Index crime rate that did not distinguish between property and violent crimes. It was based on data available for 1975, 1980, 1981, 1983, and 1984. Finally, we considered the lagged Index property crime rate and the lagged Index violent crime rate. Both measures used 1975, 1980, and 1984 figures. None of these alternatives predicted outcomes as well as the lagged Index crime rate, matched by type of offense (violent or property).

6. The increase in explained variance for type of sentence was .002 for an F ratio of 14.03 (5/27,526 df, $p \leq .005$). Interactions involving violent and drug offenders were significant, but effects differed only in magnitude. Violent offenders are slightly more likely to be incarcerated in courts with exact information than aggregated data, whereas drug offenders are slightly less likely to be incarcerated. The increase in explained variance for split sentence severity was .003 for an F value of 3.46 (5/4,179 df, $p \leq .005$), and only one interaction was significant. It indicates that the split sentences imposed on burglary offenders are slightly less severe in courts with exact information. Finally, the increase in prison sentence length was .0007 and not significant ($F = 2.17$, 5/4,930 df, $p > .005$).

7. Intercorrelations are potentially harmful if the condition index approaches or exceeds 20, the variance-decomposition proportions for two or more coefficients exceed .5, and one or more variables implicated in collinearity fail to reach statistical significance.

8. Logistic regression, used in preliminary additive analysis, typically yielded similar results. Weighted least squares was preferred for reasons of cost and interpretability of interactions. The weight is designed to increase the efficiency of the estimators. It gives greater weight to those observations whose error terms have smaller variances. The algorithm for the weight is $1/\sqrt{p * (1 - p)}$, where p = predicted value (Hanushek and Jackson, 1977:181). Predicted values greater than or equal to 1 were recoded .9999; those less than or equal to 0 were recoded .0001.

9. In the selection equation, we could also have estimated a linear probability (using weighted least squares) or a probit model. Despite different assumption about the distribution of error terms, these models tend to produce hazard rates that correlate at .9 or better with those obtained from logistic analysis (see Berk and Ray, 1982). We chose logit for reasons of cost, software availability, and ease of hazard rate computation.

3
The Community and Sentencing

In this chapter, we consider the effects that urbanization, economic conditions, and crime have on three sentencing decisions. As will become apparent, the direct influence these characteristics exert is neither strong nor consistent. Indeed, both the magnitude and direction of effects vary, depending on the sentencing decision in question. We also briefly consider an issue that has traditionally concerned criminologists, namely, the extent to which sentences vary as a function of offender attributes and behavior. Consistent with the previous literature, we find that judges give greater weight to factors that can explicitly be construed as legally relevant. Although social background attributes do affect outcomes, there is no evidence that offenders with fewer resources are consistently punished more severely. As was the case for county characteristics, the role case attributes play depends on the sentencing outcome under consideration.

Our second and more important task in this chapter is to determine whether county attributes condition the impact race and offense have on sentences. We find that some county characteristics such as the crime rate consistently and strongly affect race and offense differences in sentences, whereas others are less important conditioners of differential treatment. In most instances, however, an accurate understanding of the relationship between the community and sentencing requires that we consider county characteristics in conjunction with characteristics of the offender and the offense.

Finally, we examine the nature of the conditioning influence each county attribute exerts. The findings are complex, and many provide only isolated support for the expectations we derived from previous literature and theorizing.

The Community and Sentencing

Table 3.1 presents the results of regression equations that estimate the additive effects county variables have on sentencing. Several features of these results are noteworthy. First, county factors usually have quite modest effects on the type and severity of punishment. Most coefficients indicate relatively small changes in sentencing outcomes, and are often weaker than the effects of case characteris-

TABLE 3.1. Regression coefficients and related statistics, additive models for county contexts

Variable	Type of sentence			Split sentence severity			Prison sentence length		
	b	(SE)	β	b	(SE)	β	b	(SE)	β
Offender characteristics									
Type of crime									
Common-law violent	.04	(.01)	.048***	-1.26	(.68)	-.039	4.48	(.29)	.232***
Robbery	.24	(.01)	.241***	-1.15	(3.85)	-.032	-3.56	(.39)	-.154***
Burglary	-.02	(.01)	-.019***	-.71	(.57)	-.024	-1.82	(.20)	-.092***
Property theft/damage	-.13	(.00)	-.167***	2.89	(2.79)	.097	.36	(.25)	.019
Drug	-.13	(.01)	-.166***	.23	(1.40)	.007	.54	(.35)	.028
Offense seriousness	.02	(.00)	.510***	1.00	(.06)	.276***	.81	(.06)	.650***
Prior arrests				.35	(.07)	.089***	.08	(.02)	.037***
Prior incarceration				3.44	(.78)	.073***	1.07	(.26)	.041***
Sex	.08	(.01)	.071***	-.07	(2.23)	-.001	1.24	(.52)	.025*
Race	-.05	(.01)	-.046***	1.07	(1.05)	.027	-.38	(.26)	-.016
Age	.0007	(.00)	.014***	-.07	(.05)	-.031	.03	(.01)	.022**
Marital status				2.45	(.64)	.055***	.44	(.24)	.015
Employment status				-4.26	(.61)	-.100***	-.62	(.22)	-.024***
County variables									
Urbanization	3×10^{-7}	(.00)	.033***	-3×10^{-5}	(.00)	-.144***	-8×10^{-5}	(.00)	-.063***
Income standard deviation	2×10^{-6}	(.00)	.007	6×10^{-4}	(.00)	.067	1×10^{-4}	(.00)	.024
Racial income inequality	4×10^{-7}	(.00)	.003	-4×10^{-4}	(.00)	-.086*	-1×10^{-4}	(.00)	-.038*
Lagged unemployment rate	.005	(.00)	.019***	-1.19	(.22)	-.105***	.09	(.06)	.015
Percent black									
Under 25% vs. 25–49%	.03	(.01)	.028***	.85	(.71)	.022	-.66	(.31)	-.028*
Under 25% vs. 50+%	-.02	(.01)	-.010*	-.28	(1.40)	-.001	.06	(.48)	.002
Lagged Index crime rate	-2×10^{-6}	(.00)	-.007	-9×10^{-4}	(.00)	-.147***	4×10^{-5}	(.00)	.010***
Hazard rate				-52.36	(29.91)	-.205	-3.30	(2.89)	-.068
Intercept	.12	(.02)***		89.91	(26.19)***		-.97	(3.80)	
R^2	.196			.191			.667		
N	27,702			4,287			5,039		

*$p \le .05$; **$p \le .01$; ***$p \le .005$.

tics. There is one exception to this trend. County characteristics have noticeable effects on the severity of split sentences.

Second, the influence county factors exert is not consistent across the three sentencing decisions. For example, as counties become more urbanized, judges use imprisonment more often, but tend to impose split sentences that are less severe and prison sentences that are shorter than those imposed in rural counties. In general, the results suggest that we cannot safely extrapolate the effects of county variables from one sentencing outcome to another. A willingness to use prison, however slight, may be accompanied by a reluctance to impose long prison terms. Whether conscious or not, this strategy serves to balance notions of the punishment offenders deserve with pragmatic considerations such as prison overcrowding.

Finally, the results provide little support for expectations about the influence county factors have on sentences. As noted in Chapter 2, the previous literature led us to expect that income inequality would increase the punitiveness of sentences. We found this to be the case only for offenders sentenced to a combination of prison and probation. As county income standard deviation increases, split sentences become more severe. The more frequent trend is for inequality to have no effect on sentences or to result in more lenient sentences. For the initial decision to imprison, for example, neither indicator of inequality has a significant effect, and as racial inequality becomes more pronounced, split sentences become less severe and prison sentences slightly shorter.

Based on the previous literature, we had also expected that the presence of large economically subordinate populations would increase the punitiveness of sentences. We found only limited evidence that this is the case. As unemployment increases, so too does the use of imprisonment. Although small, this increase has its analog in aggregate-level analyses conducted by Greenberg (1977) and others (e.g., Jankovic, 1977; Yeager, 1979; Wallace, 1981; Box and Hale, 1982). However, as unemployment increases, split sentences become *less* severe and prison sentences remain unaffected. As a whole, then, there is no consistent evidence that unemployment fosters a general climate of punitiveness during sentencing.

The same conclusion applies to the size of the county's black population. Where blacks are a sizeable minority (25% to 49%), imprisonment is used more often than in counties with smaller black populations (less than 25%). In contrast, prison terms tend to be shorter in counties with a sizeable black population. Once blacks become a numerical majority, the situation changes. Imprisonment is used slightly *less* often, and neither split nor prison sentences differ from those imposed on counties with smaller black populations.

To some extent, these results are consistent with the argument that subordinate populations pose a greater threat where they are a substantial numerical minority. As Blalock (1967) suggested, once blacks become a numerical majority, their political clout may moderate punishment. In Georgia, however, political power in many predominantly black counties remains firmly in the hands of whites. As will become apparent later, vestiges of paternalism toward blacks, documented in historical works by Flynn (1983) and Ayers (1984), could account for the more sparing use of imprisonment in predominantly black counties.

Importantly, however, racial composition has a relatively modest effect on the use of prison. The size of the black population is often a less important predictor than the legally relevant factors of offense type and seriousness. Furthermore, the absence of an influence on split and prison sentences suggests that the threat hypothesis is of little use in explaining sentencing outcomes once the initial decision to imprison is made.

In sum, then, neither inequality nor large subordinate populations *consistently* foster more severe punishment. Instead, the expected harshness occurs only in isolated instances. Split sentences become more severe as income inequality increases, and the risk of imprisonment is greater in counties with a sizeable black population and high unemployment. More generally, however, inequality and large subordinate populations have either *no* effect on punishment or have a slight to moderate *negative* effect. The interactive analyses presented later in the chapter will determine the extent to which these general trends accurately reflect the sentences imposed on all offenders, regardless of race or offense.

The final community factor we considered was the county crime rate. Our general expectation was that as crime rates increase, so too will the punitiveness of sanctions. This expectation received no support. The magnitude of the county's crime problem has no significant effect on the use of imprisonment or on the length of prison terms, and as crime rates increase, split sentences tend to become less, not more, severe.

Case Characteristics and Sentencing

Table 3.1 also includes the effects offender and offense characteristics have on sentences. Note first that factors typically construed as legally relevant have a significant, if not strong, influence on sentencing. In general, judges impose more severe sanctions on offenders convicted of violent crimes or of serious offenses. In addition, split sentences are likely to be more severe and prison sentences longer for offenders who have prior records.

With the exception of burglary offenders (who typically receive more lenient than average treatment) and violent offenders, the sentences imposed on the remaining types of offenders are not uniformly severe or lenient. For example, robbery offenders are more likely to be imprisoned, primarily because of recently instituted mandatory minimums for armed robbery. Once imprisoned, however, they face split sentences that are less severe than average and prison terms that are shorter than average. Offenders convicted of drug crimes or of property theft and damage are more likely than average to be imprisoned. Yet, once incarcerated, their sentences do not differ significantly from the average.

In comparison with legally relevant factors, the social background attributes of offenders are less powerful predictors of sentencing outcomes. Although modest in magnitude, the findings do provide some evidence that offenders whose position implies fewer resources are more severely punished. Blacks are more likely than whites to be imprisoned, and unemployed offenders receive more severe split sentences and slightly longer prison sentences than their employed counterparts. It is important to emphasize, however, that harsher treatment of the relatively disadvantaged is not a consistent feature of sentencing in Georgia. Most notably, black offenders are more likely than white offenders to be incarcerated, but they apparently face no differential treatment in the severity of split sentences or in the length of prison terms.

We also found evidence that relatively advantaged offenders are more harshly punished. Older offenders are more likely to be imprisoned than younger offenders. This difference in treatment could be an artifact of the lack of controls for prior record, so it does not constitute strong evidence of discriminatory treatment. Two other findings provide stronger evidence that the relatively advantaged are treated with disproportionate harshness. Older offenders receive slightly longer prison terms than younger offenders, and married offenders tend to receive more severe split sentences than their unmarried counterparts. Both of these effects persist, even after prior record and employment status are controlled.

In sum, the effects that offense and social background attributes have on sentencing depend in part on the outcome under consideration. The legally relevant factors of offense seriousness and type generally exert a stronger influence than social background characteristics. Where social attributes affect outcomes, there is evidence that *for some sentencing decisions*, offenders with fewer resources (e.g., black, unemployed) are treated more severely. However, there is also evidence (e.g., for married and older offenders) that a comparatively advantaged position does not necessarily guarantee lenience during sentencing.

In the sections that follow, we determine whether the influence race and offense have on sentencing is relatively uniform across Georgia's communities. Put differently, we address the following questions about the relationship between the community and differential treatment: Does urbanization reduce race differences in treatment, as the previous literature suggests? Do inequality and large subordinate populations foster disproportionate harshness toward offenders who appear particularly threatening to the property interests of elites? Finally, do serious crime problems intensify punitiveness toward offenders who may be perceived as more dangerous to the community?

The Community as Context

To answer these questions, we added a set of interaction terms to the additive models that predicted each sentencing outcome. As noted in Chapter 2, these product terms were constructed by multiplying each county variable with offender race and type of offense. Table 3.2 presents the increases in explained variation produced by the addition of interaction terms, and identifies interactions that were significant at the .05 level.

TABLE 3.2. Significant county interactions and related statistics, by sentencing outcome[a]

Context	Type of sentence	Split sentence severity	Prison sentence
Urbanization	Burglary	Common-law violent	Common-law violent
	Property theft/ damage	Robbery Burglary	Robbery Burglary
Income standard deviation			Common-law violent
Racial income inequality	Common-law violent		Common-law violent
Lagged unemployment rate	Common-law violent Property theft/ damage	Drug	Common-law violent
Racial composition			
Under 25% vs. 25–49%	Common-law violent Burglary	Common-law violent Drug	
Under 25% vs. Over 50%	Common-law violent Burglary Property theft/ damage	Race Common-law violent Property theft/ damage	Common-law violent
Lagged crime rate	Race Common-law violent Burglary Property theft/ damage Drug	Property theft/ damage	Race Robbery
Additive model R^2	.1963	.1913	.6672
Interactive model R^2	.2058	.2121	.6760
F (degrees of freedom)	9.45 (35/27,651)	3.19 (35/4,231)	3.87 (35/4,983)

[a] Interactions significant at $p \leq .05$. All increments in explained variation significant at $p \leq .001$.

In this section, we compare the conditioning influence county variables have on differences in sentencing outcomes. We also identify the case and county factors involved in significant interaction. In the sections that follow, we focus on each county factor, and examine in detail the nature of its conditioning influence.

As Table 3.2 indicates, sentencing outcomes differ in their responsiveness to contextual interactions. Recall from Table 3.1 that, when considering a simple additive model, we concluded that county attributes are of limited importance in predicting the initial decision to imprison offenders, since they had little or no influence on the probability of imprisonment. A consideration of interaction reveals a quite different picture of their role during this part of the sentencing process. For the initial decision to imprison, community contexts exert their most pervasive influence *indirectly*, by conditioning the relevance of race and offense. Nearly half (15 of 35) of all possible interactions involving county variables were significant.

As noted earlier, county factors typically had modest additive effects on the severity of split sentences. As was the case for the probability of imprisonment, however, they also operate more subtly, by conditioning the relevance of race and offense. Their conditioning influence is relatively infrequent, however, and only 29% of all possible interactions reached statistical significance.

Finally, the results presented in Table 3.1 gave us the impression that county characteristics are not prominent determinants of the length of prison sentences. In contrast, Table 3.2 suggests that several county factors are nonetheless important, because they affect the magnitude of differential treatment. Again, however, interactions are relatively infrequent, and as was the case for split sentence severity, only 29% of all possible interactions were significant.

At the most general level, then, the results of interactive analyses support the conclusion that county characteristics condition the relevance of race and offense during sentencing. This is particularly the case for the initial decision to imprison offenders. Once offenders have been sentenced to prison, county factors condition differences in treatment less frequently. An accurate understanding of the role county characteristics play during sentencing requires, then, that we consider them in conjunction with characteristics of the offender and the offense. Similarly, an accurate estimate of the weight judges give to the offender's race and crime depends, at least in part, on the community where sentencing occurs.

If we shift our focus and consider which offender characteristics are typically involved in interactions, we find a surprising trend. The sentencing of common-law violent offenders is conditioned most consistently by county attributes. Thus, although one might expect a relatively high degree of consensus on the punishment these offenders should receive, analysis indicates that this is clearly not the case. Similarly, where one might expect greater diversity across communities (e.g., the sentencing of black or drug offenders), we find more uniform treatment.

We find another unexpected trend when focusing on the county contexts themselves. County factors that have received sustained theoretical and empirical attention, such as inequality and unemployment, do *not* appear to condition consistently the role race and offense play during sentencing. Rather, one of the strongest conditioners of differential treatment is the crime rate, an attribute that has typically been of theoretical importance as a phenomenon to be explained, rather than as an independent variable in its own right. Moreover, the crime rate has often been of empirical interest as a control variable that permits researchers to estimate accurately the role of theoretically more central attributes such as inequality. Here, we find that it plays a dual role during sentencing. The crime rate directly affects the severity of split sentences and, for each sentencing outcome, it affects differences in treatment based on both race and offense.

In the sections that follow, we examine the effect each county factor has on differences in punishment. Taking the interaction between the county crime rate and race as an example, we used the following procedure. First, we computed predicted sentences for four groups of offenders: (1) blacks sentenced in counties with the lowest crime rate; (2) blacks sentenced in counties with the highest crime rate; (3) whites sentenced in counties with the lowest crime rate; and (4) whites sentenced in counties with the highest crime rate. Predicted sentences are based on the metric coefficients from the interactive model for race, crime rate, and their product term. They permit us to assess the effect crime rates have on the sentences of black and white offenders, while holding constant at 0 the effects of the remaining variables and interactions.

Second, we computed the base predicted sentence offenders would receive at the mean value of the remaining variables and interactions. The base predicted sentence, which also uses metric coefficients from the interactive model, is the sum across the remaining variables, interactions, and intercept of the predicted effect of each variable, calculated at its mean. Finally, we added the four predicted outcomes derived above to this base predicted sentence. The resulting predicted sentences allow us to assess the conditioning effect crime rates have on race differences in treatment, while holding constant at the mean the effects of other variables and interactions.

The Conditioning Influence of Urbanization

Table 3.3 presents the predicted outcomes for offenders whose sentences are affected by urbanization. Column 1 shows the predicted sentences offenders receive in the least urbanized counties, and column 2 presents the predicted sentences they receive in the most urbanized counties. Column 3 is the difference between Columns 1 and 2, and indicates the direction and magnitude of the change in sentence produced by an increase in urbanization. Table 3.3 also presents the magnitude of *between-group* differences in sentences that occur in the least and the most urbanized counties. A comparison of these disparities provides an indication of whether differences in treatment increase or decrease with urbanization. We begin with an examination of differential treatment based on race, then consider differences based on type of offense.

URBANIZATION AND RACE DISCRIMINATION

Unlike previous research, we found no evidence that urbanization conditions race differences in treatment. Only one interaction approached statistical significance ($p = .06$, not presented), and it suggested two patterns. First, split sentences become less severe as urbanization increases, and the magnitude of this decline is greater for white than for black offenders (-7.5 vs. -0.6). Second, in rural counties the split sentences of white and black offenders are quite similar, whereas in heavily urbanized counties blacks receive more severe split sentences. Thus, urbanization increases race differences in treatment, and puts black offenders at a comparative disadvantage.

TABLE 3.3. Predicted outcomes for selected offenders, by urbanization[a]

Type of offender	Degree of urbanization		Effect of urbanization
	Least	Most	
Type of sentence			
Burglary	.393	.339	−.053*
Average	.429	.454	.025
Disparity	(.036)	(.115)	
Property theft/damage	.262	.424	.163***
Average	.429	.454	.025
Disparity	(.167)	(.030)	
Split sentence severity			
Common-law violent	53.450	46.175	−12.275*
Average	52.437	47.930	−4.507
Disparity	(1.013)	(1.755)	
Robbery	47.131	53.137	6.006*
Average	52.437	47.930	−4.507
Disparity	(5.306)	(5.207)	
Burglary	50.161	53.424	3.263*
Average	52.437	47.930	−4.507
Disparity	(2.276)	(5.494)	
Prison sentence length			
Common-law violent	17.953	13.971	−3.982*
Average	10.944	9.002	−1.942
Disparity	(7.009)	(4.969)	
Robbery	8.836	2.588	−6.248***
Average	10.944	9.002	−1.942
Disparity	(2.108)	(6.414)	
Burglary	8.436	9.411	1.005***
Average	10.944	9.002	−1.942
Disparity	(2.508)	(.439)	

[a] Predicted sentences capture the effects of urbanization, while holding constant at the mean the effects of the remaining variables.
*$p \leq .05$; ***$p \leq .005$.

Apart from this marginally significant result, the data analysis provides no other evidence that urbanization affects race differences in treatment. Regardless of the degree to which the county is urbanized, race differences persist, but are quite slight and are present only during the initial decision to imprison.

Several factors could account for the discrepancy between these findings and the results reported in earlier work (e.g., Pope, 1976; Hagan, 1977; Austin, 1981; Kempf and Austin, 1986; Miethe and Moore, 1986). Variation at the upper extremes of population size could have been insufficient to capture the total effect of urbanization. Sparsely populated counties are well represented in Georgia, but metropolitan areas, although densely populated, have populations that are small in comparison with Standard Metropolitan Statistical Areas (SMSAs) elsewhere. In 1980, for example, the most populous county in Georgia (Fulton) was 98% urban, but had a population of approximately 590,000 residents. The absence of very large populations may only partly account for the findings, however, since both Hagan (1977) and Austin (1981) conducted their work in comparably sized urban areas, and found that urbanization does affect race differences. It is also possible that, like inequality (Bailey, 1981) and race composition (Liska et al., 1981), urbanization has conditioning effects that differ by region or by country.

Still another explanation rests on more idiosyncratic factors. Site visits in rural and urban counties indicated that judges did not always fit the profiles typically associated with those jurisdictions. Some urban judges, for example, spoke in retributive terms, voiced discriminatory opinions about specific classes of offenders, and gave every indication of being "country magistrates." In contrast, some rural judges professed the moderate and objective stance more frequently associated with "big city" judges. It is possible that some of these personality traits could account for the patterns observed and for the fact that typical expectations were not realized in our analysis.

Relatedly, urban courts invariably consist of several judges. The resulting diffusion of responsibility may heighten the impact of personality, since individual judges may feel removed from public scrutiny and free to express more passionate and subjective decisions. In rural courts, judges function if not in isolation then in situations where responsibility is not diffused. In an effort to appear impartial, they may actually try to restrain prejudice and other, even salutary personal preferences.

A final explanation for our divergent findings involves differences in research design. We controlled for several other county factors that are confounded with urbanization. As will become apparent below, some of these factors condition race differences in sentencing. Thus, the differential treatment earlier studies found and attributed to urbanization could be due, at least in part, to the conditioning influence exerted by other community factors left uncontrolled in the analysis. Here we discovered that *net* of these other community factors, urbanization has no unique effect on race differences in sentencing. In Chapter 4, we will examine the possibility that court bureaucratization, another correlate of urbanization, exerts an independent influence and reduces race differences in treatment.

URBANIZATION AND OFFENSE DIFFERENCES

Urbanization does condition differential treatment, but these differences are based on the type of offense for which the offender was convicted. In general, we found little indication that the treatment of offenders is more evenhanded in urbanized counties. Rather, differential treatment persists or increases as counties become more urbanized. Moreover, when compared with their rural counterparts, urban counties appear to put certain offenders at an advantage, primarily by fostering greater than average lenience. This is the case in three instances: the initial decision to sentence burglary offenders to prison, the split sentences and prison terms imposed on common-law violent offenders, and the prison terms of robbery offenders.

First, as noted in Table 3.3, the average risk of imprisonment increases slightly with urbanization ($+2.5\%$). In contrast, the imprisonment risk faced by burglary offenders *decreases* slightly (-5.3%). Second, as urbanization increases, violent offenders experience greater than average decreases in both their split and prison sentences. For example, as urbanization increases, prison sentences on the average decline by 1.9 years. The corresponding decrease for violent offenders is approximately 4 years. Finally, with increasing urbanization, robbery offenders experience a greater than average decrease in prison sentences. In rural counties, their prison terms are 2.1 years shorter than the average, whereas in urban counties they receive prison terms that are nearly 6.5 years shorter than average.

Although unlikely, rural-urban differences in offense seriousness could account for this disproportionate lenience. That is, violent and property offenses may simply be less serious in urban counties. To explore this possibility, we examined the seriousness of offenses in the lowest and the highest quartiles of county urbanization. For prisoners, we also computed the mean number of charges, arrests, and prior incarceration. Appendix Table B presents these comparisons. Only for burglary did we find a slight tendency for less serious offenders to be concentrated in highly urbanized counties. The mean seriousness of burglary offenses in rural counties is 10.5, and the corresponding mean in urbanized counties is 10.3 ($p = .0001$). To control for this difference, we constructed a product term consisting of burglary, urbanization, and offense seriousness, entered it into the interactive model for type of sentence, and reanalyzed the data. Surprisingly, disproportionate lenience toward burglary offenders persists, but only for those convicted of *more* serious offenses. If sentenced in urban counties, these offenders are 15.7% less likely to be imprisoned than their counterparts sentenced in rural counties. In contrast, the risk of imprisonment faced by less serious burglary offenders, those convicted of attempts or of possessing burglary tools, increases with urbanization, and they are 10% *more* likely to be incarcerated if sentenced in an urban county.

For the remaining offenders who experience disproportionate lenience, we discovered that those sentenced in urbanized counties tend to be *more* serious than offenders sentenced in rural counties. For example, both violent and robbery offenders sentenced to prison in urban counties have significantly more conviction charges and prior arrests than those in rural counties. On the basis of legally relevant differences alone, then, we would expect their punishment to be disproportionately harsher. As noted above, however, the prison sentences imposed on these offenders become shorter with urbanization.

In general, then, the disproportionate lenience we found toward certain offenders does not appear to be due to rural-urban differences in offense and offender seriousness. The issue is far from settled, however, since rural and urban crime could differ qualitatively (e.g., victim-offender relationship) in ways that are not adequately reflected in our measure of offense seriousness.

Urbanization does not place all offenders at a comparative advantage. Indeed, it operates to the disadvantage of several types of property offenders, largely by fostering disproportionate severity. This is the case for the initial decision to imprison offenders convicted of property theft and damage, for the split sentences imposed on robbery and burglary offenders, and for the prison terms burglary offenders receive. As noted above, the average risk of imprisonment increases slightly with urbanization (+2.5%). In comparison, the risk of imprisonment for property theft and damage offenders increases much more dramatically, by 16.3%. Similarly, whereas the average split sentence becomes slightly less severe with urbanization (−4.5), it becomes more severe for offenders convicted of robbery and burglary (6.0 and 3.3, respectively). Finally, the average prison sentence declines with urbanization (−1.9 years), but increases by 1 year for burglary offenders.

Again, it is possible that these results reflect rural-urban differences in offense seriousness. More serious robbery and burglary offenders do indeed tend to be concentrated in urban counties. Robbery offenders who received split sentences in urban counties have significantly more conviction charges than similar offenders sentenced in rural counties (2.1 vs. 1.5, $p = .001$). Rural-urban differences are more common for burglary offenders sentenced to some form of imprisonment. They have significantly more charges and more arrests and are more likely to have been previously incarcerated in Georgia than their rural counterparts. On the basis of legally relevant factors, then, we would expect their punishment to be disproportionately harsher in urban counties.

To control for these differences, we followed the same procedure discussed above, and constructed product terms to capture interactions between type of crime, urbanization, and the legally relevant variables of conviction charges, prior arrests, and prior incarceration in Georgia. These product terms were added to the interactive model, and the data reanalyzed. The results remain virtually unchanged. As urbanization increases, robbery and burglary offenders continue to experience greater than average increases in their split sentences, and burglary offenders continue to experience greater than average increases in length of their prison sentences.

The findings for robbery and burglary are complex, and indicate that the precise role urbanization plays is a complicated function both of the offense and the specific sentencing outcome under consideration. Urbanization appears to foster disproportionate lenience toward burglary offenders during the initial decision to imprison, but disproportionate severity toward those for whom imprisonment was deemed appropriate. For robbery offenders, urbanization is associated with disproportionately harsh split sentences, but more lenient than average prison sentences. Although the underlying reason for these patterns is unclear, they provide clear evidence that, with the exception of violent offenders, urbanization places no group of offenders at a *consistent* advantage or disadvantage during sentencing.

The Conditioning Influence of Inequality

As noted in Chapter 2, we expected inequality to foster a disproportionate amount of punitiveness toward offenders whose criminality appears to pose a strong threat, whether symbolic or real, to established elite interests. Although not without controversy (cf. Jacobs, 1978, and Bailey, 1981), the previous literature provides some support for this expectation. Both Jacobs (1978) and Bailey (1981) found that inequality tends to increase imprisonment ratios for larceny offenders. In this section, we examine the differential treatment of property offenders. In addition, we consider the possibility that, as a group, black offenders may also appear more threatening than white offenders to the interests and hegemony of predominantly white elites and for this reason may be singled out for harsher punishment.

Despite their plausibility, these arguments received only isolated support. Moreover, the two measures of inequality condition sentences in quite different ways and are hardly interchangeable. We examine the results for income standard deviation first, then consider the conditioning influence exerted by a measure of inequality that is sensitive to race differences in income.

INCOME INEQUALITY AND DIFFERENTIAL TREATMENT

Table 3.4 presents the estimated outcomes for offenders whose sentences are affected by county income standard deviation. Contrary to expectation, this measure of income inequality has no effect on the imprisonment risk faced by either property or black offenders. Nor does it affect the split sentences and prison terms these offenders receive.

It is possible that the property theft and damage category is so broad that it obscures within-category differences in treatment. Aggregate level research (Jacobs, 1978; Bailey, 1981), for example, focused on larceny and vehicle theft. We therefore distinguished larceny offenders from three other types of property

TABLE 3.4. Predicted prison sentence length for selected offenders, by income inequality[a]

Type of offender	Amount of inequality		Effect of inequality
	Least	Most	
Common-law violent	15.009	23.062	8.053***
Average	10.319	11.619	1.300
Disparity	(4.690)	(11.443)	
White-collar theft[b]	9.292	13.780	4.488*
Average	10.241	10.766	.525
Disparity	(.949)	(3.014)	

[a] Predicted sentences capture the effects of inequality, while holding constant at the mean the effects of the remaining variables.
[b] Offenses within the category of property theft and damage for which more detailed analysis was conducted (see pp. 53–54). White-collar theft consists of forgery, fraud, and embezzlement.
*$p \leq .05$; ***$p \leq .005$.

offenses: vehicle theft; the white-collar offenses of forgery, fraud, and embezzle-ment; and a residual category of property damage and possession of stolen goods. We reanalyzed the data,[1] but found little evidence of disproportionate harshness. Inequality has no significant effect on the sentences imposed on offenders con-victed of larceny, vehicle theft, property damage, or the possession of stolen goods. Instead, it conditions only the prison terms imposed on white-collar offenders. This result, also presented in Table 3.4, confirms our original expecta-tion. As inequality increases, prison sentences increase by 6 months for the aver-age offender, but 4.5 years for white-collar offenders. In counties with low income inequality, white-collar offenders are treated little differently from the average offender. In counties experiencing high income inequality, however, their prison sentences are 3 years longer than average.

We explored the possibility that white-collar offenders are treated more harshly in unequal counties because they tend to be more serious than those sentenced in counties with low inequality. In particular, they have significantly more prior arrests (5.4 vs. 2.9, $p = .03$) and more conviction charges (2.7 vs. 1.4, $p = .0001$). Yet, even if we control for these differences, the patterns noted above persist.

In short, then, only for white-collar offenders sentenced to prison do we find evidence that inequality fosters disproportionate harshness. Inequality has no implications for the sentences imposed on the remaining types of property offenders. Furthermore, the results are also inconsistent with expectations about the punishment of common-law violent offenders. On the basis of Jacobs' (1978) argument, we thought that inequality would either have little effect on the sen-tences of these offenders or foster disproportionate lenience. Following Jacobs' reasoning, this would occur because elites presumably are relatively uncon-cerned with crimes that typically involve lower class victims and do not directly threaten their own interests and life-style.

Apparently, this is not the case. As inequality increases, so too do the prison sentences imposed on violent offenders. On the average, prison sentences increase by 1.3 years with growing inequality, but for violent offenders the com-parable increase is 8 years. This difference in treatment becomes clearer if we compare disparities in treatment within the least and the most unequal counties. In counties with relatively little inequality, common-law violent offenders receive prison sentences that are 4.7 years longer than average. In highly unequal counties, their prison sentences are nearly 11.5 years longer than average.

This counterintuitive trend could be an artifact of differences in the seriousness of violent offenses. Violent crimes committed in highly unequal counties may simply be more serious than those committed in less unequal counties. In two respects, this is indeed the case. Violent offenders in highly unequal counties are convicted of significantly more charges than those sentenced in less unequal counties (1.9 vs. 1.4, $p = .0001$), and they are also more likely to have been incarcerated in Georgia (.21 vs. .15, $p = .03$). Since these differences could account for the disproportionately harsh treatment they receive in highly unequal counties, we reanalyzed the data, after controlling for interactions between type of crime, income inequality, and the two legally relevant factors (i.e., number of conviction charges and prior incarceration). The patterns noted above persist. As income inequality increases, violent offenders continue to experience a greater than average increase in the length of their prison sentences.

As within-group inequality becomes more pronounced, then, the tolerance level for common-law violence appears to decline. In the absence of victimization data, we cannot tell whether the threat such violence poses to elites is symbolic or real, but whether grounded in reality or not, white elites in these contexts may fear victimization by lower class whites. These fears may prompt the harshness toward violent offenders we found.

In sum, we found comparatively little punitiveness where we expected it, that is, toward black and property offenders sentenced in highly unequal counties. There was only one exception to this trend: the disproportionately longer sentences imposed on white-collar offenders in counties experiencing high income inequality. Moreover, we found disproportionate harshness where we least expected it, among common-law violent offenders sentenced to prison in highly unequal counties.

RACIAL INCOME INEQUALITY AND DIFFERENTIAL TREATMENT

An inequality measure sensitive to race differences in income has been used to predict metropolitan violence (Blau and Blau, 1982:121–2) and police force size and expenditures (Jackson and Carroll, 1981; Carroll and Jackson, 1982). In this section, we examine its influence on sentencing. Where racial inequities are pronounced, we expected that the criminality of certain offenders (e.g., black, property) would appear to threaten established interests. Consequently, these offenders may be singled out for disproportionately harsher treatment than their less threatening counterparts.

Table 3.5 presents the predicted outcomes for offenders whose sentences are significantly affected by racial income inequality. As was the case for income standard deviation, most results are unanticipated. Racial inequality has no effect on the sentences of either property or black offenders. Since earlier findings led us to suspect variation within the property theft and damage category, we again distinguished larceny offenders from those convicted of vehicle theft, white-collar offenses, and a residual category of property damage and possession of stolen goods. Reanalysis of the data provides evidence of disproportionate harshness toward two groups of property offenders. These results are also presented in Table 3.5.

First, as racial inequality increases, larceny offenders experience a greater than average increase in imprisonment risk (+16.9% vs. +5.0%). As a result, the comparative leniency they experience declines as counties become more racially unequal. Second, racial inequality puts offenders convicted of damaging property or possessing stolen goods at a slight disadvantage. As racial income inequality increases, split sentences become less severe on the average (−3.2), but more severe for these property offenders (+10.2). This difference in treat-

TABLE 3.5. Predicted outcomes for selected offenders, by racial income inequality[a]

| | Amount of inequality | | Effect of |
Type of offender	Least	Most	inequality
Type of sentence			
Common-law violent	.592	.552	−.041*
Average	.422	.441	.019
Disparity	(.170)	(.111)	
Larceny[b]	.169	.316	.169*
Average	.356	.405	.050
Disparity	(.187)	(.089)	
Split sentence severity			
Damage property/possess stolen goods[b]	38.202	48.376	10.174**
Average	48.986	45.821	−3.165
Disparity	(10.784)	(2.555)	
Prison sentence length			
Common-law violent	20.463	14.335	−6.128**
Average	11.663	9.716	−1.947
Disparity	(8.800)	(4.619)	

[a] Predicted sentences capture the effects of inequality, while holding constant at the mean the effects of the remaining variables.
[b] Offenses within the category of property theft and damage for which more detailed analysis was conducted (see pp. 53–54).
*$p \le .05$; **$p \le .01$.

ment persists even after we conducted additional analyses, controlling for the slight, nonsignificant tendency for offenders convicted of damaging property or possessing stolen goods to be more serious in highly unequal counties.

As was the case for income standard deviation, the results indicate differential treatment during the sentencing of common-law violent offenders. Recall that as income inequality increased, violent offenders experienced a significantly greater than average increase in their prison sentences. Unlike income standard deviation, racial inequality does not put violent offenders at a disadvantage. Instead, where racial inequities are pronounced, violent offenders are treated with disproportionate lenience in two respects. First, as racial inequality increases, the risk of imprisonment increases slightly on the average (+1.9%), but declines (−4.1%) for violent offenders. Second, as racial inequality increases, prison sentences on the average decline by nearly 2 years, whereas for common-law violent offenders they decline by 6 years. Thus, lenience toward violent offenders increases as racial inequality becomes more pronounced.

Initially, we thought that this ostensibly preferential treatment of violent offenders could be due to differences in the seriousness of crimes they commit. To explore this possibility, we compared the seriousness of violent offenders in two groups of counties: those at the highest quartile of racial inequality and those at the lowest quartile of racial inequality. For the sample as a whole, there were no significant differences in seriousness. For offenders sentenced to prison, however, violent offenders in racially unequal counties tend to have *more* conviction charges than do violent offenders sentenced in counties with less racial inequality (1.9 vs. 1.4, $p = .0001$). On the basis of this difference, we would expect harsher treatment. In actuality, we found disproportionate lenience.

In sum, as was the case for a "color-blind" measure of inequality, there is little evidence that racial inequality operates to the disadvantage of property or black offenders. The only exceptions involve the risk of imprisonment for larceny offenders and the split sentences imposed on offenders convicted of damaging property or possessing stolen goods. As racial inequality increases, these offenders receive disproportionately more severe sanctions. These findings provide the only support we found for the argument that greater inequality lowers the tolerance level for property crime and results in harsher punishment. The data are consistent with a related argument, however, that elites are presumably indifferent to crimes involving lower class victims. Common-law violent offenders are afforded disproportionate lenience in racially unequal counties.

The Conditioning Influence of Unemployment

As noted earlier, the relationship between unemployment and punishment has been examined only at the aggregate level of analysis, where researchers (e.g., Greenberg, 1977; Jankovic, 1977) have noted a tendency for unemployment to increase the use of imprisonment. Here, we examine the effect of unemployment on the sentencing of individual offenders. In particular, we are interested in determining whether unemployment fosters disproportionate harshness toward offenders who may be perceived as potentially threatening and troublesome (e.g., black, property). As will become apparent below, unemployment operates in a more complex fashion than originally anticipated. Whereas it puts some property offenders at a disadvantage, unemployment appears to foster disproportionate *lenience* toward others.

Table 3.6 presents the predicted outcomes for offenders whose sentences are conditioned by the unemployment rate. In several respects, the results are unanticipated. County unemployment does not affect race differences in treatment. Nor does it affect the punishment imposed on offenders convicted of robbery or burglary. In fact, unemployment fosters disproportionate *lenience* toward offenders convicted of property theft and damage. In counties facing high levels of unemployment, these offenders are much *less* likely than average to be imprisoned (.310 vs. .549). As unemployment increases, the average probability of imprisonment increases by 15%, whereas the probability that property theft and damage offenders will be imprisoned increases by only 4.1%.

Given the counterintuitive nature of this result, we examined the property theft and damage category more closely. We disaggregated larceny from three other types of property offenses (vehicle theft, white-collar offenses, and property

TABLE 3.6. Predicted outcomes for selected offenders, by unemployment[a]

Type of offender	Level of unemployment		Effect of unemployment
	Lowest	Highest	
Type of sentence			
Common-law violent	.556	.635	.079*
Average	.399	.549	.150
Disparity	(.157)	(.086)	
Property theft/damage	.269	.310	.041**
Average	.399	.549	.150
Disparity	(.130)	(.239)	
Larceny[b]	.197	.426	.229*
Average	.354	.456	.102
Disparity	(.157)	(.030)	
Damage property/possess stolen goods[b]	.284	.191	−.093**
Average	.354	.456	.102
Disparity	(.070)	(.265)	
Split sentence severity			
Drug	48.741	45.791	−2.950*
Average	55.544	38.424	−17.120
Disparity	(6.803)	(7.367)	
Prison sentence length			
Common-law violent	15.045	23.729	8.684***
Average	10.338	11.691	1.353
Disparity	(4.707)	(12.038)	
Adjusted prison sentence length[c]			
Less serious violent	9.316	4.703	−4.613***
More serious violent	22.544	33.966	11.422
Disparity	(13.228)	(29.263)	

[a] Predicted sentences capture the effects of unemployment, while holding constant at the mean the effects of the remaining variables.
[b] Offenses within the category of property theft and damage for which more detailed analysis was conducted (see pp. 53–54).
[c] Adjusted prison sentences are predicted outcomes derived after controlling for the fact that violent offenders in counties with high unemployment are convicted of more serious crimes than those convicted in counties with low unemployment rates.
*$p \leq .05$; **$p \leq .01$; ***$p \leq .005$.

damage or possession of stolen goods). The results of the reanalysis, also presented in Table 3.6, indicate that the effect noted for the broad category of property theft and damage is misleading, because it does not reflect accurately the effect unemployment has on the sentences of two types of property offenders. Notice that as unemployment increases, larceny offenders face a *greater* than average risk of being imprisoned (22.9% vs. 10.2%). Thus, within the broad category of property theft and damage, larceny offenders are at a disadvantage in counties with high unemployment.

This disproportionately harsh treatment cannot be due to any tendency for larcenies committed in counties with high unemployment to be more serious than those committed in counties with low unemployment. Indeed, just the opposite is the case. The mean seriousness of larcenies in counties with little unemployment is 7.8, whereas the corresponding mean in counties at the top quartile of unemployment is slightly but significantly smaller (7.5). Despite the less serious nature of their crimes, then, larceny offenders are treated with disproportionate harshness in situations where the unemployment rate is high. This pattern is consistent with the argument that unemployment lowers the tolerance level for property crime.

In contrast, however, high unemployment puts other property offenders at an *advantage*, primarily by fostering disproportionate lenience. Although the average risk of imprisonment increases with growing unemployment (+10.2%), offenders convicted of damaging property or possessing stolen goods experience a *decline* (−9.3%). As was the case for larceny, this pattern cannot be due to differences, by unemployment, in offense seriousness because no significant differences exist.

In short, then, unemployment appears to put larceny offenders at a disadvantage. However, this pattern provides the only support we found for the argument that greater unemployment lowers the tolerance level for property crimes and results in harsher punishment. The remaining results are inconsistent with that argument. Either unemployment does not affect sentencing outcomes (e.g., for robbery or burglary) or it fosters an unexpected lenience.

Two other findings remain to be discussed, namely, the differential treatment of common-law violent and drug offenders. The prior literature offered little guidance in formulating expectations about the treatment of these offenders. Following the reasoning developed earlier for inequality, we might expect unemployment to have little effect on the sentences of violent offenders. To the extent that victims tend to be lower class or unemployed themselves, their victimization may not appear particularly threatening, even in contexts where unemployment rates are high. As shown in Table 3.6, unemployment does indeed affect the treatment of violent offenders, but in a more complex manner than originally anticipated.

As unemployment increases, the risk of being incarcerated increases for violent offenders. Importantly, however, the increase is much smaller than average (7.9% vs. 15%). To a limited extent, this difference is consistent with the presumption of elite indifference to crimes involving lower class victims. The findings for prison sentence length are not consistent with such a presumption, however, because unemployment puts violent offenders at a comparative *disadvantage*. As unemployment increases, prison sentences, on average, increase almost 1.4 years. For common-law violent offenders, the increase is nearly 9 years. In counties with relatively little unemployment, then, a willingness to imprison violent offenders is accompanied by a reluctance to impose long prison terms. A much different pattern emerges if we focus on counties that face serious unemployment problems. Here, violent offenders are only slightly more likely than average to be imprisoned, but once imprisoned, their sentences are nearly 12 years longer than average. Thus, in counties with high unemployment rates, a comparative reluctance to imprison violent offenders is accompanied by disproportionate harshness toward those offenders for whom imprisonment was deemed appropriate.

In short, regardless of the level of unemployment, we find disproportionate harshness toward violent offenders. What varies by unemployment is the *form* that harshness takes, whether a much greater risk of imprisonment or much longer than average prison terms. The reason for these patterns remains unclear. To some extent, particularly for offenders sentenced to prison, they reflect differences in the seriousness of violent offenses committed in counties with low and high unemployment. Violent offenders sentenced to prison in counties with high unemployment are significantly more serious than those sentenced in counties with relatively little unemployment. The mean seriousness of their offenses is 21.4, whereas the mean seriousness of violent offenses in counties at the lowest quartile of unemployment is significantly lower (19.2, $p = .05$). After controlling for the interaction between violent crime, unemployment, and offense seriousness, disproportionate harshness toward violent offenders changes noticeably, and is confined only to more serious violent offenders (i.e., those whose offenses are a standard deviation above the mean). The adjusted prison sentences, presented in Table 3.6, indicate two quite different patterns. As unemployment increases, the prison sentences imposed on serious violent offenders increase by 11.4 years, whereas those imposed on less serious violent offenders *decline* by 4.6 years.

Finally, what of the sentencing of drug offenders? To the extent that property crime and drug use are linked, unemployment might foster disproportionate harshness toward these offenders. This appears to be the case, but only for offenders receiving split sentences. As unemployment increases, drug offenders receive a smaller than average reduction in severity of their split sentences (-2.9 vs. -17.1). Note that in counties with the least unemployment, the split sentences of drug offenders are less severe than average, whereas in counties with serious unemployment problems, their split sentences are more severe than average. This trend is not due any tendency for more serious drug offenders to be concentrated in counties with high unemployment. Instead, drug offenders in these contexts tend to have significantly *fewer* conviction charges (1.4 vs. 1.7, $p = .02$). At least for offenders who received split sentences, then, unemployment appears to lower the tolerance level for drug offenders.

In sum, if we consider the results as a whole, they provide little support for original expectations about the relationship between unemployment and differential treatment during sentencing. The size of the unemployed population has no effect on the sentencing of black, burglary, or robbery offenders, and unemployment puts at least one group of property offenders at an advantage, namely, those convicted of damaging property or possessing stolen goods. Only the findings for larceny and, indirectly, for drug offenders support the argument that unemployment lowers the tolerance level for property crime, and fosters harsher punishment.

The limited effect of unemployment may be due in part to the levels at which analysis was conducted. Most research has focused exclusively on the aggregate level, and the relationship between unemployment and punishment may only be discernible there. For example, Berk et al. (1980) found that, although his or her own employment history affects an offender's risk of recidivating, the county unemployment rate does not. Other recent work (Marenin et al., 1983; Galster and Scaturo, 1985; Chiricos, 1987) suggests that, even within the aggregate level, the unemployment rate has quite different effects on both crime and punishment, depending on whether one focuses on the nation as a whole or on individual states. Although none of these studies deals with precisely the same issue addressed here, they nonetheless lead us to suspect that the role played by unemployment may be heavily. contingent on the level at which both it and punishment are measured.

It is also possible that unemployment has a more localized effect than we considered during the analyses. It may affect the sentences of other "troublesome" offenders, in particular those who are male, younger, single, or unemployed (Box and Hale, 1982). Unemployment may have an even more complex effect, and condition the treatment of offenders who, by virtue of their social position, may be seen as doubly problematic, for example, blacks who are also male, single, younger, or unemployed. In the next section we examine these possibilities, and find that they have some merit.

UNEMPLOYMENT AND THE TREATMENT OF OTHER PROBLEMATIC OFFENDERS

To explore in greater detail the role of county unemployment, we developed two additional interactive models. Table 3.7 presents the relevant product terms in these models, and provides an overview of the results. Interactive model I is designed to determine whether unemployment affects difference in treatment based on offender characteristics other than race and type of crime; interactive model II considers higher order interactions.

Our first interest centers on whether unemployment intensifies harshness toward other offenders who may be perceived as troublesome or problematic, namely, offenders who are male, younger, unmarried, or unemployed, have prior records, or were convicted of serious offenses. To explore this possibility, we constructed product terms between the lagged unemployment rate and the remaining characteristics of the offender and offense. For the sample as a whole, these terms test for interactions between the unemployment rate and offender sex, age, and offense seriousness. For prisoners, we were also able to construct interactions between the unemployment rate and several other characteristics, including marital status, employment status, prior arrests, and prior incarceration.

TABLE 3.7. Product terms and related statistics for additional analyses involving lagged unemployment rate

Interactive model	Type of sentence	Split sentence severity	Prison sentence length
Model I			
Unemployment rate ×	Sex*	Sex	Sex
	Age*	Age	Age
	Offense serious-ness	Employment sta-tus	Employment sta-tus
		Marital status	Marital status
		Offense serious-ness	Offense serious-ness*
		Prior arrests	Prior arrests
		Prior incarcera-tion	Prior incarcera-tion
R^2 original interactive model	.2058	.2121	.6760
R^2 interactive model I	.2061	.2133	.6768
F (degrees of freedom)	3.48* (3/27,648)	.92 (7/4,224)	1.76 (7/4,976)
Model II			
Unemployment rate ×	Race × Age*	Race × Age	Race × Age
	Race × Sex	Race × Sex	Race × Sex
	Sex × Age	Sex × Age	Sex × Age
Unemployment rate × Offender employment status ×		Sex	Sex
		Race	Race
		Age	Age
		Marital status**	Marital status***
		Offense serious-ness	Offense serious-ness
		Prior arrests*	Prior arrests
		Prior incarcera-tion	Prior incarcera-tion
		Type of crime	Type of crime***
R^2 interactive model I	.2061	.2133	.6768
R^2 interactive model II	.2064	.2179	.6787
F (degrees of freedom)	3.48* (3/27,645)	2.22** (11/4,213)	2.67** (11/4,965)

$*p \leq .05; **p \leq .01; ***p \leq .005.$

For each sentencing outcome, we added these product terms as a set to the original interactive model, and tested for the significance of the increase in explained variance. Only for type of sentence did the increase approach an acceptable level of statistical significance ($p \leq .05$). For prisoners, we found no evidence that unemployment conditions differences in treatment based on these other social background or legally relevant factors. Put differently, these factors have essentially the same effect on split and straight prison sentences, regardless of the level of unemployment in the county.

TABLE 3.8. Predicted risk of imprisonment for selected offenders, by county unemployment[a]

Type of offender	Level of unemployment		Effect of unemployment
	Lowest	Highest	
Female	.288	.289	.001*
Male	.339	.482	.143
Disparity	(.071)	(.193)	
Younger (19 years old)	.323	.490	.167*
Older (35 years old)	.344	.425	.081
Disparity	(.021)	(.065)	

[a] Predicted imprisonment probabilities capture the effects of unemployment, while holding constant at the mean the effects of the remaining variables.
*$p \leq .05$.

The same cannot be said for the initial decision to imprison, where unemployment conditions the role played by offender sex and age. Table 3.8 presents the predicted outcomes for these offenders. Both patterns suggest that high unemployment intensifies harsher treatment of troublesome populations, here, offenders who are younger or male. As unemployment increases, so too does the risk that both male and female offenders will be imprisoned. Note, however, that the increase for males is significantly more pronounced (+14.3%) than that experienced by females (+0.1%). In counties with little unemployment, males are 7.1% more likely than females to be imprisoned, whereas in counties with high unemployment they are 19.3% more likely to be imprisoned.

A similar, but weaker, pattern characterizes differences in treatment by age. We estimated the risk of imprisonment for two groups of offenders, those age 19 and those age 35 years when convicted. As unemployment increases, the risk of being incarcerated increases more for younger offenders (+16.7%) than for older offenders (+8.1%). If sentenced in counties with little unemployment, both groups of offenders run essentially the same risk of being imprisoned, but if sentenced in counties with serious unemployment problems, younger offenders are 6.5% more likely than older offenders to be incarcerated.

Taken together, these results provide evidence that, at least for the initial decision to imprison, unemployment exacerbates the disproportionately harsh treatment selected groups of troublesome offenders (i.e., male, young) receive. Again, however, the absence of controls for prior record requires that we consider these trends as tentative, rather than definitive.

In the second part of the analysis, we posed a more complex relationship between unemployment and sentencing, namely, one in which its effect on differential treatment depends on a combination of offender characteristics. For example, we sought to determine whether unemployment results in disproportionately harsh treatment of selected subgroups of offenders who, because of their social position, may be seen as doubly problematic (e.g., black males, young males, young blacks). In addition, the availability of data on the employment status of prisoners allowed us to determine whether selected subgroups of the unemployed are also singled out for harsher treatment, namely, those whose social background or previous behavior may be perceived as problematic. We are interested, then, in the sentences of unemployed offenders who are also male, single, or young, have serious prior records, or were convicted of serious offenses.

For the sample as a whole, three higher order product terms were possible. The first term tests for interactions among unemployment, race, and age. It allows us to estimate the effect the unemployment rate has on the sentences imposed on four groups of offenders: young blacks, young whites, older blacks, and older whites. The second higher order product term provides us with an indication of the effect the unemployment rate has on the sentences of black males, white males, black females, and white females. The final higher order product term tests for interactions among unemployment rate, sex, and age, and will tell us whether young males are singled out for particularly harsh treatment in counties facing serious unemployment.

We constructed several other interaction terms for offenders who received a split sentence or straight prison term. These terms test for interactions among the lagged unemployment rate, the offender's employment status, and the remaining social background and legally relevant factors (sex, race, age, marital status, offense seriousness, prior arrests, prior incarceration, and type of crime).

We added all higher order product terms as a set to interactive model I, and tested for the significance of the increase in explained variance. Table 3.7, presented earlier, includes the coefficients of determination, and notes which product terms reached statistical significance. Increases for each sentencing outcome are slight, although significant, and, due in part to multicollinearity, only a minority of product terms are significant.

Table 3.9 presents the predicted outcomes for subgroups of offenders whose sentences are conditioned by unemployment. Although there are some exceptions, harsher treatment of potentially troublesome offenders usually increases with unemployment. We discuss the findings for type of sentence first, then focus on offenders receiving split sentences and straight prison terms.

Two features of the findings for type of sentence are noteworthy. First, controlling for higher order interactions does not change the tendency for increases in unemployment to foster disproportionately harsh treatment of male offenders. Second, age differences in imprisonment risk are contingent not only on the extent of unemployment in the county, but also on the race of the offender. As expected, unemployment fosters the largest increase in imprisonment risk for younger blacks (+18.6%), and the smallest increase for older whites (+10.8%). Where unemployment is pronounced, then, young blacks are the most likely to be incarcerated, whereas older whites are the least likely to be imprisoned.

For offenders receiving split sentences, the situation differs, and there is little support for expectations. Most notably, split sentences, whether imposed on married or single, employed or unemployed offenders, become *less* severe as unemployment increases. Thus, unemployment does not appear to foster harsher

TABLE 3.9. Predicted outcomes for selected offenders, by county unemployment[a]

| Type of offender | Level of unemployment | | Effect of unemployment |
	Lowest	Highest	
Type of sentence			
Female	.375	.416	.041*
Male	.441	.591	.150
Disparity	(.066)	(.175)	
Young black	.460	.646	.186*
Young white	.400	.542	.142
Disparity	(.060)	(.104)	
Older black	.474	.588	.114*
Older white	.419	.527	.108
Disparity	(.065)	(.061)	
Split sentence severity			
Unemployed single	56.566	40.828	−15.738**
Employed single	52.037	31.959	−20.078
Disparity	(4.529)	(8.869)	
Unemployed married	56.512	42.812	−13.700**
Employed married	53.369	44.698	−8.671
Disparity	(3.143)	(1.886)	
Unemployed/prior arrests	57.277	42.098	−15.179*
Employed/prior arrests	53.477	38.893	−14.584
Disparity	(3.800)	(3.205)	
Unemployed/no prior arrests	55.947	40.837	−15.110*
Employed/no prior arrests	51.554	33.030	−18.524
Disparity	(4.393)	(7.807)	
Prison sentence length			
Less serious	3.182	1.481	−1.701**
More serious	17.700	23.688	5.988
Disparity	(14.518)	(22.207)	
Unemployed violent	16.527	24.038	7.511***
Employed violent	15.355	19.172	3.817
Disparity	(1.172)	(4.866)	
Unemployed property theft/damage	8.927	11.914	2.987*
Employed property theft/damage	8.637	13.221	4.584
Disparity	(.290)	(1.307)	

TABLE 3.9. (*Continued*)

Type of offender	Level of unemployment		Effect of unemployment
	Lowest	Highest	
Prison sentence length (*Continued*)			
Unemployed single	10.625	12.631	2.006***
Employed single	10.107	12.340	2.233
Disparity	(.518)	(.291)	
Unemployed married	11.456	15.256	3.800***
Employed married	10.472	11.702	1.230
Disparity	(.984)	(3.554)	

[a] Predicted outcomes capture the effects of unemployment, while holding constant at the mean the effects of the remaining variables, including all first- and higher-order interactions.
*$p \leq .05$; **$p \leq .01$; ***$p \leq .005$.

split sentences for any subgroup of offenders. A closer look at the results reveals further disconfirmatory evidence. Of the four groups of offenders—unemployed single, unemployed married, employed single, and employed married—we originally thought that the "doubly disadvantaged" single and unemployed offenders would fare the worst. They do not. In fact, as unemployment increases, they received more lenient treatment than both employed and unemployed married offenders. We also expected that the "double advantaged" employed and married offenders would receive the most lenience. This is also not the case. Instead, they experience the smallest reduction in severity of split sentence (-8.7).

In sum, then, judges appear to reserve the most severe split sentences for unemployed offenders and, within this category, do not distinguish strongly between those who are single or married. This is the case, regardless of the level of unemployment in the county. Conversely, judges are inclined to be more lenient toward employed offenders and, within this category, single out employed offenders who are single for the most lenient treatment. Increases in county unemployment intensify this pattern, so that differences in the treatment of employed single and employed married offenders are most pronounced in counties that face serious unemployment problems.

The second significant interaction involves the conditioning influence of unemployment on offenders who vary in prior record and employment status. It provides clearer support for expectations. As the unemployment rate increases, doubly advantaged offenders, those who are employed and have no prior arrests, experience the greatest reduction in severity of split sentences (-18.5). Regardless of unemployment, these offenders receive the least severe split sentences, but lenience toward them becomes more pronounced as county unemployment problems become more severe.

The final set of findings presented in Table 3.9 focuses on the conditioning influence unemployment exerts on differences in prison sentence length. With few exceptions, they provide additional evidence that unemployment intensifies harsher treatment of troublesome offenders. In general, prison sentences are longer in counties experiencing serious unemployment. Moreover, several groups of offenders—the more serious, violent, and unmarried—are singled out for disproportionately harsh treatment. First we examine the legally relevant factors of offense seriousness and type; then we consider interactions involving marital status.

The findings for offense seriousness represent the predicted sentences offenders would receive if their offenses were one standard deviation below or above the mean in seriousness. In counties with low unemployment, more serious offenders receive prison terms that are 14.5 years longer than those imposed on less serious offenders, whereas in counties with high unemployment rates, their prison sentences are 22 years longer. These differences in treatment became more pronounced because, as unemployment increases, the prison sentences imposed on more serious offenders increase by 6 years, while those imposed on less serious offenders *decrease* by 1.7 years.

Also as expected, unemployment intensifies the harsher treatment of unemployed common-law violent offenders. As the unemployment rate increases, the prison sentences imposed on these offenders increase by 7.5 years, while those imposed on violent offenders who are employed increase by 3.8 years.

The result for property theft and damage offenders is contrary to expectation, and suggests that unemployment puts property offenders who are employed at a comparative disadvantage. As unemployment increases, their prison sentences increase by over 4.5 years, while those imposed on unemployed property theft and damage offenders increase by only 3 years.

The final interaction involves unemployment and the marital status of offenders. As expected, we find that the doubly advantaged offender, one who is both married and employed, experiences the smallest increase in prison sentence length (+1.2 years). However, as was the case for split sentences, unemployment does *not* put the doubly disadvantaged offender, one who is both unemployed and single, at the greatest disadvantage. Instead, it is the unemployed *married* offender who experiences the largest increase in prison sentence (+3.8 years). Regardless of unemployment in the county, these offenders receive the longest prison sentences, and harshness toward them increases as counties experience more unemployment. In counties with the highest unemployment rate, their prison sentences are 3.5 years longer than those imposed on offenders who are married but unemployed.

In sum, then, the additional analysis reported above provides evidence that unemployment conditions differences in treatment based on factors other than race and type of offense (i.e., sex and offense seriousness). More importantly, the conditioning influence of unemployment often becomes apparent only after considering offender characteristics in combination with one another. Whether alone or in combination with other offender characteristics, however, unemployment does *not* appear to condition race differences consistently. That is, we found no evidence of disproportionate harshness toward blacks who occupy other potentially troublesome positions, that is, those who are also male, single, or unemployed, have prior records, or were convicted of serious offenses. The one exception is young blacks, who are more likely than older blacks or whites to be incarcerated if sentenced in counties with high unemployment.

It is more often the case that unemployment conditions differences in the treatment of certain types of unemployed offenders. Although there are exceptions, unemployed offenders are usually treated more harshly than employed offenders, and the county's unemployment rate intensifies this harsher treatment. Also as expected, we found that unemployment intensifies harsher treatment of the doubly problematic offender, that is, one who not only is unemployed but also has been convicted of violence or has a prior arrest record. Finally, we found instances where unemployment fosters more lenient treatment of the doubly advantaged, most notably, employed offenders without prior arrests who received split sentences.

These trends are far from universal, however. As the results for marital status indicate, offenders with inconsistent statuses, such as unemployed and married, risk the longest prison sentences, and this trend becomes particularly apparent in counties with high unemployment. Also, at least in one instance (split sentences), unemployment increases the amount of *lenience* accorded offenders with inconsistent statuses (employed and single).

In short, unemployment plays an important role during sentencing, but it is a complex one. To properly estimate it requires that we consider many offender characteristics, alone and in combination with one another. In general, however, unemployment tends to exacerbate disproportionate harshness toward potentially troublesome offenders, particularly the unemployed. It does so not only by fostering disproportionately more severe punishment, but also by extending these offenders comparatively less lenience.

The Conditioning Influence of Racial Composition

The size of minority populations has been linked with more serious crime (e.g., Blau and Blau, 1982; Messner, 1983) and, independently of crime, with more coercive social control responses (e.g., Jacobs, 1979; Huff and Stahura, 1980; Williams and Drake, 1980; Bailey, 1981; Liska et al., 1981). Here, we examine whether coerciveness is disproportionately imposed.

As previous work suggests (Williams and Richardson, 1976), the sentences imposed on black offenders may be disproportionately harsh in counties where they are a substantial minority and presumably more threatening to whites. In contrast, the presence of a black majority may moderate differences in treatment for two very different reasons. As Blalock (1967) suggested, the political power of blacks is likely to be greater where they constitute a numerical majority. In Georgia, blacks have political influence in few of the 19 counties that contain a majority black population. One is urban Fulton County, which comprises the major part of the city of Atlanta. In 1980, 51.5% of the county was black, as were the mayor, police commissioner, and nearly 20% of the city council. Blacks also appear to be politically influential in rural Hancock and Burke counties. Since 1984, the chair of the Hancock county commission is black, as are 37.5% of the commissioners. The majority of commissioners in Burke county are also black. In both counties, the current costs of discriminating against blacks may outweigh any benefits white elites may gain.

In most predominantly black counties, however, blacks hold few if any positions of political power. In these contexts, other factors may reduce race differences in treatment or foster lenience toward black offenders. Vestiges of paternalistic attitudes, documented in historical work (Flynn, 1983; Ayers, 1984), may lead judges to tolerate, if not expect, a certain amount of black criminality. Conversely, judges may expect more of whites, by virtue of their membership in a traditionally dominant racial group. There may be a sense, particularly in counties where whites are a numerical minority, that "they should know better." The tolerance level for white criminality may also be lower than comparable crime by blacks simply because white victims are involved (Myrdal, [1944], 1964). Presumably, the victimization of whites poses a greater threat than black intraracial crime to the position and interests of white elites. Finally, black criminality may be perceived as less threatening because black populations are both segregated and dispersed in rural counties (Spitzer, 1975; Liska et al., 1981).

In short, then, several factors — paternalism, more stringent expectations for whites, greater value placed on protecting white victims, and dispersed residential segregation — may foster disproportionate lenience toward black offenders in predominantly black counties. As will become apparent below, these arguments have some merit. First, we compare counties with low (under 25%) and moderate (25–49%) black populations. Then, we consider sentencing in predominantly black counties.

THE SIZEABLE BLACK MINORITY AND SENTENCING

Table 3.10 presents the estimated outcomes for offenders whose sentences are affected by the presence of a substantial black minority in the county. The results provide no support for the argument that black offenders are seen as particularly threatening in these counties. Indeed, there are no significant race differences in sentencing.

Moreover, the sentences of property offenders are also apparently unaffected by the presence of a sizeable black population. The one exception involves the disproportionately harsher treatment of burglary offenders, which is consistent with the expectation of a lower tolerance level for property offenders. Since these differences in treatment are relatively small, support is not particularly strong. As the size of the black population shifts from small to moderate, the imprisonment risk increases by 3.4% for the average offender, but by 7.5% for burglary offenders.

As before, we were concerned that the breadth of the property theft and damage category might obscure within-category differences in treatment. As a result, we disaggregated this category and reanalyzed the data. Disproportionate

TABLE 3.10. Predicted outcomes for selected offenders in counties with a sizeable black minority[a]

	Percent black		Effect of
Type of offender	Under 25%	25–49%	percent black
Type of sentence			
Common-law violent	.581	.577	−.004***
Average	.416	.450	.034
Disparity	(.165)	(.127)	
Burglary	.345	.421	.075***
Average	.416	.450	.034
Disparity	(.071)	(.029)	
Split sentence severity			
Common-law violent	60.158	56.166	−3.992**
Average	51.982	52.063	.081
Disparity	(8.176)	(4.103)	
White-collar theft[b]	40.101	45.118	5.017***
Average	48.111	47.738	−.373
Disparity	(8.010)	(2.620)	
Damage property/possess stolen goods[b]	49.099	41.678	−7.421***
Average	48.111	47.738	−.373
Disparity	(.988)	(6.060)	
Drug	46.515	49.746	3.231*
Average	51.982	52.063	.081
Disparity	(5.467)	(2.317)	
Prison sentence length			
White-collar theft[b]	10.097	11.299	1.202*
Average	10.415	10.010	−.405
Disparity	(.318)	(1.289)	

[a] Predicted sentences capture the effects of percent black, while holding constant at the mean the effects of the remaining variables.
[b] Offense within the category of property theft and damage for which more detailed analysis was conducted (see pp. 53–54). White-collar theft consists of forgery, fraud, and embezzlement.
$*p \leq .05; **p \leq .01; ***p \leq .005$.

harshness toward property offenders occurs only for white-collar offenders who received some form of imprisonment. As counties contain more blacks, split sentences on the average become slightly less severe (−0.4), and prison sentences become slightly shorter (−0.41 years). For offenders convicted of white-collar theft, the situation is different, because they experience an increase in both split sentence severity (+5.0) and prison sentence length (1.2 years).

These patterns do not appear to be due to the tendency for serious white-collar thefts to be concentrated in counties with sizeable black minorities. In these contexts, white-collar offenders are indeed convicted of more offenses than those

sentenced in counties with few blacks (2.0 vs. 1.4, $p = .0001$), but disproportionate harshness remained virtually unchanged after we controlled for this
difference. We constructed a product term for white-collar crime, race composition, and number of conviction charges, added it to the interactive model, and
reanalyzed the data. As the size of the black population increases, white-collar
offenders continue to experience a greater than average increase in the severity
of split sentences and the length of their prison terms.

In short, the results for burglary and white-collar theft are consistent with the
expectation of a lower tolerance level for property crime in counties with a sizeable black population. Yet the presence of such a population appears to put
another group of property offenders at an *advantage*. Recall that, on the average,
the shift from small to moderate concentrations of black residents is accompanied by a slight decline in the severity of split sentences (-0.37). In contrast,
offenders convicted of damaging property or possessing stolen goods experience
a significantly greater decline in split sentence severity (-7.4).

What of the sentencing of drug and common-law violent offenders? In the
absence of explicit guidance from theory or empirical work, we applied the argument developed for unemployment to racial composition. The link between drug
and property crime may make drug offenders appear particularly threatening in
counties with a substantial black minority, and for this reason they may receive
disproportionately harsh punishment. The findings for split sentence severity are
consistent with this reasoning. Drug offenders experience a greater than average
increase in split sentence severity as counties contain more blacks. Although
slight, this trend is particularly anomalous, since less serious drug offenders tend
to be concentrated in counties with a sizeable black minority. The average seriousness of drug offenses in counties with few blacks is 7.8, whereas in counties
containing a substantial black population, drug offenses are slightly but significantly less serious (7.1, $p = .01$).

The final set of findings involves the differential treatment of common-law violent offenders. We expected the presence of a sizeable black minority to put these
offenders at a comparative advantage for two reasons. First, violent crimes typically involve the victimization of lower class persons, which may not be perceived as a direct threat to elite interests. Second, in counties with a sizeable
black minority, a larger proportion of violent offenses may involve blacks. For
reasons noted above, perceptions about the differential value of victims and
divergent expectations about the behavior of blacks and whites may foster
lenience toward violent offenders.

In general, the results are consistent with these arguments. It is interesting to
note that the findings resemble those reported earlier for racial inequality, where
the treatment of common-law violent offenders became increasingly more
lenient as racial inequities became more pronounced. The same pattern obtains
for violent offenders sentenced in counties with a substantial black population.
They experience greater than average declines in both the risk of imprisonment
and the severity of split sentences. For example, as counties contain more blacks,
the average imprisonment risk increases by 3.4%, but decreases slightly (-0.4%)

for violent offenders. It merits emphasis that, although these findings are consistent with the reasoning presented above, they represent very small differences in treatment.

This lenience toward violent offenders does not appear to be due to any tendency for less serious violent offenders to be concentrated in counties with a sizeable black minority. For the total sample, as well as the subset of offenders receiving split sentences, there are no significant differences in the seriousness of violent offenses committed in the two groups of counties.

As expected, then, the presence of a sizeable black minority in the county fosters disproportionately harsh punishment for selected property offenders (e.g., burglars, white-collar thieves) and for drug offenders. Also as expected, offenders convicted of violent crime are at a slight advantage. In contrast, the size of the black population does not affect the sentences imposed on most property offenders, and for offenders convicted of damaging property or possessing stolen goods, the presence of a substantial black population fosters disproportionate lenience, rather than the expected severity.

SENTENCING IN PREDOMINANTLY BLACK COUNTIES

Table 3.11 presents the predicted outcomes for offenders whose sentences are affected by the presence of a black numerical majority in the county. Note first that there are significant race differences in treatment, with the presence of a black majority fostering a slight, although disproportionate, lenience toward black offenders. Also as expected, the presence of a black majority puts certain property offenders at a disadvantage, and fosters disproportionate lenience toward common-law violent offenders.

First, the findings provide evidence of disproportionate lenience toward black offenders. In comparison with counties having few blacks, the split sentences of whites in predominantly black counties are slightly more severe ($+1.6$), whereas those imposed on blacks are slightly less severe (-3.8). This pattern cannot be due to the tendency for less serious black offenders to be concentrated in predominantly black counties, because *both* black and white offenders tend to have significantly fewer conviction offenses than their counterparts sentenced in counties with relatively few blacks.

Second, the findings indicate disproportionate harshness toward several types of property offenders. As noted above, burglary offenders are at a slight disadvantage in counties with moderate black populations. The same is true in predominantly black counties. As counties become predominantly black, the average risk of imprisonment decreases by 2.1%, while burglary offenders experience a 2% *increase* in imprisonment risk.

Similarly, offenders convicted of property theft and damage receive disproportionately more severe split sentences in predominantly black counties. If we focus only on counties with few blacks, we see that their split sentences are slightly less severe than average (3.8), whereas in predominantly black counties their split sentences are *more* severe than average (1.9). After disaggregating this

TABLE 3.11. Predicted outcomes for selected offenders in predominantly black counties[a]

	Percent black		Effect of
Type of offender	Under 25%	Over 50%	percent black
Type of sentence			
Common-law violent	.581	.531	−.050*
Average	.416	.394	−.021
Disparity	(.165)	(.137)	
Burglary	.345	.367	.021*
Average	.416	.394	−.021
Disparity	(.071)	(.027)	
Property theft/damage	.268	.205	−.062**
Average	.416	.394	−.021
Disparity	(.148)	(.189)	
Larceny[b]	.228	.130	−.098***
Average	.356	.313	−.042
Disparity	(.128)	(.183)	
Split sentence severity			
Black	53.126	49.280	−3.846*
White	50.455	52.039	1.584
Disparity	(2.671)	(2.759)	
Common-law violent	60.158	51.842	−8.316**
Average	51.982	51.255	−.727
Disparity	(8.176)	(.587)	
Property theft/damage	48.187	53.186	4.999*
Average	51.982	51.255	−.727
Disparity	(.456)	(5.270)	
Damage property/possess stolen goods[b]	42.704	55.806	13.102***
Average	47.577	49.050	1.473
Disparity	(4.873)	(6.756)	
Prison sentence length			
Common-law violent	17.999	17.029	−.970*
Average	10.991	11.827	.836
Disparity	(7.008)	(6.202)	

[a] Predicted sentences capture the effects of percent black, while holding constant at the mean the effects of the remaining variables.
[b] Offense within the category of property theft and damage for which more detailed analysis was conducted (see pp. 53–54).
*$p \leq .05$; **$p \leq .01$; ***$p \leq .005$.

category, we found that significant differences in treatment occur only for offenders convicted of damaging property or possessing stolen goods. These offenders experience a greater than average *increase* in the severity of their split sentences (+13.1 vs. +1.5). As is typically the case, this result cannot be attributed to differences in the seriousness of property offenses committed in predominantly black counties. Indeed, these offenders tend to have slightly but significantly *fewer* conviction charges in predominantly black counties (1.3 vs. 1.6, $p = .001$). Hence, we would expect judges to sentence these offenders more leniently. In actuality, they sentenced more severely.

It is important to emphasize that only for decisions about split sentences does the presence of a black majority put property offenders at a disadvantage. For the initial decision to imprison, these offenders are at a slight *advantage*. As noted earlier, the average risk of imprisonment declines slightly (-2.1%) as blacks become the majority in the county. The corresponding decline for offenders convicted of property theft and damage is 6.2%.

Again, we took a closer look at subgroups within the broad category, and found that this general difference reflects the differential treatment of one subgroup, namely, those convicted of larceny. This result, also presented in Table 3.11, indicates that, as blacks become a numerical majority, larceny offenders experience a greater than average decrease in imprisonment risk (-9.8% vs. -4.2%). Initially, we thought this result might be due to the tendency for less serious larceny offenders to be concentrated in predominantly black counties. In counties with few blacks, the mean seriousness of larcenies is 7.7, whereas in predominantly black counties, larcenies are slightly but significantly less serious (7.5, $p = .01$). To control for this difference, we constructed a product term consisting of the larceny vector, offense seriousness, and race composition, added it to the interactive equation, and reanalyzed the data. The results (not presented) indicate that the lenience reported in Table 3.11 is confined to the sentences imposed on more serious larceny offenders. As counties become predominantly black, the risk that serious larceny offenders will be imprisoned declines by 15.4%, whereas the risk faced by less serious larceny offenders remains unchanged.

The presence of a black majority also has implications for the sentencing of violent offenders. As noted in the previous section, moderate-sized black populations put these offenders at an advantage, primarily by fostering greater than average lenience. The same is true for violent offenders sentenced in predominantly black counties. They experience significantly greater than average declines in imprisonment risk (-5.0% vs. -2.1%), split sentence severity (-8.3 vs. -0.73), and length of prison sentences (-0.97 vs. $+0.84$ years).

We would expect these trends if violent crimes committed in predominantly black counties are less serious than those committed in counties with few blacks. To some extent, this might be the cases. For the sample as a whole, the crimes violent offenders commit in predominantly black counties are significantly less serious than those committed in counties with few blacks (10.3 vs. 12.7, $p = .0001$). For split prisoners, violent offenders in predominantly black counties are convicted of less serious crimes (7.7 vs. 11.0, $p = .0001$) and fewer offenses (1.2 vs. 1.5, $p = .003$) than their counterparts in counties with few blacks. The same patterns describe violent offenders sentenced only to prison. To control for these differences, we constructed product terms consisting of the violent crime vector, race composition, and offense seriousness. For prisoners, we also included a product term involving the number of conviction charges. In

subsequent reanalysis of the three sentencing decisions, we found that disproportionate lenience toward violent offenders in predominantly black counties does
not diminish. Indeed, it appears to be slightly *greater* for more serious than less
serious violent offenders.[2]

In sum, then, when compared with their counterparts sentenced in counties
with few blacks, black and violent offenders sentenced in predominantly black
counties are at an advantage. However, although the presence of a black majority
puts selected property offenders (e.g., burglars, offenders convicted of property
damage or possession of stolen goods) at a slight disadvantage, disproportionate
harshness toward property offenders is the exception rather than the rule. The
presence of a black majority typically has no effect on the sentencing of property
offenders (e.g., robbers, vehicle thieves, white-collar thieves). Furthermore, for
the initial decision to imprison, we found evidence of disproportionate *lenience*
toward serious larceny offenders in predominantly black counties. In short, then,
there is no strong evidence of a lower tolerance level for property offenders in
counties with large black populations.

Three general trends emerge from this consideration of the link between racial
composition and sentencing. First, the size of the black population affects race
differences only in predominantly black counties and only for offenders sentenced to a combination of prison and probation. As expected, the presence of a
black majority operates to the advantage of black offenders, by fostering more
lenient treatment.

Second, as counties contain more blacks, certain property offenders (e.g., burglars, white-collar thieves) experience disproportionately harsh sentences. This
is particularly the case in counties where blacks are a sizeable minority. The
differential treatment of property offenders is less pronounced once blacks
become a numerical majority. Differences in treatment are usually small, and
must be placed within the broader context of sentences imposed on the remaining
property offenders. For example, offenders convicted of robbery and vehicle
theft are treated no differently than the average offender. Furthermore, in at least
two instances, the presence of a large black population fosters disproportionate
lenience. Taken as a whole, then, the findings provide no strong or consistent evidence that a large black population fosters disproportionately harsh treatment of
most types of property offenders.

The final trend involves the sentences imposed on common-law violent
offenders. As counties contain more blacks, these offenders are at a comparative
advantage because they receive greater than average lenience. This comparative
advantage becomes particularly strong once blacks become a numerical majority,
and it persists regardless of differences, by racial composition, in the seriousness
of violent offenses.

The Conditioning Influence of County Crime

As noted earlier, researchers have been interested in studying crime rates for
two reasons: to predict them from structural conditions in the community or to
control for their effects in predicting social control responses. Here, we empha-

size crime as a potential determinant of differential treatment during sentencing. Expectations were fairly simple: we thought that differences in treatment would be greater in counties that experience serious crime problems, and that high crime rates would foster disproportionate harshness toward offenders who may appear particularly threatening (e.g., black, violent).

As will become apparent, these expectations were far too simple. Rising crime rates increase race differences in treatment, but do not invariably put blacks at a disadvantage. In addition, although crime rates also intensify differences in treatment based on offense, the nature of these differences is a complicated function of the specific offense and the sentencing outcome under consideration. Table 3.12 presents the predicted outcomes for offenders whose sentences are affected by county crime rates. We discuss interactions involving race first, then consider interactions based on offense.

CRIME AND RACE DIFFERENCES

Although never large, race differences in the use of prison are more pronounced in counties with high crime rates. As crime rates increase, the risk of imprisonment increases for both white and black offenders, but this increase is greater for blacks (+16.7% vs. +8.0%). Note that in counties with little crime, blacks and whites run similar risks of being imprisoned. For counties that face serious crime problems, however, blacks are nearly 13% more likely than whites to be imprisoned.

These patterns are particularly interesting in light of race differences in the seriousness of offenders sentenced in high crime counties. As shown in Table 3.13, the offenses committed by both black and white offenders are significantly *less* serious in counties with high crime rates, which leads us to expect that treatment will be more lenient in high crime counties. In actuality, treatment becomes harsher, and this is particularly the case for black offenders.

The situation is quite different once offenders have been sentenced to prison. High crime rates put white, not black, offenders at a comparative disadvantage. Focusing for a moment on counties with relatively little crime, note that the sentences imposed on whites are 1.2 years *shorter* than those imposed on blacks. In contrast, where crime rates are high, the sentences of whites are approximately 1.5 years longer than those of comparable blacks. In two senses, then, white offenders are at a disadvantage. Their prison sentences are slightly longer than those imposed on blacks in the same high crime contexts, as well as being longer than those imposed on both black and white offenders in low crime rate jurisdictions.

We would expect these trends if more serious offenders are concentrated in counties with high crime rates. In most instances, this is not the case. As Table 3.13 indicates, both black and white offenders in high crime counties tend to be *less* serious than those sentenced in counties with low crime rates, and the one exception (more prior arrests) is true for both black and white offenders.

In short, then, judges in counties with little crime are consistently, although slightly, harsher toward black offenders: they are more likely to imprison blacks

TABLE 3.12. Predicted outcomes for selected offenders, by crime rate[a]

| | Crime rate | | Effect of |
Type of offender	Lowest	Highest	crime rate
Type of sentence			
Black	.368	.535	.167***
White	.326	.406	.080
Disparity	(.042)	(.129)	
Common-law violent	.437	1.115	.678***
Average	.395	.574	.178
Disparity	(.042)	(.541)	
Burglary	.373	.443	.070*
Average	.395	.574	.178
Disparity	(.022)	(.131)	
Property theft/damage	.299	.195	−.104***
Average	.395	.574	.178
Disparity	(.014)	(.268)	
Larceny[b]	.290	.069	−.221***
Average	.382	.368	−.014
Disparity	(.092)	(.299)	
Vehicle theft[b]	.522	.486	−.036*
Average	.382	.368	−.014
Disparity	(.140)	(.118)	
Drug	.262	.777	.515***
Average	.395	.574	.178
Disparity	(.133)	(.203)	
Split sentence severity			
Property theft/damage	48.725	52.603	3.878**
Average	50.839	56.237	5.398
Disparity	(2.114)	(3.634)	
Vehicle theft[b]	57.968	38.829	−19.139*
Average	49.091	45.932	−3.159
Disparity	(8.877)	(7.103)	
White-collar theft[b]	48.162	31.088	−17.074***
Average	49.091	45.932	−3.159
Disparity	(.929)	(14.844)	
Damage property/possess stolen goods[b]	39.105	51.491	12.386***
Average	49.091	45.932	−3.159
Disparity	(9.986)	(5.559)	

TABLE 3.12. (*Continued*)

Type of offender	Crime rate		Effect of crime rate
	Lowest	Highest	
Prison sentence length			
Black	10.929	14.374	3.445***
White	9.694	15.857	6.163
Disparity	(1.235)	(1.483)	
Robbery	8.314	7.170	−1.144**
Average	10.109	13.640	3.531
Disparity	(1.795)	(6.470)	
White-collar theft[b]	11.615	10.379	−1.236***
Average	10.118	12.903	2.785
Disparity	(1.497)	(2.524)	

[a] Predicted sentences capture the effect of the crime rate, while holding constant at the mean the effects of the remaining variables.
[b] Offenses within the category of property theft and damage for which more detailed analysis was conducted (see pp. 53–54). White-collar theft consists of forgery, fraud, and embezzlement.
*$p \leq .05$; **$p \leq .01$; ***$p \leq .005$.

than whites, and they tend to impose longer prison sentences on blacks than on comparable whites. Judges in counties with serious crime problems also treat blacks differently when making these two decisions, but blacks are at a disadvantage only for the first decision, when they are more likely than white to be imprisoned. They are at a comparative advantage for decisions about sentence length, when they are sentenced to slightly shorter terms in prison than whites.

TABLE 3.13. Race differences in seriousness, by county crime rate

Race of offender	Measure of seriousness	County crime rate[a]			
		Lowest quartile		Highest quartile	
Type of sentence					
Black	Offense seriousness	10.35	(3540)	8.52	(2628)***
White	Offense seriousness	10.00	(3338)	8.00	(4287)***
Prison sentence length					
Black	Offense seriousness	16.86	(1049)	10.97	(529)***
	Number of conviction charges	2.07	(1049)	1.36	(529)***
	Prior arrests	2.39	(1019)	3.07	(509)***
	Prior incarceration	.24	(1049)	.24	(529)
White	Offense seriousness	17.82	(767)	10.33	(515)***
	Number of conviction charges	2.05	(767)	1.44	(515)***
	Prior arrests	2.75	(747)	3.41	(498)**
	Prior incarceration	.21	(767)	.19	(515)

[a] Number of offenders in parentheses.
T-test significant at $p \leq .01$; *T-test significant at $p \leq .005$.

CRIME AND OFFENSE DIFFERENCES IN TREATMENT

As crime rates increase, so too does the risk of imprisonment, the severity of split sentences, and the length of prison terms. However, several types of offenders are at a particular disadvantage. Most notably, as counties face more serious crime problems, violent and drug offenders experience significantly greater than average increases in their risk of being imprisoned. The situation is different for property offenders. For example, an increase in crime rates has little effect on the imprisonment risk faced by burglary offenders. Indeed, serious crime problems foster disproportionate *lenience* toward offenders convicted of property theft or damage. As crime rates increase, the risk of imprisonment on the average increases by 17.8%, while the risk of imprisonment that property theft and damage offenders face *decreases* by 10.4%. A slightly more detailed picture emerges if we examine the broad category of property offenses more closely. Although disproportionate lenience accurately describes the treatment of most offenders within this category, some offenders receive more lenience than others. This is true for the initial decision to imprison larceny offenders and it occurs as well as for the split sentences imposed on white-collar and vehicle theft offenders. The final instance of lenience toward property offenders involves robbery offenders sentenced to prison. As crime rates increase, prison sentences on the average increase as well, by nearly 3.5 years. The prison sentences imposed on robbery offenders, in contrast, *decline* by 1 year.

There is one notable exception to this general trend for rising crime rates to foster disproportionate lenience toward property offenders. Those convicted of damaging property or possessing stolen goods are at a comparative *disadvantage* if sentenced in counties with high crime rates because their split sentences become more severe ($+12.4$).

We examined the possibility that these differences in treatment, whether involving lenience or harshness, might reflect differences in the seriousness of crimes committed in counties with high crime rates. Offenses seldom differ significantly in seriousness, and the most existing differences in no way jeopardize the findings noted above.[3] The one exception involves larceny offenders in the sample as a whole, whose offenses are slightly but significantly less serious in counties with high crime rates (7.4 vs. 7.6, $p = .001$). To a great extent, this legally relevant difference accounts for the disproportionate lenience these offenders experience in counties with high crime rates. We added a product term to the interactive model that consisted of the larceny vector, crime rate, and offense seriousness, and reanalyzed the data. The disproportionate lenience attenuates markedly, and as crime rates increase the imprisonment risk faced by larceny offenders declines by only 3.6% rather than 22%.

In sum, high violent crime rates appear to create a punitive climate toward violent offenders. In contrast, high property crime rates do not have as simple an influence on sentencing. Although high property crime rates appear to put drug offenders at a disadvantage, particularly for the initial imprisonment decision, few property offenders experience the harshness we expected. Indeed, most experience greater than average lenience. Since we could not match crime rates with the offender's conviction charge exactly, instances of lenience could reflect variation in specific crime rates. For the moment, however, we have evidence that increases in the general property crime rate are seldom accompanied by disproportionately harsh punishment, unilaterally applied against all types of property offenders.

Summary

In this chapter, we addressed two general questions about the relationship between the community and sentencing: first, what effects do county attributes have on punishment, and second, to what extent do these attributes determine the relevance of race and the offense during sentencing? As we have seen, the answers to these questions are complex and depend, in part, on the sentencing decision under consideration. In this section of the chapter, we summarize the major findings and offer some comments on their significance.

The most commonly studied sentencing outcomes, imprisonment probability and prison sentence length, were only occasionally affected in a direct way by county characteristics, and the direction of that effect varied by decision. Most notably, judges in urban counties were slightly more willing than their rural counterparts to use prison, but reluctant to impose long prison terms on those incarcerated. County characteristics had consistent, direct effects only on the severity of split sentences, and for several reasons this is not surprising. In comparison with other sentencing decisions, split sentences seemed to be the most susceptible to the influence of local preferences and perceptions. In site visits, some judges and other court authorities indicated that the split sentence was symbolically important. Recognizing that prisons were overcrowded, judges specified harsh terms with the knowledge that the bulk of the punishment would be carried out on probation. The press, however, frequently emphasized the total term, thus giving the impression that the sentence was quite punitive. Not all authorities, however, thought that this symbolic benefit was important enough to outweigh the practical difficulties of implementation. In the final analysis, it appeared that court authorities disagreed about the utility of combining imprisonment and probation. It is possible, then, that varying opinion on the symbolic benefit ascribed to, and the practical problems associated with, the split sentence accounts for the direct effects that county variables had on this sentencing outcome.

In analyzing the direct relationship between sentencing and the community, we expected that sanctions would be more severe in counties characterized by pronounced inequality, a sizeable percentage of black or unemployed residents, and relatively high crime rates. In actuality, we found little evidence to support these expectations. Using two indicators of inequality (income standard deviation and racial income inequality), we found no consistent relationship with punitiveness in sentencing. Nor did the presence of large economically subordinate populations, whether black or unemployed, foster more severe sanctions.

Also contrary to expectations, crime rates also had little direct bearing on most decisions, and fostered unexpectedly lenient split sentences.

Some of these results can be explained with insights gleaned from site visits to selected courts. For example, the absence of direct effects for crime rates is not surprising, because court authorities rarely exhibited a comprehensive understanding of the scope of crime in their counties. When asked about its extensiveness, judges and district attorneys invariably referred to the problem of burglary and/or to particular cases that evoked intense, personal concern. In most instances, conclusions about crime rested on anecdotal evidence as authorities referred to isolated cases and generalized these to the broader community. The same lack of comprehensive information about economic conditions could also account for the limited direct role that inequality played during sentencing.

Characteristics of the case also had direct effects on sentencing outcomes, and in this part of the analysis we were interested in obtaining a preliminary indication of the nature and extent of differential treatment. Given previous research, it was not surprising that the legally relevant factors of offense type and seriousness exerted stronger influences than the social background characteristics of offenders. Of greater interest was the finding that the impact of legally relevant factors depended on the sentencing outcome under consideration. Offenders who experienced more severe treatment for one sentencing decision (e.g., probability of imprisonment) were sometimes treated with comparative lenience once that decision was made. Thus, the initial sentencing decision appeared to condition the second sentencing decision (length of sentence). For example, robbery offenders were more likely than average to be imprisoned, but received shorter than average prison terms. An adequate understanding of sentencing hinges, then, both on an empirical examination of several sentencing options and on controls, if only partial, for biases introduced by exercising one of these options.

In comparison with legally relevant factors, offender attributes had relatively weak effects on sentencing outcomes. Although there was some evidence of punitiveness for offenders with fewer resources (e.g., blacks were slightly more likely to be imprisoned than whites), harsher treatment of relatively disadvantaged offenders was not consistent. Surprisingly, we found evidence of lenience toward relatively disadvantaged persons and even some suggestion that relative advantage fostered punitiveness in sentencing. The fact that all of these direct social background effects were small, however, suggests that judges are fairly rational in sentencing, relying primarily on those individual-level characteristics that are legally relevant. As we shall see, their judgment of legal relevance is conditioned by the contexts in which they function.

As we have emphasized in this book, a study of the direct determinants of sentencing outcomes is both incomplete and potentially misleading. Accordingly, the second question posed in this chapter focused on indirect effects, namely, the degree to which county attributes condition the significance of the legally relevant and social background characteristics of the offender. To examine this issue, we used interactive models to determine if the weight judges attach to race and offense depends on the community where sentencing occurs.

At the most general level, the results of interactive analysis support the conclusion that county characteristics do, indeed, condition the relevance of race and offense in sentencing. Once again, however, this conditioning effect varied by decision. County attributes influenced the relevance of race and offense most strongly for the initial decision to incarcerate offenders, and their interactive effects contrasted sharply with the additive pattern, where county attributes had little or no direct influence on the decision to imprison offenders. Once offenders had been sentenced to prison, county factors conditioned differences in treatment less frequently.

The difference between additive and interactive models becomes particularly apparent when considering crime rates. As noted earlier, additive models gave the impression that crime rates had no effect on the use of prison or on the length of prison terms. This is clearly not the case. As we learned in interactive analysis, crime rates interacted with both the race of the offender and the offense committed both for the initial decision to imprison, where they fostered disproportionate harshness toward black offenders, and in the sentence length decision, where high crime rates put white offenders at a disadvantage.

Despite the indirect impact of crime rates, it is important to note that not all county attributes are equally pervasive or powerful conditioners of differential treatment. Characteristics that have received more sustained theoretical and empirical attention, particularly inequality, are neither consistent nor powerful conditioners of differential treatment.

At the most general level, the results also suggest that an accurate estimate of the weight judges attach to the offender's race and crime depends in part on the community where sentencing occurs. This becomes obvious when we compare the effect race and offense have in additive and interactive models. For example, the results of additive analysis suggested that race differences existed, but only for the initial decision to imprison, where blacks were slightly more likely to be imprisoned than whites. Interactive analysis demonstrated that certain county attributes (e.g., crime rates) exacerbated this difference.

Similar comparisons can be drawn for certain types of offenders. Additive models gave the impression that violent offenders were more likely to be imprisoned and, if imprisoned, to receive longer prison terms. This statement is both misleading and incomplete. In some contexts, such as counties with high violent crime rates, violent offenders were indeed more likely to be imprisoned than nonviolent offenders. Violent offenders were also likely to receive longer than average prison sentences if sentenced in counties with high income inequality and unemployment. In other contexts, however, violent offenders were at a comparative advantage. Most notably, their prison sentences were shorter than average where the surrounding community was heavily urbanized, racially unequal, or predominantly black.

In summarizing specific interactions, we will concentrate on the questions derived from previous research and theory that directed our analyses. Does urbanization reduce race differences in sentencing? Do inequality and large subordinate populations foster disproportionate harshness toward property offenders? Can the argument linking inequality with the punishment of property offenders be extended to black offenders as well? Do economic conditions have any effect on the sentences of violent offenders? Do high crime rates foster a climate of punitiveness toward offenders whose criminality may be perceived as particularly threatening? We will briefly examine each question, draw on site visit observations where pertinent, and highlight significant findings.

Consistent with previous research, we found that urbanization did condition differences in treatment, but the nature of its conditioning influence was quite different from that documented in the previous literature. Urbanization neither intensified nor reduced race differences in sentencing. It simply had no effect on differential treatment based on race. Given previous research (e.g., Hagan, 1977), this finding was particularly unanticipated, and could have a number of sources, including insufficient variation in urbanization, regional differences in its conditioning influence, and a more sophisticated research design.

Urbanization did affect the impact of offense, however. Differential treatment usually *increased* with urbanization, and some serious offenders (e.g., violent) were at a comparative advantage if sentenced in urban counties. With the exception of violent offenders, however, urbanization placed no group of offenders at a consistent advantage or disadvantage during sentencing. Instead, its precise role was a complex function of both the offense and the specific sentencing outcome under consideration. For example, urban judges appeared reluctant to imprison burglary offenders, but were particularly harsh with those they chose to incarcerate.

The second question examined in the interactive part of the analysis centered on the indirect effects of income inequality and subordinate populations. Here we thought that both inequality and large subordinate populations would foster greater punitiveness toward property offenders. We expected this because property crime could appear especially threatening to established interests in contexts where inequality is pronounced, unemployment is high, and a sizeable minority of the county is black. In some instances, our results supported these expectations. For example, in counties with high income inequality, judges imposed disproportionately longer prison terms on white collar offenders. In racially unequal counties, judges were more likely than average to imprison larceny offenders and to impose more severe split sentences on offenders convicted of damaging property or possessing stolen goods.

These examples of disproportionate harshness must be placed within the broader context of all possible significant interactions. For many property offenders (e.g., robbers) and sentencing decisions, we found no evidence of harsher than average treatment, and an unexpected amount of comparative lenience. As unemployment increased, for example, certain property offenders (i.e., those convicted of property damage or possession of stolen goods) were much less likely than average to be imprisoned. Serious larceny offenders also ran a less than average risk of imprisonment if sentenced in predominantly black counties. In short, then, we found little evidence that inequality and the presence of large economically subordinate populations *consistently* put property offenders at a disadvantage during sentencing. This negative finding suggests that court officials' professed preoccupation with property offenses did not translate into sentencing punitiveness.

The third question addressed in interactive analysis was whether the argument linking inequality with the punishment of property offenders could be extended to black offenders as well. We expected black offenders to appear particularly threatening in contexts where elites were in a defensive posture and had the resources to demand harsh punishment. As noted earlier, we assumed this because blacks are culturally dissimilar from whites, have traditionally been economically disenfranchised, and have been linked with both criminal stereotypes and the fear of crime. Despite the plausibility of these arguments, the results provided virtually no support for them. Neither of the two measures of inequality we used affected race differences in punishment, and the size of the subordinate population had either extremely limited or unanticipated implications for the criminal penalties imposed on black offenders. The presence of a black majority affected differential treatment by race, but it operated to the *advantage* of black offenders who received split sentences.

As noted earlier, several factors could account for this comparative lenience toward black offenders: the political clout of blacks, which makes discrimination too costly for white elites; vestiges of paternalistic attitudes that tolerate, if not expect, a certain amount of black criminality; more stringent expectations for whites, who by virtue of their membership in a traditionally superordinate racial group "should know better"; greater value placed on protecting white victims; and the dispersed residential segregation of blacks in rural counties, which may reduce their apparent threat. Some of these factors were illustrated in site visit observations. District attorneys, for example, frequently indicated that black-on-black crimes did not merit much concern because they simply consisted of "one nigger cutting up another." Similarly, one judge expressed considerable frustration with aggravated assaults, observing that "these [black] people had guns all their lives and they get into a fight every Friday and Saturday night."

Importantly, additional analysis of the unemployment rate highlighted the value of considering race in conjunction with other attributes, for only then did we discover that young blacks are at a particular disadvantage if sentenced in counties with high unemployment. This additional analysis also suggested that the unemployment rate operates as an important conditioner of the role played by attributes other than race and offense (e.g., marital status, prior arrests, employment status). To some extent, the results corroborated site visit information, which indicated the court's sensitivity toward crimes committed "by the nonproductive against the productive." Furthermore, additional analysis indicated that high unemployment exacerbates harshness toward certain doubly problematic offenders, that is, those who are doubly disadvantaged or dangerous (e.g., violent offenders with prior arrests). In short, the results revealed that the unemployment rate plays a more complex role during sentencing than originally anticipated, and it is possible that other indicators of economic conditions (e.g., percent black, income inequality) operate in a similar manner.

The fourth question addressed in interactive analysis was whether economic conditions had any effect on the sentencing of violent offenders. Given the paternalistic attitudes and lack of concern described above about some violent crimes, we expected that elites would be relatively indifferent toward these crimes. Given the comparable status of offender and victim, we also did not expect this indifference to change as inequality became more pronounced, or as black and unemployed populations became larger. Our findings were more complex than anticipated. Economic conditions profoundly affected the sentences imposed on common law violent offenders. In contexts where racial inequities were pronounced and black populations were large, common-law violent offenders were at the comparative advantage our hypothesis led us to expect. To the extent that violence in these counties tends to involve lower class blacks, elites may be relatively indifferent, if not tolerant. This was definitely not the case, however, in counties where income inequality and unemployment were high. The presence of pronounced *within-group* income inequities and a large unemployed population appeared to lower the tolerance level for violence and foster punitiveness. Unfortunately, we lacked the data needed to gauge fear of victimization by lower class whites.

The final question examined in interactive analysis concerned crime rates, and we were interested in discovering whether high rates fostered a climate of punitiveness toward offenders whose criminality was perceived as particularly threatening. Although the direct effect of crime rates was minimal, their indirect impact was more substantial, and crime rates emerged as consistent and often powerful determinants of race and offense differences in treatment. This finding is one of the most striking in the chapter, because it illustrates the potential importance of crime rates as an independent, and not only dependent, variable.

As an independent variable in interactive analysis, high violent crime rates appeared to foster a climate of punitiveness toward violent offenders, whose criminality may have been perceived as particularly threatening. In contrast, high property crime rates did not affect the punishment of property offenders as straightforwardly, and the more common trend was for high crime rates to foster disproportionate lenience. It must be remembered, however, that we lacked information about crime rates for specific kinds of property crimes. The disproportionate lenience we observed, then, may simply reflect variation in the general category. For the moment, however, it is reasonable to conclude that general increases in property crime appear to foster lenience toward most types of property offenders.

Conclusion

Our often complex answers to questions that motivated interactive analyses illustrate quite clearly that the county context plays an important, although complicated, role in sentencing. Contextual effects are neither constant across all sentencing decisions, nor consistent for each dimension of the community we considered. We turn now to the court, and examine the direct and indirect effects that this more proximate context exerts on criminal sentencing.

Notes

1. Multicollinearity problems prevented us from creating an eight-category measure of offense and adding an additional 21 interactions to the model. Instead, we recoded type of crime into eight categories, and added three more product terms to the interactive model. Income standard deviation was multiplied by each additional offense vector: vehicle theft, white-collar theft (forgery, fraud, and embezzlement), and a residual category of property damage/possession of stolen goods. We then examined these three product terms for significance. We also examined the product term for larceny, which in the original model had estimated interactions for the entire property theft and damage category.

   We used this strategy separately for each county variable. Findings of reanalysis are reported only where one or more of the product terms for an offense within the broad category reached statistical significance ($p < .05$).

2. For example, in comparison with less serious violent offenders sentenced in counties with few blacks, those sentenced in predominantly black counties are 3.8% less likely to be incarcerated. If sentenced in predominantly black counties, more serious violent offenders are 7.5% less likely than their counterparts in counties with few blacks to be incarcerated. As counties shift from few blacks to a black majority, the severity of split sentences imposed on violent offenders with a single conviction charge decrease by 5.8, while those imposed on violent offenders with several charges decrease more sharply (-10.9). Finally, as counties become predominantly black, the prison sentences of less serious violent offenders increase by a year (1.07), whereas those imposed on more serious offenders *decrease* by nearly a year (-0.92).

3. The first noteworthy difference in seriousness involves white-collar offenders receiving split sentences in high crime counties. They have significantly fewer conviction charges than their counterparts sentenced in counties with less crime (1.3 vs. 4.3, $p = .0001$), and this difference could account for the marked tendency for their split sentences to become less severe as crime rates increase. To examine this possibility, we included two additional variables in the interactive model predicting split sentences. The first variable was number of conviction charges, and the second was an interaction term between the crime rate, white-collar crime, and conviction charges. The results remained virtually unchanged after subsequent reanalysis of the data. As crime rates increase, white-collar offenders continue to experience a greater than average decline in split sentence severity.

   The final differences in seriousness involve robbery and white-collar offenders sentenced to prison. Robbery offenders in high crime counties have significantly fewer charges than those convicted in counties with much less crime (1.5 vs. 3.7, $p = .0001$), and in several respects, white-collar offenders in counties with high crime rates are also less serious offenders. They have significantly fewer conviction charges (1.2 vs. 4.1, $p = .0001$) and fewer prior arrests (4.1 vs. 6.1, $p = .05$) , and are less likely to have been incarcerated in Georgia (.24 vs. .45, $p = .003$). Disproportionate lenience toward both groups of offenders persists, however, even after we introduced product terms in the interactive model to control for these differences.

4
The Court and Sentencing

In this chapter, we explore the role court organization and personnel play during sentencing. Again, we are interested in two issues: whether bureaucratization and characteristics of the sentencing judge directly affect outcomes and whether they operate more subtly to condition the effect race and offense have on sentences. As we shall see, characteristics of the court and sentencing judge resemble county variables in several respects. They often have unanticipated, but very slight, effects on the three sentencing outcomes. Moreover, the weakness of these direct effects does not appear to be due to the imprecision introduced by aggregating judge information (see Appendix A). Instead, like county factors, court variables play a more indirect but nonetheless prominent role as conditioners of the effect race and offense have on sentencing. Some attributes of the sentencing judge, such as age, religion, and circuit of origin, are particularly influential conditioners, whereas others are less important (e.g., membership in community organizations). As a group, however, court variables affect differences in treatment for each of the three sentencing outcomes. Race differences in treatment are particularly noticeable, as are differences in the sentencing of common-law violent and burglary offenders.

First, we consider the direct effects court bureaucratization and judge characteristics have on the three sentencing decisions. In particular, we examine whether judges sentence more punitively if their background characteristics and experiences suggest conservatism or involvement in the community. We then consider the effect case characteristics have on sentences, once both court and county variables are controlled.[1] The remaining sections of the chapter focus on each court variable as a conditioner of the role race and offense play during sentencing. The final section summarizes and discusses the results.

Court Variables and Sentencing

Table 4.1 presents the results of additive models that estimate the direct effects court variables have on sentences. As was the case for county variables, these effects are quite slight. Most standardized coefficients do not exceed .10, and many are not statistically significant.

TABLE 4.1. Regression coefficients and related statistics, additive models for court contexts

Variable	Type of sentence			Split sentence severity			Prison sentence length		
	b	(SE)	β	b	(SE)	β	b	(SE)	β
Offender characteristics									
Type of crime									
Common-law violent	.05	(.01)	.070***	−.76	(.72)	−.024	4.76	(.26)	.247***
Robbery	.24	(.01)	.245***	5.36	(1.31)	.150***	−3.18	(.29)	−.138***
Burglary	−.02	(.01)	−.023***	−.43	(.52)	−.015	−1.95	(.20)	−.099***
Property theft/damage	−.13	(.01)	−.172***	−2.04	(.99)	−.069*	.16	(.22)	.008
Drug	−.13	(.01)	−.178***	−2.13	(.69)	−.066***	.19	(.28)	.010
Offense seriousness	.02	(.00)	.463***	1.00	(.06)	.278***	.88	(.04)	.707***
Prior arrests				.33	(.07)	.084***	.08	(.02)	.038***
Prior incarceration				3.61	(.78)	.077***	1.09	(.26)	.042***
Sex	.09	(.01)	.081***	3.13	(1.15)	.044***	1.66	(.45)	.033***
Race	−.05	(.01)	−.052***	−.44	(.66)	−.011	−.55	(.23)	−.023*
Age	.001	(.00)	.017***	.002	(.04)	.001	.03	(.01)	.021*
Marital status				2.31	(.64)	.052***	.36	(.24)	.013
Employment status				−4.09	(.62)	−.097***	−.48	(.22)	−.019*
Court bureaucratization									
Caseload pressure	3×10^{-5}	(.00)	.005	−.02	(.00)	−.092***	−.003	(.00)	−.027**
Court specialization	2×10^{-4}	(.00)	.007	−.01	(.02)	−.008	−.03	(.01)	−.038***
Judge characteristics									
Sex composition	−.02	(.03)	−.003	−3.62	(4.37)	−.012	−4.22	(1.55)	−.024**
Age	−.002	(.00)	−.025***	.03	(.06)	.009	.03	(.02)	.015

Religion	.02	(.01)	.016***	.56	(1.11)	.008	.08	(.38)	.002
Years as prosecutor	.01	(.00)	.056***	.32	(.10)	.053***	−.07	(.03)	−.020*
Circuit of origin	.02	(.01)	.019***	−.53	(.89)	−.011	−.24	(.31)	−.009
Membership in community organizations	.04	(.00)	.010**	.67	(.23)	.049***	−.18	(.08)	−.022*
Years in local government	−.001	(.00)	−.014***	.09	(.08)	.017	.03	(.03)	.011
Opponents in primary	−.04	(.01)	−.021***	−4.43	(1.27)	−.056***	.46	(.41)	.011
Election history	.05	(.00)	.050***	.27	(.69)	.007	−.10	(.26)	−.004
County variables									
Urbanization	6×10^{-7}	(.00)	.050***	-2×10^{-5}	(.00)	−.072*	-1×10^{-5}	(.00)	−.078***
Income standard deviation	-8×10^{-7}	(.00)	−.004	5×10^{-4}	(.00)	.052	2×10^{-4}	(.00)	.039*
Racial income inequality	2×10^{-6}	(.00)	.014*	-2×10^{-4}	(.00)	−.044	-1×10^{-4}	(.00)	−.037*
Lagged unemployment rate	.01	(.00)	.028***	−.97	(.18)	−.086***	.07	(.06)	.012
Percent black									
Under 25% vs. 25–49%	.01	(.01)	.010*	.87	(.75)	.022	−.20	(.28)	−.008
Under 25% vs. 50+%	−.05	(.01)	−.030***	−.13	(1.41)	−.003	.83	(.49)	.026
Lagged Index crime rate	-3×10^{-6}	(.00)	−.010	-5×10^{-4}	(.00)	−.075***	2×10^{-5}	(.00)	.003
Hazard rate	.18			−.81	(8.22)	−.004	.38	(1.71)	.008
Intercept	.18	(.04)***		46.55	(9.28)***		.94	(3.21)	
R^2	.204			.202			.670		
N	27,613			4,271			5,022		

$*p \leq .05; **p \leq .01; ***p \leq .005.$

The first set of court variables consists of caseload pressure and specialization, and measures the degree to which courts are bureaucratized. Neither indicator of bureaucratization affects the initial decision to imprison offenders. However, judges with heavy caseloads tend to impose slightly less severe split sentences and shorter prison terms than judges with smaller caseloads. Judges also impose shorter prison sentences if they receive assistance from lower courts and specialize in felony cases. Thus, although bureaucratization does not affect the initial use of prison, it tends to foster more lenient terms of imprisonment.

The remaining court variables measure characteristics of the sentencing judge. Previous research, often at the appellate court level, led us to formulate two expectations about the relationship between these characteristics and sentencing. First, we thought that certain types of judges would be more conservative and for this reason sentence more punitively. In particular, we expected this kind of sentencing behavior from judges who are male, older, Baptist, or had previously been a county or circuit prosecutor. The results presented in Table 4.1 provide very limited support for this expectation. Baptist judges are indeed more likely than non-Baptist judges to imprison offenders. Also as expected, former prosecutors are more likely to incarcerate and to impose more severe split sentences on those they choose to imprison (cf. Frazier and Bock, 1982). During site visits, these patterns were substantiated by perceptions of district attorneys. According to one judge:

The D.A.s are police oriented and want to drink half a pint of blood . . . . They want to lock them up and throw away the key.

And at least one defense attorney thought that the "judge still thinks he is the D.A. from the bench — it is funny when you feel like you have got the judge and the D.A. trying against you."

The remaining findings are inconsistent with the expectation noted above. First, rather than being more lenient, courts with female judges tend to impose longer prison terms than exclusively male courts. Although slight, this harshness could reflect a concern not to appear "soft" in an environment where sexism exists or is perceived to exist.

Second, older judges are less likely to incarcerate offenders than their younger colleagues. During site visit interviews, we noted several instances of tolerance on the part of older judges. For example, one older judge admitted:

I have a lot of empathy with young offenders. I would have to candidly say that as a young fellow I probably did some things that I should have been arrested for and could have been sent to prison for myself. But most everyone else that I know has been in similar circumstances. But the young buck in the growing process is exposed to temptations, troubles, and that sort of thing. A great deal of the normal conduct particular to young American males, is of a type that if the circumstances are presented right, could result in a criminal charge.

Finally, although they are more punitive in their initial use of prison and split sentences, former prosecutors tend to impose shorter prison terms than judges without prosecutorial experience. Thus, the perception of district attorneys quoted above is only partly accurate: former prosecutors are more willing to "lock (offenders) up," but do not necessarily "throw away the key." Reliance on shorter prison terms may reflect an often-cited awareness of prison overcrowding, and this awareness may moderate the punitive attitudes of former prosecutors.

Our second expectation focused on the relationship between the sentencing judge and the community. We thought that several types of judges would be more responsive to community demands for punitiveness and would sentence more harshly. In particular, we expected more punitive sentencing behavior by judges who had been born in the circuit, were politically or socially involved in the community, or were electorally vulnerable. The results provide isolated support for these expectations. Judges born in the circuit are indeed more likely to imprison offenders than are judges born outside the circuit. Similarly, as membership in community organizations increases, so too does the use of prison and the severity of split sentences.

Although these findings suggest a link between community involvement and punitiveness, others indicate that the relationship is neither strong nor consistent. Judicial links with the community often have no discernible effect on sentencing behavior and, in several instances, foster leniency during punishment. Although they are more likely to incarcerate offenders, judges involved in community organizations impose slightly *shorter* prison terms than their less involved colleagues. Judges with previous involvement in local government are less likely to incarcerate offenders. So too are judges who had faced opposition in primaries; they also impose less severe split sentences than judges who had not faced opposition. Finally, less established judges (i.e., those serving less than three terms) are less likely to imprison offenders than judges who are more established.

In sum, then, there is little evidence that judges who are involved in the community or electorally vulnerable consistently impose harsher sentences on offenders. Some of these judges are slightly more lenient, and others (e.g., former prosecutors) balance lenience with harshness by combining a willingness to imprison offenders with a reluctance to impose long prison sentences. Finally, as is the case for local or established judges, punitiveness is limited to one sentencing decision only, typically the initial decision to incarcerate.

Case Characteristics and Sentencing

Characteristics of the case continue to exert a significant influence on sentencing, even after the effects of both county and court variables are controlled. This is particularly true for factors that can be construed as legally relevant. Judges impose more severe sanctions on offenders who were convicted of violent or more serious offenses. Offenders with prior records also tend to receive more severe split sentences and longer prison terms than offenders without prior records. In contrast, burglary offenders are punished more leniently. They are less likely to be imprisoned, and if imprisoned receive shorter than average prison terms. Finally, the treatment of robbery offenders depends on the sentencing decision. They are more likely to be imprisoned and to receive more severe split sentences. Yet for robbery offenders sentenced to a straight term of incarceration, prison sentences are shorter than average.

Social background attributes of the offender continue to have slight effects on sentencing outcomes. Once again, harsher treatment of relatively disadvantaged persons does not appear to be a consistent feature of sentencing. For example, black offenders are treated more harshly than whites, but this harshness is slight and significant for the initial decision to imprison and the length of prison sentences. Unemployed offenders are also punished more severely, but this effect is noteworthy only for offenders who received a split sentence. Finally, at least two groups of relatively disadvantaged offenders are punished more leniently. Younger offenders run a slightly smaller risk than older offenders of being imprisoned and also receive shorter prison terms. Unmarried offenders are at a slight advantage if sentenced to a combination of prison and probation, because their split sentences tend to be less severe than those imposed on married offenders.

The Court as Context

As we saw in Chapter 3, contextual variables may have very slight direct effects, yet still operate as powerful determinants of the sentences imposed on certain types of offenders. We explored this possibility for court variables by estimating interactive models that included product terms between each court variable and the case characteristics of race and offense. Table 4.2 presents an overview of significant interactions. For each of the three sentencing outcomes, the addition of interaction terms produced a significant, although often slight, increase in the proportion of explained variance. Unlike county characteristics, which had a pervasive conditioning influence only for the initial decision to imprison, court variables consistently condition the importance of race and offense for all three decisions under consideration. For the initial decision to imprison, 36% of all possible interactions reached statistical significance. For split sentence severity, 32% of all interactions were significant, and the corresponding figure for prison sentence length is 27%.

To some extent, all court variables are implicated in race and offense differences in treatment. Three factors figure quite prominently, however: judge age, religion, and circuit of origin. These factors condition differential treatment based on both race and offense for all three sentencing decisions. In contrast, membership in community organizations conditions differential treatment less frequently. It has no implications for race differences in treatment, and only affects the sentences imposed on violent offenders.

TABLE 4.2. Significant court interactions and related statistics, by sentencing outcome[a]

Context	Type of sentence	Split sentence severity	Prison sentence
Court bureaucratization			
Caseload pressure		Common-law violent Robbery Property theft/damage	Drug
Court specialization	Race Robbery	Common-law violent Burglary	Race Common-law violent
Judge characteristics			
Sex composition	Robbery Burglary Drug		Race Robbery
Age	Race Burglary Property theft/damage Drug	Race Common-law violent Property theft/damage	Common-law violent
Religion	Race	Race Common-law violent Burglary Property theft/damage	Race
Years as prosecutor	Race Common-law violent Burglary Drug	Robbery Drug	Robbery
Circuit of origin	Common-law violent Burglary	Race Robbery Drug	Robbery Burglary
Membership in community organizations	Common-law violent		Common-law violent
Years in local government	Race Robbery Property theft/damage	Common-law violent Burglary Property theft/damage	Common-law violent
Opponents in primary	Race		Common-law violent Robbery Burglary Property theft/damage

TABLE 4.2. (Continued)

Context	Type of sentence	Split sentence severity	Prison sentence
Election history	Common-law violent Burglary Property theft/ damage	Burglary	Race Common-law violent
Additive model R^2	.204	.202	.670
Interactive model R^2	.213	.249	.682
F (degrees of freedom)	6.22 (54/27,532)	4.93 (54/4,185)	3.45 (54/4,936)

[a] Interactions significant at $p \leq .05$. All increments in explained variation significant at $p \leq .0001$.

Focusing attention on the case characteristics themselves, notice that they differ in their responsiveness to variation in court bureaucratization and judicial composition. Recall that when considering county factors, we found relatively few instances where race differences depended on the community where sentencing occurred. When considering court factors, particularly those indicating bureaucratization and judicial conservatism, we encounter race differences more frequently. As will become apparent, the nature of those differences does not always support expectations derived from previous research.

As was the case for county variables, characteristics of the court also consistently condition the sentences imposed on common-law violent offenders. In some courts these offenders are at a distinct disadvantage, whereas in others they are at a comparative advantage. The sentences imposed on other types of offenders (e.g., drug) do not depend as heavily on court characteristics, however. Yet even for offenders who receive relatively uniform treatment, there are still situations where the harshness of their punishment depends on court bureaucratization and judicial characteristics.

The following sections focus on each aspect of the court and sentencing judge. Using the previous literature as a point of departure, we consider whether and how each dimension of the court conditions differential treatment based on race and offense.

The Conditioning Influence of Bureaucratization

Previous theorizing offers quite different hypotheses about the relationship between bureaucratization and differential treatment. The Weberian perspective (Weber, 1954) leads us to expect that as courts become more bureaucratized, the role played by legally relevant factors will become more prominent. Factors that cannot be explicitly construed as legally relevant will become less important, and differences in treatment based on such factors should decline.

Conflict theory, particularly the early work of Chambliss and Seidman (1971), offers a divergent expectation. As bureaucratization increases, so too does official concern with maintaining court efficiency. As a result, officials must develop strategies that minimize organizational costs and maximize organizational and professional gain. One strategy is the use of legally irrelevant criteria such as social background to decide whether and how to enforce the law. Punitiveness toward the relatively advantaged is more costly, in part because they are able to resist official responses. As a result, officials may single out offenders who lack the ability to resist harsh treatment. On the basis of this reasoning, we would expect court bureaucratization to increase differential treatment based on race, and to have fewer implications for differential treatment based on offense. As we shall see below, bureaucratization does not eliminate race differences in treatment, and it puts black offenders at a disadvantage. We begin with the effect of bureaucratization on the sentences of white and black offenders. Then we examine differences in treatment based on offense.

BUREAUCRATIZATION AND RACE DIFFERENCES

Table 4.3 presents the predicted outcomes for black and white offenders whose sentences are affected by court bureaucratization. Note first that only court specialization affects race differences in treatment. Caseload pressure, in contrast, is irrelevant. Second, differential treatment by race persists, regardless of specialization, but generally is relatively small. Finally, growing specialization puts black offenders at a comparative *disadvantage* in two respects. As courts become more specialized, the risk of imprisonment increases for blacks ($+10.1\%$), but decreases slightly for white offenders (-2.6%). Also, as courts become more specialized, black offenders sentenced to prison receive less lenience than comparable white offenders. That is, the prison sentences imposed on white offenders decline by 4.4 years, whereas those imposed on black offenders decline by nearly 2 years.

In short, blacks sentenced in less specialized courts are *less* likely than whites to be imprisoned, and they also receive shorter prison sentences than white

TABLE 4.3. Predicted outcomes for black and white offenders, by court specialization[a]

Race of offender	Level of specialization		Effect of specialization
	Lowest	Highest	
Type of sentence			
Black	.342	.443	.101***
White	.398	.372	−.026
Disparity	(.056)	(.071)	
Prison sentence length			
Black	11.770	9.782	−1.988*
White	13.559	9.114	−4.445
Disparity	(1.789)	(.668)	

[a] Predicted outcomes capture the effects of varying specialization, while holding constant at the mean the effects of the remaining variables.
* $p \le .05$; *** $p \le .005$.

offenders. In contrast, if sentenced by judges who are assisted by lower courts and able to confine most of their attention to felonies, blacks are slightly *more* likely than whites to be imprisoned. Their prison sentences also tend to be longer than those imposed on white offenders. In the following section, we consider the possibility that these trends reflect differences in the kind of black and white offenders judges in specialized courts sentence.

ALTERNATIVE SOURCES OF RACE DIFFERENCES

First, we examined the differential effect specialization has on the probability that black and white offenders will be incarcerated. Recall that as courts become increasingly specialized, judges are more likely to imprison blacks but less likely to imprison whites. We would expect this pattern if more serious black offenders and less serious white offenders are concentrated in highly specialized courts. We therefore examined race differences in the seriousness of offenders sentenced in courts at the lowest and the highest quartiles of specialization. We found that black offenders are indeed convicted of significantly more serious offenses in highly specialized courts (9.4 vs. 9.1, $p = .05$). To control for this difference, we constructed a product term involving race, court specialization, and offense seriousness, entered it into the interactive model, and reanalyzed the data. The increased imprisonment risk for black offenders, as well as the decline for whites, persist with virtually no change.

Next, we examined the tendency for specialization to reduce prison sentences, particularly for white offenders. This pattern may reflect a greater concentration of less serious offenders, particularly those who are white, in highly specialized courts. We therefore examined race differences along four legally relevant dimensions: offense seriousness, number of conviction charges, prior arrests, and prior incarceration in Georgia. We found that both black and white offenders in specialized courts were convicted of significantly less serious offenses than those sentenced in less specialized courts. For example, in highly specialized courts, the mean seriousness of offenses committed by blacks is 12.8, whereas in less specialized courts, the mean is significantly higher (14.4). The comparable figures for whites are 12.0 and 13.4, respectively. Hence, we would expect a decline in prison sentences for both offenders as specialization increases. Yet when we included a product term for the interaction between race, specialization, and offense seriousness, the decline persisted and continued to be greater for white offenders, particularly those convicted of serious offenses.[2]

In sum, then, the effect that specialization has on race differences in sentencing does not appear traceable to differences in the seriousness of offenders, whether black or white, that judges in bureaucratized courts must sentence.

BUREAUCRATIZATION AND OFFENSE DIFFERENCES

Bureaucratization also has implications for treatment based on the legally relevant factor of offense. Table 4.4 presents the predicted outcomes for offenders whose sentences are affected by caseload, and Table 4.5 presents predicted

TABLE 4.4. Predicted outcomes for selected types of offenders, by caseload pressure[a]

Type of offender	Caseload level		Effect of caseload
	Lowest	Highest	
Split sentence severity			
Common-law violent	61.876	41.163	−20.713***
Average	44.270	35.017	−9.253
Disparity	(17.606)	(6.146)	
Robbery	44.862	45.350	.488*
Average	44.270	35.017	−9.253
Disparity	(.592)	(10.333)	
Property theft/damage	40.159	37.095	−3.064*
Average	44.270	35.017	−9.253
Disparity	(4.111)	(2.078)	
Prison sentence length			
Drug	5.833	9.480	3.647***
Average	15.632	15.015	−.617
Disparity	(9.799)	(5.535)	

[a] Predicted outcomes capture the effects of varying caseload, while holding constant at the mean the effects of the remaining variables.
*$p \leq .05$; ***$p \leq .005$.

TABLE 4.5. Predicted outcomes for selected types of offenders, by court specialization[a]

Type of offender	Level of specialization		Effect of specialization
	Lowest	Highest	
Type of sentence			
Robbery	.585	.715	.130***
Average	.415	.461	.046
Disparity	(.170)	(.254)	
Split sentence severity			
Common-law violent	76.060	51.182	−24.878***
Average	42.695	41.280	−1.415
Disparity	(33.365)	(9.902)	
Burglary	30.673	42.555	11.882***
Average	42.695	41.280	−1.415
Disparity	(12.022)	(1.275)	
Prison sentence length			
Common-law violent	21.749	16.047	−5.702***
Average	10.375	7.893	−2.482
Disparity	(11.374)	(8.154)	

[a] Predicted outcomes capture the effects of varying court specialization, while holding constant at the mean the effects of the remaining variables.
***$p \leq .005$.

outcomes for significant interactions involving court specialization. Note, first, that bureaucratization tends to condition offense differences after the initial decision to imprison has been made. Moreover, although differences in treatment often decline, they continue to persist in highly bureaucratized courts. Indeed, for several types of offenders (e.g., robbers), differences in treatment become more pronounced. Finally, bureaucratization appears to foster disproportionate lenience toward some offenders (e.g., violent), while placing others (e.g., property) at a comparative disadvantage.

Caseload and specialization exert their most consistent influence on the sentences of common-law violent offenders. As courts face heavier caseloads and become more specialized, these offenders experience greater than average declines in both split and prison sentences. For example, as courts become more specialized, prison sentences decline by 2.5 years for the average offender, and 5.7 years for violent offenders. Put differently, sentencing becomes more lenient as courts become bureaucratized, and violent offenders receive a disproportionate amount of this lenience.

A possible reason for this lenience could be the concentration of less serious violent offenders in bureaucratized courts. To consider this possibility, we compared violent offenders sentenced in courts at the lowest and highest quartiles of caseload and specialization. Only one difference was significant, and it involved offenders sentenced to prison. In highly specialized courts, violent offenders are convicted of significantly less serious crimes than violent offenders sentenced to prison in less specialized courts (19.2 vs. 23.1, $p = .005$). To control for this difference, we included a product term consisting of the violent crime vector, specialization, and offense seriousness. After reanalyzing the data, the disproportionate lenience we noted above persists unchanged.

The remaining instances of disproportionate lenience toward violent offenders are particularly anomalous. Violent offenders receiving split sentences in specialized courts tend to be *more* serious than their counterparts in less specialized courts. In particular, they are convicted of more serious crimes and have more charges than violent offenders in less specialized courts. On the basis of these differences, we would expect punishment in bureaucratized courts to be disproportionately harsh. In actuality, we found the opposite to be the case.

We must place this disproportionate lenience toward violent offenders in perspective, however. When compared with the average offender, violent offenders receive more severe split sentences and longer prison terms, and this is the case regardless of the extent to which the court is bureaucratized. What changes with bureaucratization, however is the *magnitude* of differential treatment. It decreases with, but is not eliminated by, growing bureaucratization. Differential treatment decreases because as courts become overloaded and more specialized, violent offenders receive more lenience than the average offender.

In contrast with the increasingly more lenient treatment of violent offenders, bureaucratization puts several types of property offenders at a comparative disadvantage. It does so by fostering either disproportionate harshness or less than average lenience. We consider the findings for caseload pressure first, then discuss the effect of specialization.

As noted above, judges impose less severe split sentences as their caseload increases. Property theft and damage offenders experience a smaller than average decrease in severity of split sentence (-3.1 vs. -9.3), whereas the split sentences of robbery offenders become slightly more severe ($+.5$). Similarly, as caseload increases, the average prison sentence declines by over 7 months. Drug offenders, in contrast, experience a noticeable increase of 3.6 years. None of these patterns can be attributed to the concentration of more serious robbery, property, or drug offenders in courts with heavy caseloads, since such tendencies are not present in these data.

Although somewhat different offenders are involved, specialization also tends to foster disproportionate harshness toward property offenders. As courts become more specialized, robbery offenders experience a significantly greater than average increase in imprisonment risk (13% vs. 4.6%). Burglary offenders experience an increase in the severity of their split sentences ($+11.9$). We compared the seriousness of both types of offenders in the least and most specialized courts, and found a tendency for burglary offenders in specialized courts to have significantly more conviction charges than those sentenced in less specialized courts (1.7 vs. 1.4, $p = .005$). Yet, disproportionate harshness toward burglary offenders persists unchanged, even after we controlled for the interaction between specialization and number of conviction charges.

In sum, bureaucratization affects differential treatment based on offense. It appears to foster disproportionate lenience toward violent offenders, and disproportionate harshness toward property and drug offenders. These results persist, despite differences in the seriousness of offenders sentenced in bureaucratized courts.

The Sex Composition of the Bench

Few studies have examined the relationship between the sex of judges and their sentencing behavior. In large part, this neglect reflects the absence of information about the sentencing behavior of female judges. The situation in Georgia is no different. As noted in Chapter 2, most judges are male, and comparatively few offenders were sentenced by female judges.[3] The results reported in the following sections must therefore remain tentative.

In the past, researchers have focused on interactions between the sex of the sentencing judge and two case characteristics: the conviction offense and the sex of the defendant. We examine both issues, as well as the extent to which male and female judges sentence black and white offenders differently.

First, we review previous studies on sex differences in sentencing behavior. We then determine whether there is any support for the expectation that female judges are more lenient than male judges, particularly toward black offenders. We find that, contrary to expectation, the prison sentences of both black and white offenders tend to be longer in courts where female judges preside.

The next issue we consider is whether female judges treat certain types of offenders differently than do males judges. The general expectation was that, with the exception of rape, female judges would sentence more leniently than male judges. In actuality, we find considerable similarity in the sentences imposed by male and female judges. Where significant differences exist, they suggest that female judges may be more severe than male judges toward both violent and property offenders.

On the basis of previous work, we expected female judges to sentence rape offenders more harshly than male judges. Despite small sample sizes, the data provide some support for this expectation. Rape offenders are more likely to be imprisoned and to receive longer prison sentences if sentenced in courts with at least one female judge presiding. Surprisingly, however, they receive more lenient split sentences in these courts.

Finally, we were interested in discovering whether male judges treat female offenders more leniently than female judges. We found that they do not. Indeed, male judges appear to sentence female offenders more harshly than do female judges, and there is also some evidence that male judges may sentence male offenders more leniently than female judges. Again, however, samples were small, and these differences are suggestive rather than definitive.

PREVIOUS RESEARCH ON FEMALE JUDGES

The most detailed information about sex differences in sentencing behavior is based on research conducted in "Metro City," a Northeastern urban area. For our purposes, two outcomes examined in previous work are relevant: the decision to incarcerate and sentence severity, as measured by the 93-point scale discussed in Chapter 2. The first work (Kritzer and Uhlman, 1977), using data from 1968 to 1974, developed competing expectations about the sentencing behavior of female judges. First, the authors argued that female judges may be more threatened than male judges by normative violations, and for this reason be more punitive. On the other hand, because of differences in sex role socialization, female judges may be more empathetic and compassionate than males. For this reason, they may sentence more leniently. Previous evidence of chivalrous or paternalistic attitudes toward female offenders led Kritzer and Uhlman to expect that male judges would punish female offenders more leniently than their female colleagues.

Kritzer and Uhlman (1977) found virtually no support for these expectations. In general, the sentencing behavior of male and female judges was more alike than different. Most notably, there were no significant differences in the way male and female judges treated female (or male) offenders. Male judges did not appear to be paternalistic toward female offenders, nor did female judges appear to be more empathetic. Although female judges treated rape offenders more harshly than did male judges, the differences were not significant. Only one difference in sentencing behavior was noteworthy: female judges punished larceny offenders more harshly than did male judges. Other differences in sentencing behavior existed, but could be traced to legally relevant differences. That is, female judges tended to receive offenders who were convicted of more serious offenses or who had more conviction charges than those sentenced by male judges. On these grounds, it was not surprising that female judges sentenced more harshly than male judges.

More recent work on "Metro City" used a larger sample and covered a longer time period (1971–79). Although there were still few female judges ($N = 7$), they accounted for nearly 6,000 cases. Using previous work on elites as their point of departure, Gruhl and his colleagues (1981) expected that female judges would be more liberal than male judges, more receptive to lower class interests, and as a result more lenient during sentencing. They noted two exceptions to this pattern. Female judges would punish rape offenders more harshly than male judges, and in part because of paternalistic attitudes, male judges would sentence female offenders more leniently than female judges.

Support for these expectations was mixed. As did we, Gruhl and his colleagues found a slight, but substantively insignificant, tendency for female judges to use prison more than male judges. Although sentencing behavior differed depending on the type of offender, there was no consistent tendency for female judges to be lenient or male judges to be more severe. For example, female judges were more likely than male judges to imprison some property offenders (e.g., burglars, forgers), whereas for other property offenses (e.g., auto theft, embezzlement, stolen property), female and male judges did not differ. Similarly, female judges imposed more lenient sentences than male judges on violent offenders, but imposed harsher sanctions than male judges on offenders convicted of certain property crimes (e.g., robbery, burglary, forgery). Also contrary to expectation, female judges were *less* likely to imprison rapists.

Only one expectation received support. Male judges sentenced female offenders more leniently than did female judges. They were less likely to send female offenders to prison, and imposed slightly less severe sentences. In contrast, female judges treated male and female offenders similarly.

In sum, the previous literature provides some indication that male and female judges sentence certain offenders differently. These differences are not always strong, however, and occur within a general backdrop of similarity in sentencing behavior. The following sections expand previous inquiries into sex differences in sentencing behavior. First, we examine whether male and female judges differ in their treatment of black and white offenders. We then consider whether the sex of the sentencing judge has implications for the sentences imposed on violent, property, and drug offenders. Next, we focus attention on rape offenders in an effort to determine whether female judges sentence these offenders more severely than male judges. Finally, we address an issue of perennial concern, whether male judges are paternalistic and sentence female offenders more leniently than do female judges.

RACE AND OFFENSE DIFFERENCES IN SENTENCING

Table 4.6 presents the predicted outcomes for offenders whose sentences are affected the sex composition of the bench. First we focus on race differences in treatment, then consider differences based on the offense.

For two of the three sentencing decisions, there appears to be an underlying similarity in the sentences imposed by female and male judges. That is, the sex composition of the bench has no implications for race differences in treatment.

TABLE 4.6. Predicted outcomes for selected offenders, by sex composition of bench[a]

Type of offender	Proportion male		Effect of sex composition
	Least	Most	
Type of sentence			
Robbery	.765	.690	−.075*
Average	.461	.452	−.009
Disparity	(.304)	(.238)	
Burglary	.604	.419	−.185***
Average	.461	.452	−.009
Disparity	(.143)	(.033)	
Drug	.085	.158	.073***
Average	.461	.452	−.009
Disparity	(.376)	(.295)	
Prison sentence length			
Black	10.634	10.070	−.564**
White	14.417	9.653	−4.764
Disparity	(3.783)	(.417)	
Robbery	13.697	5.499	−8.198***
Average	11.273	8.181	−3.092
Disparity	(2.424)	(2.682)	

[a] Predicted outcomes capture the effects of varying sex composition of bench, while holding constant at the mean the effects of the remaining variables.
*$p \leq .05$; **$p \leq .01$; ***$p \leq .005$.

However, for offenders sentenced to prison, the results suggest that female judges may be harsher than male judges, particularly toward white offenders. As the bench becomes predominantly male, the prison sentences of blacks decrease by over 6 months, and those imposed on whites decrease by 4.8 years. As a result, white offenders are at a particular disadvantage if sentenced in courts with female judges. Their prison sentences are 3.8 years longer than those imposed on black offenders. In contrast, white offenders are at a slight *advantage* if sentenced in courts composed exclusively of male judges. Their prison sentences are about 5 months *shorter* than those imposed on black offenders.

We would expect male and female judges to sentence offenders differently if they received different types of black and white offenders. That is, courts with female judges may be faced with more serious offenders than courts composed only of male judges. To consider this possibility, we distinguished all-male courts from those that are between 25% and 50% female. We then compared black and white offenders sentenced in the two groups of courts along four dimensions: the seriousness of their offenses, the number of charges of which they were convicted, the number of prior arrests, and whether previously incarcerated in Georgia (see Appendix Table C).

In general, all-male and partially female courts appear to be sentencing the same kinds of offenders, whether black or white. Yet there are two significant differences. The first involves black offenders sentenced in courts composed exclusively of males. They are more likely to have been incarcerated in Georgia than their counterparts sentenced in courts where female judges preside. This difference leads us to expect that male judges would be harsher toward blacks than female judges. As noted above, however, they appear to be more lenient. The second difference involves white offenders sentenced in courts where female judges preside. They have significantly more prior arrests than whites sentenced in exclusively male courts. To determine whether this difference could account for our findings, we added a product term consisting of race, sex of sentencing judge, and prior arrests to the interactive model predicting prison sentence length. The results remain unchanged. Female judges appear to be harsher than male judges, particularly toward white offenders.

Turning attention to specific types of offenders, we also find an underlying similarity in the sentences imposed by female and male judges. Split sentences do not differ and, for other sentencing decisions, differences are limited. They suggest, however, an unexpected tendency for female judges to sentence more harshly than male judges. Indeed, several groups of offenders are at a clear disadvantage if sentenced in courts where female judges preside. Both robbery and burglary offenders are more likely to be imprisoned, and the prison terms imposed on robbery offenders are 8.2 years longer than those imposed by courts composed only of males. Only for drug offenders do we find the expected lenience. As courts become partially female in composition, the probability that drug offenders will be imprisoned decreases by 7.3%.

As was the case for race, we thought that differential treatment might be an artifact of the concentration of more serious offenders in courts where female judges preside. This is clearly not the case. Within each offense category (common-law violent, burglary, robbery, and drug), we found no significant association between the sex composition of the bench and the seriousness of the offender (i.e., offense seriousness, prior record, number of conviction charges).

It is possible that the breadth of our offense categories obscures other sex differences in sentencing. In the next section, we distinguish rape offenders from other violent offenders, and determine whether female judges sentence these offenders more severely. Here, we consider the possibility that male and female judges sentence offenders within the broad property theft and damage category differently.

The previous literature provided at least preliminary evidence that female judges are more intolerant than male judges of larceny and white-collar crime (e.g., forgery). There was no evidence that this is the case in Georgia. To explore this possibility, we followed the same procedures discussed in Chapter 3. We recoded the property theft and damage category to distinguish larceny offenders from those convicted of vehicle theft, white-collar theft, and a residual category of possessing stolen goods and damaging property. The resulting measure for type of crime was a seven-vector variable. We multiplied each vector by the sex of sentencing judge, added these product terms to the interactive model, and reanalyzed the data. Table 4.7 presents the results of this reanalysis.

Recall that the original analysis of the data uncovered no evidence of sex differences in the imposition of split sentences. Closer inspection of the broad property theft and damage category reveals the existence of two significant differences within that category. Consistent with the general trend, courts where female judges preside impose more severe split sentences on offenders convicted of possessing stolen goods or damaging property. Unlike previous work, however, we discovered that female judges may be more lenient than male judges toward offenders convicted of larceny. Courts where female judges preside impose significantly less severe split sentences on larceny offenders than courts composed only of males. In both instances, the number of offenders who may have been sentenced by female judges is extremely small (9 and 15, respectively). Hence, these differences are suggestive rather than definitive.

In sum, then, the sex composition of the bench has few implications for the sentences imposed on most types of offenders. Yet for some decisions and offenders, sex differences exist. With few exceptions, female judges appear to sentence more severely than their male colleagues, particularly offenders convicted of robbery and burglary.

THE SENTENCING OF RAPE OFFENDERS

To determine whether this general pattern of harshness characterizes the sentencing of rape offenders, we differentiated rapists from other violent offenders, and added another product term to each interactive model. Table 4.8 presents the results of the reanalysis. Again, since the number of rape offenders who could have been sentenced by female judges is extremely small ($N = 31$), these results must be cautiously accepted.

TABLE 4.7. Predicted split sentences for selected property offenders, by sex composition of bench[a]

Type of offender	Proportion male		Effect of sex composition
	Least	Most	
Larceny	24.676	34.569	9.893*
Average	42.034	36.184	−5.850
Disparity	(17.358)	(1.615)	
Property damage/possess stolen goods	63.191	32.911	−30.280***
Average	42.034	36.184	−5.850
Disparity	(21.157)	(3.273)	

[a] Predicted split sentences capture the effects of varying sex composition, while holding constant at the mean the effects of the remaining variables.
*$p \leq .05$; ***$p \leq .005$.

TABLE 4.8. Predicted outcomes for rape offenders, by sex composition of bench[a]

Type of offender	Proportion male		Effect of sex composition
	Least	Most	
Type of sentence			
Rape	.878	.647	−.231***
Average	.546	.515	−.031
Disparity	(.332)	(.132)	
Split sentence severity			
Rape	20.715	26.050	5.335*
Average	38.738	28.421	−10.317
Disparity	(18.023)	(2.371)	
Prison sentence length			
Rape	24.549	14.717	−9.832***
Average	14.190	10.712	−3.478
Disparity	(10.359)	(4.005)	

[a] Predicted outcomes capture the effects of varying sex composition of bench, while holding constant at the mean the effects of the remaining variables.
*$p \leq .05$; ***$p \leq .005$.

We found significant sex differences in the predicted direction for two of three sentencing decisions. Courts where female judges preside are about 23% more likely to imprison rape offenders than courts consisting only of male judges. We can tentatively rule out the possibility that this result occurs because female judges receive more serious rape offenders, since there is no evidence this is the case. However, since we lacked information on a number of legally relevant factors (e.g., prior record), we have not definitely excluded the possibility that, for the sample as a whole, female judges sentence differently because they receive more serious rape offenders than male judges.

Courts where female judges preside also impose prison terms on rape offenders that are longer than those imposed by male judges (9.8 years). To determine whether this result is an artifact, we distinguished all-male courts from courts that contain between 25% and 50% female judges. Then, we compared rape offenders in the two groups of courts along four legally relevant dimensions: offense seriousness, conviction charges, prior arrests, and previous incarceration. Rape offenders sentenced to prison in courts with some female judges tend to have more conviction charges than their counterparts sentenced by male judges (2.6 vs. 1.7, $p = .01$). To control for this difference, we added a product term consisting of the vector for rape, judge sex, and number of conviction charges, and reanalyzed the data. The results remain virtually unchanged. Courts with female judges continue to impose substantially longer prison sentences on rape offenders than do exclusively male courts, and this is the case for rape offenders with one charge as well as for rape offenders with multiple charges.

The final set of findings is particularly unanticipated. They suggest that female judges impose slightly *less* severe split sentences on rape offenders than do male judges. This result becomes even more anomalous, once we consider the types of rape offenders sentenced in courts where female judges preside. They tend to be *more* serious than those sentenced in courts composed only of males. Their sexual assaults are more serious, and they have longer prior records and more conviction charges. For example, the average number of prior arrests is 5.1 for offenders sentenced by courts with female judges, but only 1.8 for offenders sentenced by male judges. On legally relevant grounds alone, then, we would expect courts with female judges to impose more severe split sentences on rape offenders. In actuality, we find that split sentences in these courts are more lenient than those imposed in courts composed exclusively of males. For this sentencing decision, it appears that male, not female, judges may be more intolerant of rapists.

We are left, then, with mixed support for the original expectation. Female judges appear to be more likely than male judges to imprison rape offenders and to impose longer prison sentences. Yet they exhibit lenience toward those rape offenders for whom a split sentence was deemed appropriate. As noted above, these differences are based on a small sample of rape offenders sentenced in courts with female judges, and are suggestive rather than definitive.

MALE JUDGES AND FEMALE OFFENDERS

The most common explanation for lenience toward female offenders is the paternalism male judges experience when sentencing them. Although seldom defined rigorously (for reviews, see Nagel and Hagan, 1983; Daly, 1986), paternalism refers to a general protective and benevolent attitude toward women (Moulds, 1980), an attitude presumably held by male but not female judges. In several respects, recent research has eroded the utility of paternalism as an explanation for sex differences in sentencing behavior. Paternalistic attitudes appear to be shared by males and females alike (Steffensmeier, 1977; Kruttschnitt, 1985), and a number of factors unrelated to the sex of the sentencing judge may account for lenience toward women. Among these are the presence of informal social control mechanisms, which obviate the need to invoke harsh formal sanctions (Hagan et al., 1979; Kruttschnitt, 1984; Kruttschnitt and Green, 1984; Daly, 1987) and protectionist attitudes toward the family as a whole (Daly, 1987).

Also influential during sentencing are sex-based stereotypes about the rehabilitative potential of female offenders (Steffensmeier and Kramer, 1982), their relative dangerousness (Steffensmeier and Kramer, 1982), and the kinds of conduct—whether normal or deviant—that are appropriate for women (Simon, 1975; Nagel and Hagan, 1983; Schur, 1984). To date, we do not know whether male and female judges differ in the emphasis they place on these stereotypes. Nevertheless, notions about the appropriateness of female criminality in general and of specific kinds of female criminality (e.g., violence) yield a quite different expectation about the treatment of female offenders. Females convicted of serious felonies violate traditional expectations about what constitutes appropriate normal *and* deviant behavior by women. Male judges may be more threatened than female judges by these violations and, accordingly, may sentence female offenders more harshly.

To examine the relationship between the sex of sentencing judge and the sex of the offender, we constructed a product term between the two variables and entered it into each interactive model. Table 4.9 presents the results of this analysis. The most striking finding is the consistent and unexpected tendency for courts composed exclusively of males to punish female offenders more harshly than those consisting in part of female judges. Although the pattern of results is identical for all three outcomes, only the result for type of sentence is statistically significant and, although significant, the difference is relatively small (8.2%).

In addition to treating female offenders differently, judges also differ in their treatment of male offenders. Courts composed only of male judges are more likely to imprison male offenders than courts with one or more female judges. In contrast, they are slightly, although not significantly, more lenient toward male offenders receiving some form of imprisonment.

In sum, we found little indication that male judges are paternalistic toward female offenders. With one exception, they sentence female offenders more harshly and male offenders more leniently than do female judges. Importantly, however, these trends are not statistically significant for prisoners, and they are not particularly strong for the sample as a whole.

TABLE 4.9. Predicted outcomes for male and female offenders, by sex composition of bench[a]

| | Proportion male | | Effect of |
Sex of offender	Least	Most	sex composition
Type of sentence			
Female	.240	.322	.082*
Male	.641	.823	.182
Disparity	(.401)	(.501)	
Split sentence severity			
Female	33.174	40.274	7.100
Male	48.463	41.943	−6.520
Disparity	(15.289)	(1.669)	
Prison sentence length			
Female	6.936	8.483	1.547
Male	12.609	10.065	−2.544
Disparity	(5.673)	(1.582)	

[a] Predicted outcomes capture the effects of varying sex composition of the bench, while holding constant at the mean the effects of the remaining variables.
*$p \leq .05$.

Differential Treatment and the Age of Judges

Based on appellate court research, we expected older judges to sentence more harshly than their younger colleagues, and to be particularly punitive toward black offenders. We found only slight tendencies for older judges to be harsher (or less lenient) toward blacks than younger judges, and considerable evidence of lenience.

TABLE 4.10. Predicted outcomes for selected offenders, by age of sentencing judge[a]

| Type of offender | Age of sentencing judge | | Effect of judge age |
	Youngest	Oldest	
Type of sentence			
Black	.439	.408	−.031***
White	.450	.291	−.159
Disparity	(.011)	(.117)	
Burglary	.562	.259	−.303***
Average	.502	.394	−.108
Disparity	(.060)	(.135)	
Property theft/damage	.324	.321	−.003***
Average	.502	.394	−.108
Disparity	(.178)	(.073)	
Drug	.150	.164	.014***
Average	.502	.394	−.108
Disparity	(.352)	(.230)	
Split sentence severity			
Black	38.439	43.351	4.912*
White	42.495	38.849	−3.646
Disparity	(4.056)	(4.502)	
Common-law violent	64.189	45.945	−18.244***
Average	41.963	41.048	−.915
Disparity	(22.226)	(4.897)	
Property theft/damage	35.072	44.134	9.062**
Average	41.963	41.048	−.915
Disparity	(6.891)	(3.086)	
Prison sentence length			
Common-law violent	17.793	15.969	−1.824*
Average	7.769	8.827	1.058
Disparity	(10.024)	(7.142)	

[a] Predicted outcomes capture the effects of varying the age of sentencing judge, while holding constant at the mean the effects of the remaining variables.
*$p \leq .05$; **$p \leq .01$; ***$p \leq .005$.

Table 4.10 presents the predicted outcomes for offenders whose sentences are affected by the age of the sentencing judge. Note that in two respects, older judges are more lenient than younger judges toward white offenders. As judges become older, they are less likely to imprison whites and to impose severe split sentences. Their treatment of black offenders is different. Although older judges are also less likely than younger judges to imprison black offenders, their leniency toward blacks is not nearly as pronounced as the leniency they exhibit toward white offenders. Moreover, older judges tend to impose more severe split sentences on black offenders. As a result, blacks are at a comparative disadvantage if they receive split sentences from older judges, and at a comparative advantage if sentenced by younger judges.

When considering differences in treatment based on offense, the findings suggest that older judges are generally less likely that younger judges to incarcerate offenders, particularly those convicted of burglary. Similarly, older judges tend to impose less severe split sentences than younger judges, and exhibit pronounced lenience toward violent offenders. However, although they are generally reluctant to use prison or to impose severe split sentences, older judges do appear intolerant of certain offenders and single them out for harsher sanctions. Most notably, they are slightly more likely to incarcerate drug offenders than are younger judges, and they impose much more severe split sentences on offenders convicted of property theft or damage. Moreover, lenience during the initial decision to incarcerate is accompanied by a willingness to impose slightly longer prison terms. On the average, the prison sentences imposed by older judges are a year longer than those imposed by younger judges. Violent offenders are an exception to this rule and, as was the case for split sentences, older judges treat these offenders more leniently than do younger judges. They impose prison sentences that are nearly 2 years *shorter* than those imposed by younger judges.

In sum, then, older judges are not invariably more punitive than their younger colleagues. Indeed, the results suggest a general reluctance to incarcerate offenders, particularly if they are white or convicted of burglary, as well as a reluctance to impose severe split sentences, particularly on violent offenders. Punitiveness is quite selective, and limited to drug offenders, who are more likely to be incarcerated; blacks and property offenders, who tend to receive more severe split sentences; and offenders sentenced to prison, who, with the exception of those convicted of violence, receive slightly longer prison terms.

None of these patterns is attributable to differences in the seriousness of offenders that older judges must sentence. Either these differences do not exist, or differential treatment persists once they are controlled (i.e., by adding a product term between judge age and legally relevant variables such as number of conviction charges). Indeed, the leniency we found toward violent offenders is particularly anomalous. In comparison with their younger colleagues, older judges sentence violent offenders who have significantly more prior arrests (2.3 vs. 1.4, $p = .01$) and conviction charges (1.6 vs. 1.4, $p = .02$).

Religion and Differential Treatment

As noted earlier, most previous research has compared either Protestant and non-Protestant judges (Goldman, 1975; Tate, 1981) or Fundamentalists and non-Fundamentalists (Gibson, 1978b). Both distinctions produced meaningful differences in judicial behavior, but neither could be drawn here because of insufficient variation. Instead, we distinguished between presumably conservative Southern Baptists and less conservative non-Baptists. We expected Southern Baptists to be more punitive in general, and more punitive toward blacks in particular. The findings of interactive analyses, presented in Table 4.11, provide mixed support for this expectation. Baptists do indeed punish several types of offenders (violent, property thieves and damagers) more severely than non-Baptists. Surprisingly, however, they are more lenient than non-Baptists toward blacks, as well as toward offenders convicted of burglary.

TABLE 4.11. Predicted outcomes for selected offenders, by religion of sentencing judge[a]

Type of offender	Religion of sentencing judge		Effect of judge religion
	Non-Baptist	Baptist	
Type of sentence			
Black	.431	.413	−.018***
White	.364	.402	.038
Disparity	(.067)	(.011)	
Split sentence severity			
Black	41.710	38.937	−2.773*
White	40.241	41.818	1.577
Disparity	(1.469)	(2.881)	
Common-law violent	53.175	60.336	7.161***
Average	41.332	41.908	.576
Disparity	(11.843)	(18.428)	
Burglary	43.056	35.623	−7.433***
Average	41.332	41.908	.576
Disparity	(1.724)	(6.285)	
Property theft/damage	37.131	43.000	5.869*
Average	41.332	41.908	.576
Disparity	(4.201)	(1.092)	
Prison sentence length			
Black	10.387	9.471	−.916**
White	9.455	10.498	1.043
Disparity	(.932)	(1.027)	

[a] Predicted outcomes capture the effects of varying the religion of sentencing judge, while holding constant at the mean the effects of the remaining variables.
*$p \leq .05$; **$p \leq .01$; ***$p \leq .005$.

One of the more unexpected features of the findings is the tendency for Baptist judges to be more lenient toward black offenders. In comparison with their non-Baptist colleagues, Baptist judges are slightly less likely to imprison black offenders. They also impose slightly less severe split sentences and shorter prison terms. In contrast, Baptist judges sentence white offenders more severely than do non-Baptist judges. They are more likely to imprison white offenders, and to impose more severe split sentences and longer prison terms on white than non-Baptist judges. All these differences in treatment are slight, and suggest that the effect of religion on race differences is significant but not strong.

Still, we thought it essential to consider factors other than religion that could account for these unexpected patterns. The first possibility is that Baptist judges are more punitive than non-Baptists toward white offenders because they tend to sentence more serious white offenders. This does not appear to be the case, since there were no differences in the seriousness of white offenders sentenced by Baptist and non-Baptist judges.

The second possibility is that Baptist judges are more lenient toward blacks because they tend to sentence less serious black offenders. We found some evidence this is the case. For the sample as a whole, blacks sentenced in Baptist courts were convicted of significantly less serious offenses than blacks sentenced in non-Baptist courts (9.1 vs. 9.4, $p = .05$). For the subsample of prisoners, blacks sentenced by Baptist judges had significantly fewer charges (1.4 vs. 1.8, $p = .0001$) and prior arrests (2.1 vs. 2.8, $p = .0001$). They were also less likely than their counterparts sentenced to prison by non-Baptist judges to have been incarcerated in Georgia (.21 vs. .26, $p = .003$).

We controlled for these differences by including product terms between race, religion, and the legally relevant dimensions along which courts varied. For each sentencing outcome, race differences persisted virtually unchanged. Thus, the effect of religion on race differences in treatment does not appear to be due to the tendency for less serious black offenders to be concentrated in courts composed of Southern Baptists.

Religion has few implications for differences in treatment based on offense. Indeed, offense differences in treatment are limited only to one of the three sentencing outcomes (split sentences). With one exception, we found the anticipated tendency for Baptist judges to be more punitive than non-Baptists. They impose more severe split sentences than non-Baptist judges on offenders convicted of common-law violence and property theft and damage. The one exception to this trend involves the split sentences imposed on burglary offenders, where Baptist judges are more lenient than non-Baptists.

In sum, then, we found some tendency for Baptist judges to punish more severely, but it was noteworthy only for the split sentences imposed on two groups of offenders: violent and property thieves/damagers. More importantly, we found lenience where we least expected it. For each sentencing outcome, Baptist judges are more lenient than non-Baptists toward black offenders and harsher toward white offenders. With the exception of prison sentences, though, these differences in treatment are comparatively small, and suggest that, while religion has an unanticipated moderating effect on the punishment of black offenders, it is not a strong one.

The Sentencing Behavior of Former Prosecutors

Research on the judicial behavior of former prosecutors has tended to focus on appellate court decisions. It suggests that former prosecutors are more likely to vote conservatively on civil liberties and economic issues (Johnston, 1976; Tate, 1981). More recent research at the trial court level, based on seven judges within a single circuit in Florida, found no direct effect of prosecutorial experience on the use of prison (Frazier and Bock, 1982).

We thought former prosecutors would be more punitive, particularly toward black and more dangerous offenders. The results of our analysis, presented in Table 4.12, partly support this expectation. For certain sentencing decisions and offenders, former prosecutors are noticeably harsher than judges without prosecutorial experience. Particularly surprising, though, is the comparative harshness former prosecutors extend toward white offenders. In comparison with nonprosecutors, judges with prosecutorial experience are more likely to imprison *both* blacks and whites, but the increased risk of imprisonment is greater for white than for black offenders (+15.9% vs. +10.4%). Judges with the greatest amount of experience as a prosecutor appear to treat black offenders no differently than white offenders. In contrast, judges without prosecutor experience are slightly more likely to incarcerate black offenders.

Initially, we thought that these race differences were the result of a tendency for former prosecutors to be faced with more serious offenders than nonprosecutors. Among judges without prosecutor experience, for example, the mean seriousness of offenses committed by blacks is 9.2 and by whites, 8.5. Comparable figures among former prosecutors are slightly but significantly larger (9.5 and 8.7, respectively). We reanalyzed the data, adding a product term consisting of race, offense seriousness, and prosecutor experience. The original pattern remained unchanged. Former prosecutors are more likely than judges without prosecutor experience to imprison both black and white offenders, but are more punitive toward white offenders, particularly those convicted of serious offenses. Again, however, since we could not determine whether black offenders with prior records are concentrated in courts where former prosecutors preside, differences in the initial decision to imprison must be accepted cautiously.

In comparison with nonprosecutors, former prosecutors are also more likely to incarcerate offenders, particularly those convicted of burglary; to impose more severe split sentences, particularly on drug offenders; and to imprison robbery offenders for longer periods of time. Three of these differences are particularly noticeable. First, if sentenced by former prosecutors, burglary offenders are 28.5% more likely to be imprisoned than if they had been sentenced by judges without prosecutorial experience. Second, as prosecutor experience increases, the split sentences imposed on drug offenders become markedly more severe

TABLE 4.12. Predicted outcomes for selected offenders, by judicial prosecutorial experience[a]

Type of offender	Prosecutor experience		Effect of prosecutor experience
	None	Most	
Type of sentence			
Black	.410	.514	.104*
White	.355	.514	.159
Disparity	(.055)	(.000)	
Common-law violent	.434	.495	.061***
Average	.436	.556	.120
Disparity	(.002)	(.061)	
Burglary	.384	.669	.285***
Average	.436	.556	.120
Disparity	(.052)	(.113)	
Drug	.149	.201	.052***
Average	.436	.556	.120
Disparity	(.287)	(.355)	
Split sentence severity			
Robbery	45.454	42.550	−2.904*
Average	40.466	47.432	6.966
Disparity	(4.988)	(4.882)	
Drug	39.396	57.786	18.390***
Average	40.466	47.432	6.966
Disparity	(1.070)	(10.354)	
Prison sentence length			
Robbery	5.364	7.788	2.424**
Average	8.510	7.007	−1.503
Disparity	(3.146)	(.781)	

[a] Predicted outcomes capture the effects of varying prosecutorial experience, while holding constant at the mean the effects of the remaining variables.
*$p \leq .05$; **$p \leq .01$; ***$p \leq .005$.

(+18.4). As a result, if sentenced by a former prosecutor, drug offenders are treated more severely than the average offender. In contrast, if sentenced by judges without prosecutor experience, drug offenders receive split sentences that differ little from those imposed on the average offender.

Finally, the prison sentences that former prosecutors impose on robbery offenders are nearly 2.5 years longer than those imposed by judges without prosecutor experience. When compared with the average offender, robbery offenders are at an advantage if sentenced by nonprosecutors because their sentences are 3 years *shorter* than the average sentence. They are at a *disadvantage*, however, if sentenced by a former prosecutor, because their prison sentences are about 9 months *longer* than the average prison sentence.

The punitiveness of former prosecutors toward robbery offenders can be traced in part to their tendency to sentence more serious robbery offenders. In comparison with nonprosecutors, former prosecutors sentence robbery offenders who have significantly more prior arrests (3.0 vs. 2.1, $p = .03$) and who are more likely to have been incarcerated in Georgia (.26 vs. .17, $p = .03$). We added product terms consisting of the vector for robbery, the two legally relevant factors, and prosecutor experience to the interactive model. After reanalyzing the data, we found little difference in the sentences imposed on robbery offenders without prior arrests or incarceration. Instead, former prosecutors impose much longer prison sentences than nonprosecutors on robbery offenders with prior arrests (9.2 years longer) and prior incarceration in Georgia (7.4 years longer).

In sum, the results provide evidence that former prosecutors are more punitive than their colleagues without prosecutor experience. They are more willing to incarcerate offenders, particularly those convicted of burglary, and to impose more severe split sentences, particularly on drug offenders. Former prosecutors balance this harshness, however, with a reluctance to impose long prison terms. On the average their prison sentences are 1.5 years shorter than those imposed by nonprosecutors. The one exception to this pattern is their apparent intolerance of robbery offenders with prior records, who receive significantly longer prison sentences than their counterparts sentenced by judges without prosecutor experience. Finally, former prosecutors do not single out black offenders for disproportionately harsh treatment. Rather, they are more likely to imprison both black and white offenders, and appear to be particularly harsh toward *white* offenders.

Community Involvement and Differential Treatment

The following sections explore the possibility that differential treatment depends on the extent to which judges are politically or socially involved in the community. As noted earlier, the county and court officials we interviewed were unanimous in perceiving the public as critical of what they (the public) considered lenient (i.e., nonprison) sentences. As a result, we thought that as judges become more involved in their communities, they would also become more responsive to public demands for harsh punishment. Put concretely, they would be more likely than less involved judges to sentence offenders to prison. In addition, they would impose more severe split sentences and longer prison terms on offenders for whom they consider prison appropriate. We also expected offenders who may be perceived as particularly dangerous to the community (e.g., black, violent, drug) to bear a disproportionate share of this punitiveness.

In general, we found the expected harshness from judges who are involved in the community. Yet, these tendencies are quite slight, and are consistent only for violent offenders. One of the more striking features of the findings was the absence of any tendency for heavily involved judges to be particularly harsh toward black offenders. Moreover, we found a few instances where involved judges are more *lenient* toward certain offenders (e.g., black), particularly those who receive some form of imprisonment.

The following sections discuss in greater detail the findings for three measures of local involvement: whether the judge was born in the circuit, the number of community organizations of which the judge is a member, and the years of previous experience in local government.

The Sentencing Behavior of Local Judges

Table 4.13 presents predicted outcomes for offenders whose sentences are affected by whether the judge was born in the circuit in which he or she currently presides. Note first the unanticipated findings for the split sentences imposed on black and white offenders. Rather than sentence blacks more harshly, local judges tend to be more lenient toward both black and white offenders. Put differ-

TABLE 4.13. Predicted outcomes for selected offenders, by judicial circuit of origin[a]

| | Circuit of origin | | |
Type of offender	Born outside circuit	Born in circuit	Effect of circuit of origin
Type of sentence			
Common-law violent	.403	.468	.065*
Average	.401	.486	.085
Disparity	(.002)	(.018)	
Burglary	.341	.477	.136***
Average	.401	.486	.085
Disparity	(.060)	(.009)	
Split sentence severity			
Black	49.774	34.933	−14.841***
White	46.987	36.880	−10.107
Disparity	(2.787)	(1.947)	
Robbery	56.756	37.525	−19.231***
Average	49.650	36.378	−13.272
Disparity	(7.106)	(1.147)	
Drug	30.579	49.653	19.074**
Average	49.650	36.378	−13.272
Disparity	(19.071)	(13.275)	
Prison sentence length			
Robbery	6.340	5.400	−.940***
Average	10.387	7.049	−3.338
Disparity	(4.047)	(1.649)	
Burglary	8.901	4.487	−4.414*
Average	10.387	7.049	−3.338
Disparity	(1.486)	(2.562)	

[a] Predicted outcomes capture the effects of varying circuit of origin, while holding constant at the mean the effects of the remaining variables.
*$p \leq .05$; **$p \leq .01$; ***$p \leq .005$.

ently, as courts become increasingly composed of local judges, split sentences, particularly those imposed on blacks, become less severe.

The remaining findings focus on offense differences in treatment. As expected, local judges punish presumably more dangerous offenders more severely than do nonlocal judges. They are more likely than their nonlocal colleagues to imprison violent and burglary offenders, and to impose more severe split sentences on drug offenders. None of these findings is traceable to differences in the offenders local judges are likely to sentence. We compared offenders sentenced by local and nonlocal judges along several legally relevant dimensions (e.g., offense seriousness, prior record, conviction charges) and found no significant differences.

There are two important exceptions to this general trend of punitiveness, however. First, local judges impose more lenient split and straight prison sentences on robbery offenders than do nonlocal judges, and the prison sentences they impose on burglary offenders are nearly 4.5 years shorter than those imposed by nonlocal judges. Given public sensitivity to property crimes, both findings are particularly surprising. To rule out the possibility that the lenience of local judges is due to the fact that they receive less serious robbery and burglary offenders than nonlocal judges, we compared the robbery and burglary offenders sentenced by local and nonlocal judges along several legally relevant dimensions. Local judges are indeed faced with less serious robbery and burglary offenders than nonlocal judges. For example, burglary offenders sentenced to prison by local judges tend to have significantly fewer charges (1.4 vs. 1.8, $p = .0001$) and prior arrests (2.2 vs. 2.8, $p = .01$) than those sentenced to prison by nonlocal judges. Yet the lenience of local judges persists, even after we control for these differences by adding interaction terms involving burglary, circuit of origin, and the two legally relevant variables.

The findings for burglary suggest that both local and nonlocal judges balance lenient with harsher treatment, but use different sentencing strategies. Local judges are more willing than nonlocal judges to imprison burglary offenders, but relatively reluctant to impose long prison terms. This sentencing strategy may reflect a willingness to balance public demands for imprisonment with administrative injunctions not to aggravate the overcrowding problem. Nonlocal judges, in contrast, are more reluctant to imprison burglary offenders, but willing to impose longer prison terms on those for whom prison was deemed appropriate. These judges may be less sensitive to public demands for harshness, more concerned with the overcrowding problem, or both.

As noted above, local judges sentence robbery offenders more leniently than nonlocal judges, and this lenience could be an outcome of differences in the seriousness of robbery offenders. They tend to be less serious in local courts, that is, convicted of fewer (1.3 vs. 1.8, $p = .0001$) and less serious (17.0 vs. 18.6, $p = .03$) offenses than their counterparts sentenced by nonlocal judges. After controlling for the interaction between robbery, circuit of origin, and these legally relevant factors, significant differences in split sentences persist. Lenience is particularly pronounced, however, for less serious robbery offenders. Their split sentences decline by -25.1, whereas those imposed on more serious robbery offenders do not decline as sharply (-17.7). In contrast, whereas local judges impose shorter prison terms than nonlocal judges on robbery offenders convicted of a single charge, they levy slightly *longer* sentences (2 years) on robbery offenders convicted of multiple offenses.

In sum, the findings suggest that, with some exceptions, local judges balance public demands for punitiveness with administrative concerns about prison overcrowding. Although more likely than nonlocal judges to incarcerate offenders, they combine this harshness with the imposition of less severe split sentences, particularly on blacks, as well as shorter prison terms. Their strategy is clearest for the sentencing of burglary offenders, who are much more likely than average to be incarcerated by local judges, but also receive prison terms that are nearly 4.5 years shorter than those imposed by nonlocal judges. The severe split sentences imposed on drug offenders are important exceptions to this pattern, and could reflect the priority attached to growing concerns about the drug problem, concerns that have fueled several revisions and extensions of laws governing controlled substances.

COMMUNITY ORGANIZATIONS AND DIFFERENTIAL TREATMENT

In comparison with most judicial characteristics, membership in community organizations has little effect on differential treatment. It has no implications for race differences in punishment, and only affects the sentences imposed on violent offenders. Table 4.14 presents the results of significant interactions.

As was the case for local judges, involved judges appear to use a different sentencing strategy than less involved judges. In general, they are more likely than uninvolved judges to incarcerate offenders, and they balance this harshness with a tendency to impose prison sentences that average about 2 years shorter than

TABLE 4.14. Predicted outcomes for violent offenders, by judicial membership in community organizations[a]

| | Community organization memberships | | Effect of |
Type of offender	None	Most	community involvement
Type of sentence			
Common-law violent	.452	.404	$-.048$***
Average	.440	.507	.067
Disparity	(.012)	(.103)	
Prison sentence length			
Common-law violent	16.530	18.410	1.880***
Average	8.698	6.665	-2.033
Disparity	(7.832)	(11.745)	

[a] Predicted outcomes capture the effects of varying membership in community organizations, while holding constant at the mean the effects of the remaining variables.
*** $p \leq .005$.

TABLE 4.15. Predicted outcomes for selected offenders, by judicial experience in local government[a]

Type of offender	Local government experience		Effect of government experience
	None	Most	
Type of sentence			
Black	.431	.354	−.077*
White	.379	.359	−.020
Disparity	(.052)	(.005)	
Robbery	.687	.744	.057*
Average	.454	.440	−.014
Disparity	(.233)	(.304)	
Property theft/damage	.332	.220	−.112***
Average	.454	.440	−.014
Disparity	(.122)	(.220)	
Split sentence severity			
Common-law violent	53.556	80.801	27.245***
Average	41.156	45.893	4.737
Disparity	(12.400)	(34.908)	
Burglary	40.740	36.127	−4.613*
Average	41.156	45.893	4.737
Disparity	(.416)	(9.766)	
Property theft/damage	39.936	31.546	−8.390**
Average	41.156	45.893	4.737
Disparity	(1.220)	(14.347)	
Prison sentence length			
Common-law violent	16.576	21.383	4.807*
Average	8.226	8.886	.660
Disparity	(8.350)	(12.497)	

[a] Predicted outcomes capture the effects of varying judicial experience in local government, while holding constant at the mean the effects of the remaining variables.
*$p \leq .05$; **$p \leq .01$; ***$p \leq .005$.

those imposed by judges who are not members of local community organizations. Their treatment of violent offenders departs from this pattern, however. They are slightly less willing than noninvolved judges to imprison violent offenders, but more willing to impose longer prison terms. It merits emphasis, however, that these differences are slight, suggesting that community involvement does not operate as a particularly strong conditioner of differential treatment.

LOCAL GOVERNMENT EXPERIENCE AND DIFFERENTIAL TREATMENT

The final dimension of community involvement measures judicial experience in local government prior to becoming a judge. The results of interactive analysis, presented in Table 4.15, suggest that judges with previous experience in local government are selectively punitive. Their treatment of violent offenders is particularly noteworthy. As experience in local government increases, judges impose increasingly more severe split sentences and longer prison terms on these offenders. For example, if sentenced by a judge with government experience, violent offenders receive prison sentences that are 4.8 years longer than those imposed by judges without any experience.

When we consider the sentencing of black and property offenders, a strikingly different pattern emerges. Judges with government experience are less likely than their colleagues without experience to incarcerate blacks and offenders convicted of property theft and damage. They also impose less severe split sentences on offenders convicted of burglary and property theft and damage.

On the one hand, experience in local government appears to intensify harsher treatment of violent offenders, whereas on the other, it intensifies the comparative lenience directed toward black and selected property offenders.

Electoral Vulnerability and Differential Treatment

Our analysis included two measures of the electoral vulnerability of judges: whether they had faced opposition in their most recent primary and whether they had been elected three or more times. Based in part on Alpert et al.'s (1979) discussion of stages in judicial careers, we expected electorally vulnerable judges to be more responsive to public demands for harsh punishment. As was the case for judicial involvement in the community, we also expected these judges to be particularly harsh toward offenders the community considers most threatening (e.g., violent, black, drug).

Support for these expectations was quite limited. Only opposition in primaries fosters the expected harshness toward black offenders. We found an unanticipated tendency for presumably vulnerable judges to sentence violent offenders more *leniently* and, as was the case for judges with experience in local government, electorally vulnerable judges are unexpectedly lenient toward certain property offenders. First we examine the effect of opposition in primaries on differences in treatment, then the importance of election history.

THE SENTENCING BEHAVIOR OF OPPOSED JUDGES

Table 4.16 compares the sentencing behavior of judges who faced opposition in primaries with those who were unopposed. Notice that opposition in primaries is a significant consideration primarily for offenders who have been sentenced to prison. The results provide some support for the argument that black and common-law violent offenders are at a disadvantage if sentenced by electorally vulnerable judges. Opposed judges are more likely than their unopposed counterparts to imprison blacks and less likely to imprison white offenders. This trend toward punitiveness persists, despite the fact that black offenders sentenced by opposed judges tend to be convicted of significantly more serious offenses than those sentenced by unopposed judges (8.8 vs. 9.2, $p = .05$).

TABLE 4.16. Predicted outcomes for selected offenders, by judicial opposition in primaries[a]

Type of offender	Opposition in primaries		Effect of opposition in primaries
	None	Most	
Type of sentence			
Black	.419	.507	.088***
White	.383	.289	−.094
Disparity	(.036)	(.218)	
Prison sentence length			
Common-law violent	16.293	29.006	12.713***
Average	8.193	9.826	1.633
Disparity	(8.100)	(19.180)	
Robbery	5.916	2.468	−3.448***
Average	8.193	9.826	1.633
Disparity	(2.277)	(7.358)	
Burglary	6.222	3.894	−2.328*
Average	8.193	9.826	1.633
Disparity	(1.971)	(5.932)	
Property theft/damage	8.361	6.854	−1.507**
Average	8.193	9.826	1.633
Disparity	(.168)	(2.972)	

[a] Predicted outcomes capture the effects of varying opposition in primaries, while holding constant at the mean the effects of the remaining variables.
*$p \leq .05$; **$p \leq .01$; ***$p \leq .005$.

For two of the three sentencing decisions, opposition in primaries has no implications for differential treatment based on offense. Thus, there appears to be an underlying similarity in the sentencing behavior of opposed and unopposed judges. Furthermore, differences between the two types of judges are particularly striking only for the prison sentences imposed on violent offenders. Regardless of judicial opposition in primaries, violent offenders receive longer than average sentences. They are at a particular disadvantage, however, if sentenced by judges who have been opposed in primaries, because their prison sentences are 12.7 years longer than those they would have received from an unopposed judge.

It is important to emphasize, however, that judges who faced opposition in primaries are not invariably harsher than their less vulnerable colleagues. Several types of property offenders receive significantly *shorter* prison terms if sentenced by an opposed judge. Among these are offenders convicted of both serious (e.g., robbery, burglary) and comparatively minor property crimes (e.g., property theft and damage). To see whether these unanticipated trends reflect a concentration of less serious property offenders among opposed judges, we compared the offenders that opposed and unopposed judges sentence along several legally relevant dimensions (e.g., offense seriousness, prior record, conviction charges). Surprisingly, we found that opposed judges tend to sentence robbery offenders with significantly *more* conviction charges than those sentenced by unopposed judges (2.7 vs. 1.7, $p = .03$). This difference leads us to expect that judges who have faced opposition will impose *longer* prison sentences on robbery offenders. In actuality, their sentences are 1.5 years shorter than those imposed by judges who were elected without opposition.

In sum, the findings for violent offenders sentenced to prison and the presence of race differences in imprisonment risk are consistent with the notion that opposition fosters selective responsiveness to public pressure for harsher punishment. Importantly, however, the expected harshness toward serious property offenders (e.g., robbers, burglars) failed to materialize.

THE ROLE OF ELECTION HISTORY DURING SENTENCING

Table 4.17 presents the findings for election history. Without exception, differences in treatment are quite modest, and suggest that electoral history is not a strong conditioner of differential treatment. Further, although election history

TABLE 4.17. Predicted outcomes for selected offenders, by judicial election history[a]

Type of offender	Judicial election history		Effect of election history
	0–2 Elections	3 + Elections	
Type of sentence			
Common-law violent	.444	.442	−.002***
Average	.418	.482	.064
Disparity	(.026)	(.040)	
Burglary	.354	.482	.128***
Average	.418	.482	.064
Disparity	(.064)	(.000)	
Property theft/damage	.305	.337	.032***
Average	.418	482	.064
Disparity	(.113)	(.145)	
Split sentence severity			
Burglary	41.780	39.171	−.609*
Average	41.684	41.419	−.265
Disparity	(.096)	(2.248)	
Prison sentence length			
Black	10.472	9.880	−.592*
White	9.557	9.925	.368
Disparity	(.915)	(.045)	
Common-law violent	16.496	17.152	.656*
Average	8.405	8.203	−.202
Disparity	(8.091)	(8.949)	

[a] Predicted outcomes capture the effects of varying the election history of judges, while holding constant at the mean the effects of the remaining variables.
*$p \le .05$; ***$p \le .005$.

has the anticipated effect on race differences in treatment, it is slight and limited to offenders sentenced to prison. Less established judges impose longer prison sentences on blacks and shorter sentences on whites.

With one exception (the split sentences of burglary offenders), most of the findings suggest that it may be established judges who are responsive to public demands for harsh punishment. They tend to impose slightly longer prison sentences on violent offenders, and they are also more likely than less established judges to imprison offenders convicted of property offenses (burglars, property thieves/damagers). True, established judges are usually faced with more serious violent and property offenders. For example, they sentence offenders whose violent crimes are significantly more serious than those sentenced by less established judges (12.5 vs. 11.6, $p = .01$). Yet differences in treatment persist, even after the interaction between seriousness and election history is controlled.

Summary

The analysis reported in this chapter provides two quite different images of the relationship between the court and sentencing. Regression models that assessed the direct effect of court and judge characteristics conveyed the impression that these factors are relatively unimportant. Their effects were often not statistically significant, and were usually smaller than those exerted by characteristics of the offender and the offense. Moreover, additive effects provided no strong or consistent support for the expectation, based on previous research, that judges who are conservative, involved in the community, or electorally vulnerable would be more punitive during sentencing.

Interactive models allowed us to determine the existence of a more complex relationship between the court and sentencing. Rather than ask whether court characteristics affect sentences, these models enabled us to determine whether court characteristics affect the role race and offense play during sentencing. We found that, in contrast to their limited direct effects, court variables operate as impressive conditioners of differential treatment for all three sentencing decisions analyzed. An accurate understanding of the relationship between the court and sentencing requires, then, that we use an analytic strategy that considers court variables in conjunction with characteristics of the offender and the offense.

Similarly, an accurate indication of the effect that case characteristics have on sentences hinges on the consideration of the court context where sentences are imposed. Recall from additive analyses that blacks are slightly more likely than whites to be imprisoned and to receive longer prison sentences. A consideration of the court context reveals the presence of many situations where black offenders receive noticeably more *lenient* treatment than whites, whether in the form of a smaller risk of being incarcerated (e.g., in less specialized courts; among younger judges) or shorter prison sentences (e.g., where female judges preside; in Baptist courts). Finally, a consideration of context reveals the

Finally, there was no evidence that male judges are paternalistic and sentence female offenders more leniently than their female colleagues. Indeed, male judges appeared to sentence female offenders more harshly than did courts with female judges. This pattern may reflect an intolerance toward the criminality of convicted female felons, because it violates two sets of traditional expectations: those that define the appropriate normal behavior for women and expectations about their typical criminal behavior (e.g., less serious, nonviolent). With the exception of the initial decision to imprison, female judges sentenced male offenders more severely than did their male colleagues. This pattern may reflect sex-based stereotypes about the greater dangerousness of male offenders, as well as greater sympathy or paternalism toward female offenders.

The final set of questions centered on the relationship between the judge and the community. We thought that if judges were politically and socially involved in the community or electorally vulnerable, they would sentence more punitively, particularly offenders who may be perceived as very threatening to the community. Several findings fit the expected pattern. Involved judges tended to sentence violent and drug offenders more harshly than less involved judges. For burglary offenders, about which public concern in Georgia is high, involved judges also appeared responsive for public demands to "get offenders off the streets": they were more likely to imprison burglary offenders than less involved judges. On the other hand, involved judges also appeared to be aware of prison overcrowding, and compensated for their willingness to imprison by imposing shorter prison terms. In contrast, less involved judges combined a reluctance to imprison burglary offenders with a willingness to impose longer prison terms. This strategy suggests less sensitivity toward public opinion or a preference for reserving prison only for those few burglary offenders who deserve it.

Although social and political involvement in the community intensified harshness toward certain types of offenders, it did not intensify harshness toward black offenders. Indeed, involvement either had no effect on race differences or fostered a disproportionate lenience toward black offenders.

What can we say of the behavior of electorally vulnerable judges? On the one hand, vulnerable judges such as those who faced opposition in primaries were harsher than less vulnerable judges toward black and violent offenders. At the same time, however, they were surprisingly lenient toward several types of property offenders, including those who are relatively serious (e.g., robbers, burglars). Furthermore, judges whose election history led us to expect they would be isolated from public demands for punitiveness nonetheless treated several types of offenders (e.g., violent, burglars, property thieves/damagers) more harshly than less established judges.

Conclusion

As was the case for attributes of the surrounding community, the more proximate court context had little direct bearing on sentencing outcomes. Instead, several aspects of the court, in particular the background characteristics of the judge, operated as relatively powerful conditioners of differential treatment based on race and offense. As a result, an accurate indication of the role both court and offender attributes play during sentencing requires that we consider them simultaneously. In the next chapter, we focus on the final context of interest, the element of time. We identify changes in sentencing outcomes over time, and explore the extent to which these changes reflect litigation on the issue of race discrimination as well as substantive changes in the penal code that occurred during the period of this study.

Notes

1. As noted in Chapter 2, intercorrelations among contextual variables make it difficult to estimate the unique effect each variable has on sentencing. This was particularly the case when estimating the effects of county variables, some of which tended to be highly correlated. Court and county variables are less strongly associated, in large part because the levels at which the two sets of variables were measured differ. Although statistically significant, correlations seldom exceeded .20. Nevertheless, we found during preliminary analysis that many court variables had slightly different effects when the county factors of urbanization, economic conditions, and crime were included in regression models. As a result, in all analyses reported in this chapter, we controlled for the effects of county variables by including them in additive and interactive equations.
2. As court specialization increases, the prison sentences imposed on less serious white offenders (i.e., those one standard deviation below mean seriousness) decline by 3.9 years, whereas those imposed on more serious offenders (i.e., those one standard deviation above mean seriousness) decline by 5.1 years.
3. Since female judges presided in circuits with between two and seven judges, judicial information on sex was aggregated. As a result, we do not know exactly how many offenders were sentenced by female judges. However, 1,024 offenders were sentenced in courts where female judges preside.

5
The Context of Time

In the previous two chapters, we documented the ways in which the sentences imposed on convicted felons vary as a function of the county and the court where sentencing occurs. We also demonstrated that both the magnitude and direction of differential treatment are contingent on the court and surrounding community. In this chapter, we consider the context of time, and its implications for outcomes and for differential treatment during sentencing.

The first section describes major trends in sentences for the period January 1976 through May 1985. Next, we explore several correlates or possible causes of these trends, in particular changes in the types of offenders judges sentence (e.g., the seriousness of their offenses). We then estimate the effect of time, holding constant these changes.

The final section examines trends in differential treatment by race and offense. The analysis addresses two major questions. First, to what extent has the significance of race changed over time? That is, has litigation appeared to foster more evenhanded treatment? Second, to what extent does the sentencing behavior of judges reflect legislative concern with specific types of crimes?

Sentencing Trends Over Time

Figure 5.1 plots the annual percentage of offenders who were sentenced to prison or to a combination of prison and probation. The use of prison declined from 45.7% to 31% between 1976 and 1979; increased gradually to a peak of 39% in 1982; and since then has declined. Although based on the first 5 months of 1985, the most recent data reveal a continued decline: only 23.6% of all convicted offenders were incarcerated. During the time period of this study, then, the use of imprisonment has declined sharply, from nearly half to less than a quarter of all offenders.

Figure 5.2 shows similar although much weaker trends for split sentences. They became slightly less severe between 1976 and 1980, increased in 1981 and 1982, and declined somewhat sharply thereafter. In comparison with changes in the use of prison, these trends are modest. Split sentences ranged in severity from

FIGURE 5.1. Percent offenders sentenced to prison.

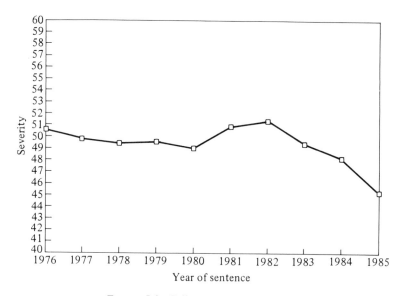

FIGURE 5.2. Split sentence severity.

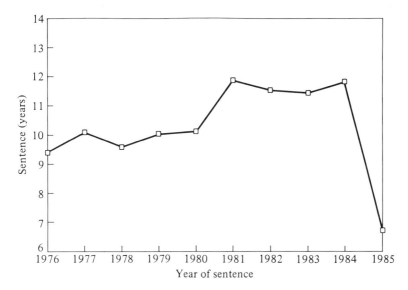

FIGURE 5.3. Prison sentence length.

a high of 51.3 in 1982 to a low of 45.2 in 1985, a difference that is less than a third of a standard deviation from the grand mean.

A different pattern describes the imposition of straight prison sentences. Figure 5.3 indicates that prison sentences became longer between 1976 and 1981, from a low of 9.4 years to a high of nearly 12 years. They remained at elevated levels until 1985, when they declined sharply from an average of 11.9 years to 6.7 years. Since the number of offenders receiving prison sentences by May of 1985 was relatively small ($N = 100$), this decline may misrepresent annual trends, and must remain tentative.

In sum, sentencing in Georgia, particularly the use of prison and split sentences, has become more lenient in recent years. Indeed, as of mid-1985 the risk of imprisonment was the smallest, split sentences the most lenient, and prison sentences the shortest of the entire period. In the following section, we consider whether these patterns can be traced to changes in the kinds of offenders eligible for sentencing.

Trends in the Characteristics of Offenders

One possible explanation for recent lenience is a change in the composition of convicted offenders judges must sentence. The most obvious possibility is that judges are faced with less serious offenders, or with offenders for whom severe sentences may be considered inappropriate. Appendix Table D presents the annual means for legally relevant factors and the social background attributes of offenders. In this section, we focus on attributes for which noticeable changes over time occurred.

The clearest changes entailed the seriousness and type of crimes of which offenders were convicted. Figure 5.4 presents the mean seriousness of offenses for the sample as a whole, for split prisoners, and for offenders receiving straight prison terms. Note first that the trend for the sample as a whole mirrors changes in the use of prison. Between 1977 and 1979, offenses became less serious. Thereafter, they gradually increased in seriousness, and after 1981 again declined to a record low of 7.64 by mid-1985. Although similar, these trends do not correspond exactly to the use of prison, because offenses began to decline in seriousness about a year before subsequent declines in the percentage of offenders receiving some form of incarceration.

Although offense seriousness and the use of prison closely correspond, the same cannot be said for split sentences. Except for a slight decline between 1977 and 1979, there has been relatively little change over time in offense seriousness. Thus, the sharp increase in split sentence severity between 1980 and 1982, as well as later declines, have no counterpart in the seriousness of offenses of which split prisoners were convicted. As will become apparent later, trends in split sentences are also not simple reflections of changes in the distribution of offenses.

For the final outcome, prison sentence length, we see only a partial correspondence between offense seriousness and the length of prison sentences. Until 1981, the gradual increase in seriousness coincided with an increase in prison

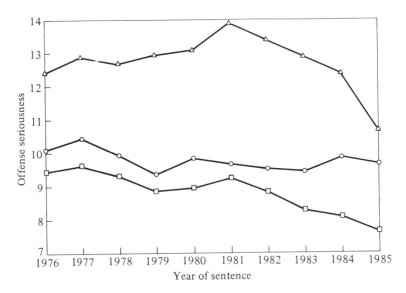

FIGURE 5.4. Offense seriousness.
□, Total sample; ○, split sentence; △, prison sentence.

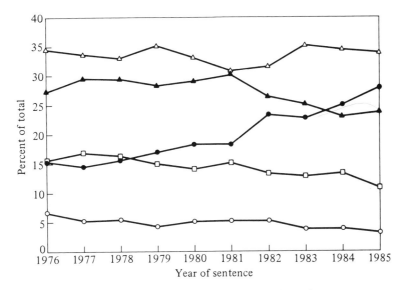

FIGURE 5.5. Offense distribution for total sample.
□, Violent; ○, robbery; ▲, burglary; △, property; ●, drugs.

sentences. After 1981, offenses became increasingly less serious, while prison sentences remained elevated until the sharp decline of 1985.

Changes in sentencing patterns, then, correspond to or follow changes in offense seriousness only to a limited extent. The next set of figures examines the distribution of offenses over time. We begin with Figure 5.5, which considers the entire sample and helps account for the declining use of prison noted earlier. First, since 1981 the percentage of offenders convicted of burglary has declined. As one of the more serious offenses, burglary carries a penalty of between 1 and 20 years for a first offense, 2 to 20 years for the second, and 5 to 20 years for the third. Probation or suspended sentences are not permitted for offenders with prior convictions. Since 1981, then, a decline in the proportion of burglary offenders to some extent reduced the number of offenders eligible for imprisonment.

Second, during the same time period, the percentage of offenders convicted of property theft and damage increased. Much of this increase occurred within the white-collar offense category. In 1981, 8.8% of all offenders were convicted of forgery, fraud, or embezzlement, whereas in 1984, the figure was 14.8%. This increase does not represent growth in the more serious crimes of embezzlement or forgery, which carry maximum penalties of 15 and 10 years, respectively. Rather, the largest increases occurred in the comparatively minor category of fraud, particularly welfare fraud, which mandates a penalty of only 1 to 5 years. Convictions for welfare fraud increased dramatically from 3.7% of all offenders in the fraud category to 61.3% in 1984. To some extent, then, recent declines in the use of prison correspond with an increase in the proportion of relatively minor white-collar offenders.

Finally, the percentage of offenders convicted of drug crimes increased throughout the time period, and sharply since 1981. A closer examination of this category is depicted in Figure 5.6. For the sake of clarity, the figure excludes attempts (a minority of all drug offenses), and combines offenses involving more serious drugs (e.g., narcotics, stimulants, and depressants) into a single category. The figure reveals precipitous declines since 1981 in possession offenses, particularly of marijuana. Correspondingly, convictions for violating Georgia's Controlled Substances Act have increased sharply since 1981. This act prohibits and specifies penalties for the possession, sale, and distribution of a wide variety of drugs, categorized in Schedules I through V. Particularly after 1980, the Department of Corrections appears to have used this general category both for marijuana possession and for the possession of specific but undesignated drugs in Schedules III through V (e.g., diazepam). Unlike penalties for Schedule I and II drugs, which involve mandatory minimums up to 5 years and maximums of 30 years or life, the penalties stipulated for marijuana and drugs in Schedules III through V lie between 1 and 10 years. Of the total number of offenders convicted of violating this act ($N = 663$), most (93.4%) received probation. Thus, the declining use of prison to some extent reflects a growth in the proportion of offenders convicted of drug offenses for which imprisonment is very unlikely to occur.

To a much more limited extent, the same conclusions apply to split sentences. As Figure 5.7 indicates, the percent of offenders convicted of burglary and, to a

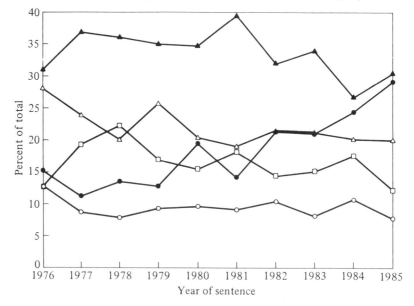

FIGURE 5.6. Distribution of drug offenses.
□, Possess marijuana; ○, possess other drugs; ▲, sell marijuana;
△, sell other drugs; ●, violate Georgia's Controlled Substances Act.

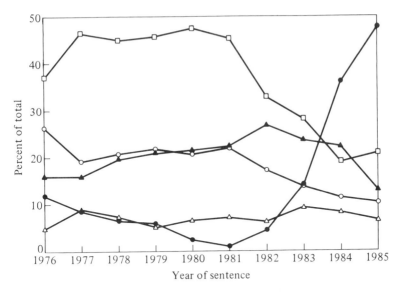

FIGURE 5.7. Offense distribution, split sentence.
□, Violent; ○, robbery; ▲, burglary; △, property; ●, drugs.

lesser degree, violent crimes has declined unevenly since 1981. These declines could account for the tendency for split sentences to become less severe since then. The percent of offenders convicted of drug crimes increased during most of the time period of the study, especially in the more serious categories of sale, distribution, and trafficking in other drugs. For example, the percentage convicted of selling, distributing, or trafficking in illegal drugs, cocaine, or methaqualone increased from 9 in 1981 to 33.3 by mid-1985. The proportion involved in marijuana possession correspondingly declined. In 1981, 39.7% of drug offenders were convicted of possessing marijuana, whereas by 1984, only 19.4% had been so convicted. The increasing seriousness of drug offenses, in itself an outcome of trafficking legislation, partly accounts for the tendency for split sentences between 1980 and 1982 to become more severe. Interestingly, however, despite the continued growth of convictions for serious drug crimes since 1982, split sentences as a whole, and for most drug offenders in particular, have become less severe since then.

As noted in the previous section, prison sentences have gradually become longer during the course of this study, and have declined only recently. Figure 5.8 shows the distribution of offenses for offenders sentenced to prison between 1976 and 1985. Part of the increase in prison sentences can be accounted for by two trends: increases in the percentage convicted of burglary and drug offenses, and a corresponding decline in the percent of offenders convicted of violent offenses. Within the drug category, a growing percentage have been convicted of offenses with mandatory minimums or long prison terms (i.e., trafficking, the sale and

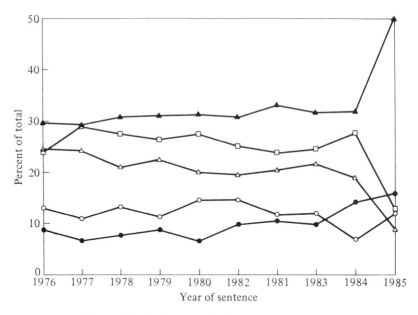

FIGURE 5.8. Offense distribution, prison sentence.
□, Violent; ○, robbery; ▲, burglary; △, property; ●, drugs.

distribution of narcotics), from 42.6 in 1981 to 58.9 in 1984. This increase helps account for the tendency for prison sentences to remain elevated during those years. In 1985, however, convictions for these offenses became less common and only constituted 37.5% of all drug convictions. The recent tendency for most drug offenders to be convicted of less serious possession offenses could account in part for marked declines in prison sentences that occurred in 1985.

In comparison with trends in offense seriousness and type, changes in other characteristics of convicted offenders have either been less dramatic or less sustained. The percent of female offenders convicted of felonies has increased, from 9.2 in 1976 to 16 by mid-1985. This increase reflects their growing involvement in property crimes and, to a much lesser extent, in burglary and robbery. In 1976, 13% of offenders convicted of property theft and damage were female; by 1985, it was 24.2%. Female involvement tended to be concentrated in the white-collar category, in particular, welfare fraud and passing bad checks. Not surprisingly, then, throughout the period of this study, their offenses were significantly less serious than those committed by males (7.2 vs. 9.1, $p \le .0001$). Hence, the growing prosecution of females could contribute to recent declines in both offense seriousness and the use of prison for the sample as a whole.

Although trends for the remaining characteristics have changed little with time, occasional departures from the norm occurred. The percent of blacks in the sample as a whole hovers between 40.5 and 45. The greatest concentration occurred in 1976 and 1985, and subsequently declined in the interim. The percentage of blacks receiving prison sentences also has a narrow range over time (between 50.6 and 59.6), and its distribution resembles that for the sample as a whole. That is, the largest concentrations were in 1977 and 1983, with declines in the interim. Finally, the use of split sentences as a sentencing option for blacks increased fitfully since 1978, when 43.7% of those receiving such sentences were black. By mid-1985, over half (55.2%) of those receiving split sentences were black.

Recent years witnessed a dramatic change in the employment status of offenders. Before 1983, over 70% of offenders sentenced to prison reported being employed. Between 1983 and 1984, however, fewer than half were employed. Among prisoners, for whom we had information about prior record, the average number of prior arrests remained relatively stable over time, and the proportion of offenders who had previously been incarcerated in Georgia declined slightly. For both measures, the year 1983 was a marked departure from the norm. The mean number of prior arrests increased sharply (from 2.1 to 3.1), as did the proportion previously incarcerated in Georgia (from 0.14 to 0.24). These increases might have helped keep prison sentences at an elevated level in 1983, despite declines in offense seriousness.

In short, the characteristics of convicted offenders have changed over time, and several of these changes, particularly those involving offense seriousness and type, help account for the patterns we observed earlier. In the following section, we control for these changes and assess the net effect the year of sentence has on outcomes.

The Effect of Time on Sentences

To estimate the effect of time on sentencing outcomes, we included a set of effect-coded variables representing year of sentence in an equation that included all case, county, and court variables. The year 1976, which included Fulton and DeKalb county data from 1974 and 1975, was designated the excluded category and assigned a score of -1. Its effects were estimated by designating another year (1977) the excluded category, and reanalyzing the data. Since data for only part of 1985 were available, the years 1984 and 1985 were combined.

Table 5.1 presents the results of additive models for the three sentencing outcomes. Without exception, offender, county, and court variables continue to have essentially the same effects as reported earlier. Some variables (e.g., judicial membership in community organizations) no longer significantly affect outcomes, but in earlier additive models their influence on outcomes was always substantively trivial. Conclusions reported in earlier chapters remain valid, then, and we confine our attention to year effects only.

After holding constant variation in the characteristics of offenses and offenders, year of sentence exerts a very small influence on sentencing outcomes. In this respect, the context of time resembles both court and county factors. Its

TABLE 5.1. Regression coefficients and related statistics, additive models for court contexts

Variable	Type of sentence			Split sentence severity			Prison sentence length		
	b	(SE)	β	b	(SE)	β	b	(SE)	β
Offender characteristics									
Type of crime									
Common-law violent	.05	(.01)	.073***	-.66	(.74)	-.021	4.56	(.26)	.237***
Robbery	.24	(.01)	.254***	5.34	(1.33)	.150***	-3.14	(.29)	-.137***
Burglary	-.03	(.01)	-.027***	-.48	(.52)	-.016	-1.92	(.20)	-.097***
Property theft/damage	-.13	(.00)	-.189***	-2.13	(1.01)	-.071*	.24	(.22)	.013
Drug	-.13	(.01)	-.171***	-2.08	(.69)	-.064***	.26	(.28)	.013
Offense seriousness	.02	(.00)	.447***	.99	(.06)	.275***	.86	(.04)	.690***
Prior arrests				.32	(.07)	.083***	.08	(.02)	.038***
Prior incarceration				3.55	(.78)	.076***	1.19	(.26)	.046***
Sex	.09	(.01)	.080***	2.91	(1.16)	.041**	1.55	(.45)	.031***
Race	-.05	(.00)	-.053***	-.42	(.66)	-.011	-.43	(.24)	-.018
Age	.001	(.00)	.014***	.01	(.04)	.004	.02	(.01)	.019*
Marital status				2.42	(.65)	.054***	.34	(.24)	.012
Employment status				-4.22	(.65)	-.102***	-.31	(.22)	-.012
Temporal Context									
1974–76	.01	(.01)	.007	1.17	(.90)	.026	-1.02	(.27)	-.047***
1977	.04	(.01)	.033***	-.61	(1.01)	-.013	-.77	(.28)	-.036**
1978	.02	(.01)	.015***	.54	(1.02)	.011	-.35	(.29)	-.015
1979	-.02	(.01)	-.018***	-.09	(.89)	-.002	-.89	(.30)	-.039***
1980	.02	(.01)	.018***	-.26	(.87)	-.006	-.51	(.29)	-.023
1981	.01	(.01)	.004	2.44	(.87)	.056***	.82	(.32)	.034**
1982	.03	(.01)	.026***	-.77	(.82)	-.019	.30	(.31)	.013
1983	-.05	(.01)	-.048***	-1.22	(.94)	-.030	.72	(.37)	.030*
1984–85	-.05	(.01)	-.057***	-1.20	(.92)	-.032	1.69	(.37)	.068***

	(1) b (SE)	(1) β	(2) b (SE)	(2) β	(3) b (SE)	(3) β
Court bureaucratization						
Caseload pressure	3×10^{-5} (.00)	.006	-.02 (.00)	-.097***	-.003 (.00)	-.030**
Court specialization	-3×10^{-4} (.00)	-.008	-.04 (.02)	-.030	-.02 (.01)	-.020
Judge characteristics						
Sex composition	-.06 (.03)	-.006*	-5.11 (4.44)	-.018	-3.30 (1.56)	-.019*
Age	-.001 (.00)	-.014***	.03 (.06)	.010	.01 (.02)	.007
Religion	.02 (.01)	.013***	.42 (1.11)	.006	.04 (.38)	.001
Years as prosecutor	.01 (.00)	.053***	.32 (.10)	.054***	-.06 (.03)	-.019*
Circuit of origin	.01 (.01)	.010*	-.56 (.90)	-.011	-.23 (.31)	-.008
Membership in community organizations	3×10^{-4} (.00)	.001	.63 (.23)	.046**	-.06 (.08)	-.007
Years in local government	-.001 (.00)	-.013***	.10 (.08)	.020	.04 (.03)	.016
Opponents in primary	-.02 (.01)	-.011**	-4.18 (1.28)	-.053***	.61 (.41)	.015
Election history	.03 (.01)	.033***	.20 (.72)	.005	.44 (.28)	.019
County variables						
Urbanization	5×10^{-7} (.00)	.041***	-2×10^{-5} (.00)	-.068*	-9×10^{-6} (.00)	-.065***
Income standard deviation	7×10^{-8} (.00)	.0003	4×10^{-4} (.00)	.050	2×10^{-4} (.00)	.034
Racial income inequality	2×10^{-6} (.00)	.016***	-2×10^{-4} (.00)	-.042	-8×10^{-5} (.00)	-.029
Lagged unemployment rate	.01 (.00)	.043***	-.97 (.21)	-.085***	.05 (.07)	.008
Percent black						
Under 25% vs. 25–49%	.01 (.00)	.014**	.91 (.75)	.023	-.20 (.28)	-.008
Under 25% vs. 50+%	-.04 (.01)	-.026***	.37 (1.42)	.007	.94 (.50)	.030
Lagged Index crime rate	-2×10^{-7} (.00)	-.001	-4×10^{-4} (.00)	-.070***	-5×10^{-5} (.00)	-.011
Hazard rate			-.98 (8.35)	-.005	-.54 (1.74)	-.011
Intercept	.21 (.04)***		51.02 (9.45)***		.35 (3.23)	
R^2	.209		.204		.673	
N	27,613		4,271		5,022	

$*p \leq .05; **p \leq .01; ***p \leq .005.$

direct influence is usually smaller than the influence of legally relevant factors and social background attributes.

Offenders faced a slightly greater than average risk of being incarcerated if they were sentenced in 1977, 1978, 1980, and 1982. Their risk of being imprisoned was smaller than average in 1979, 1983, and 1984. Split sentences, in contrast, depend little on year of sentence. Only one vector is significant, and indicates that split sentences tended to be significantly more severe than average in 1981. The clearest patterns emerge in our analysis of prison sentences. Prior to 1981, prison sentences were shorter than average, and since then they have become longer than average.

In sum, once we control for obvious determinants of outcomes, sentences continue to vary as a function of the year the offender was sentenced. Effects are quite modest, however, and noteworthy only in recent years (since 1983).

The Context of Time

In the sections that follow, we explore the presence of more subtle temporal effects, and estimate the extent to which both the amount and direction of differential treatment have changed during the period of this study. First, we consider whether, in the face of litigation, race has declined in significance over time. Then we consider whether the treatment of offenders within each crime category fluctuates, and whether these fluctuations reflect the legislative activity described earlier in Chapter 2.

To consider these issues, we constructed a set of product terms between the effect-coded variable representing year of sentence and two case characteristics: race and type of crime. As shown in Table 5.2, the addition of these terms to additive models produces slight, but significant, increases in explained variance. The

TABLE 5.2. Comparison of additive and interactive time models[a]

Model	Type of sentence	Split sentence severity	Prison sentence length
Additive model R^2	.2094	.2040	.6726
Interactive model R^2	.2157	.2281	.6798
Increment	.63%	2.41%	.72%
F ratio	5.67***	3.36*	2.85
(degrees of freedom)	(39/27,539)	(39/4,192)	(39/4,943)
Expanded interactive model R^2	.2173	.2315	.6804
Increment	.16%	.34%	.06%
F ratio	7.04***	2.31	1.16
(degrees of freedom)	(8/27,531)	(8/4,184)	(8/4,935)

[a] The additive model includes all variables listed in Table 5.1. The interactive model adds product terms between year of sentence, race, and offense. The expanded interactive model adds to the original interaction model a set of product terms between year of sentence and offense seriousness.
*$p \le .05$; **$p \le .01$; ***$p \le .005$.

effect race and offense have on outcomes depends, then, on the year the offender was sentenced. To control for the possibility that observed differences are spurious and reflect the temporal changes in offense seriousness noted above, we added a set of product terms between year of sentence and offense seriousness to the interactive model. For two of the three outcomes, the increase in explained variation is significant, and suggests that the weight given to offense seriousness also varies with time. Results for sentence type and split sentence severity are therefore taken from expanded interactive models, that is, models that control for interaction between year of sentence and offense seriousness. The results for prison sentences are based on the original interactive model.[1]

Race Differences Over Time

Table 5.3 presents the predicted sentencing outcomes for black and white offenders. Race differences were computed by subtracting the predicted sentences of whites from the predicted sentences of blacks. Positive values indicate that blacks receive more severe sentences than whites. The average race difference, which corresponds to the unstandardized regression coefficient for race in the interactive model, holds constant at 0 the effects of the remaining variables, including year of sentence. T-tests for this race difference tell whether it differs significantly from 0. T-tests for year-specific race differences indicate whether they diverge significantly from the average race difference.

As reported earlier, significant overall race differences occur, but only for the initial decision to incarcerate offenders. Throughout the time period, blacks were slightly more likely than whites to be imprisoned. These differences were significantly greater than average in 1981, and smaller than average in 1979 and 1984. It bears repeating that all differences are slight (less than 7%), and in the absence of controls for prior record, must be accepted cautiously.

Table 5.3 also indicates no clear trends in differential treatment once the initial decision to imprison is made. Overall race differences, which take no account of the year the offender was sentenced, do not differ significantly from 0. To a great extent, however, these overall averages are misleading, because race differences vary dramatically in both magnitude and direction over time. Between 1977 and 1982, blacks usually received more lenient split sentences than whites, particularly in 1980 and 1982. In contrast, in 1976 and since 1983, the split sentences imposed on blacks were more severe than those imposed on whites.

Race differences in prison sentences also vary over time. Until 1982, blacks often received longer sentences than whites, and harshness was particularly pronounced in 1976 and 1980. The year 1979 was an exception to this pattern, because the prison sentences of blacks were slightly over a year shorter than those imposed on whites. Since 1982, however, the prison sentences of blacks have become shorter than those of whites, and this was particularly the case in 1984. All differences in prison sentences are less than 2 years and, although not trivial, are comparatively slight.

TABLE 5.3. Predicted race differences in sentences over time[a]

Year of sentence	Race of offender		Difference
	White	Black	
Type of sentence			
1976	.334	.391	.057
1977	.379	.436	.057
1978	.382	.395	.013*
1979	.317	.357	.040
1980	.349	.399	.050
1981	.329	.398	.069*
1982	.343	.407	.064
1983	.270	.328	.058
1984	.280	.288	.008***
Average	.337	.380	.043***
Split sentence severity			
1976	45.495	54.700	9.205***
1977	48.121	48.101	−.020
1978	49.877	49.001	−.876
1979	49.828	49.743	−.085
1980	50.857	47.648	−3.209***
1981	51.028	51.380	.352
1982	48.561	46.564	−1.997*
1983	45.721	48.877	3.156
1984	45.892	50.112	4.220*
Average	48.371	49.565	1.194
Prison sentence length			
1976	9.601	11.110	1.509***
1977	10.963	10.467	−.496
1978	10.832	11.784	.952
1979	11.364	10.029	−1.335**
1980	10.244	11.984	1.740***
1981	11.592	12.673	1.081
1982	12.144	11.361	−.783
1983	12.309	12.047	−.262
1984	14.043	12.825	−1.218*
Average	11.455	11.587	.132

[a] Predicted outcomes capture the effects of varying year of sentencing, while holding constant at the mean the effects of the remaining variables.
*$p \le .05$; **$p \le .01$; ***$p \le .005$.

In general, then, race differences have not declined with time. Regardless of the sentencing outcome being considered, evidence of differential treatment is scattered throughout the time period of the study. Most differences are quite small, and they do not invariably imply that blacks are more harshly treated than whites. Indeed, for offenders receiving imprisonment, we found some evidence that blacks are more leniently treated. Thus, differential treatment varies not only by time, but also by sentencing outcome. The most recent data (1984–85) suggest virtually no race differences in imprisonment risk, harsher treatment of blacks who received split sentences, and more lenient treatment of blacks sentenced only to prison.

We examined the possibility that these race differences, however slight, might be spurious. For example, race differences in sentences could vary with time because the magnitude of race differences in legally relevant factors also varies with time. On the surface, this possibility has some merit. Figure 5.9 indicates that for the sample as a whole race differences in offense seriousness are far from constant. Although blacks are always convicted of significantly more serious offenses than whites, this race difference was particularly pronounced in 1981, a year when race differences in imprisonment risk were also quite pronounced. Similarly, race differences in offense seriousness tended to be smaller during those years when race differences in treatment were minimal (i.e., 1978 and 1984).

To remove the confounding influence of temporal variation in the magnitude of race differences in offense seriousness, we constructed second-order interaction terms consisting of race, offense seriousness, and year of sentencing. We added these product terms to the interactive model, and reanalyzed the data. The increase in proportion of explained variation was trivial but significant.[2] It provides evidence that race differences depend simultaneously on the year of sentencing and on the seriousness of the conviction offense. We therefore used metric coefficients from this model to recompute estimated race differences in imprisonment risk.

Table 5.4 presents these recomputed race differences for offenders whose felonies were either less serious than average (one standard deviation below the

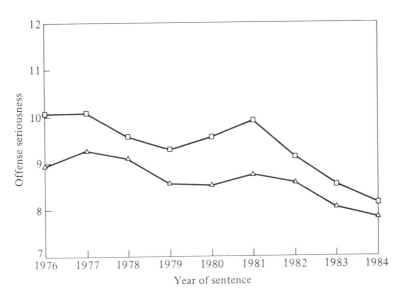

FIGURE 5.9. Race differences in offense seriousness.
□, Black; △, white.

TABLE 5.4. Race differences in imprisonment probability, by offense seriousness[a]

	Less serious offenders			More serious offenders		
Year	White	Black	Difference	White	Black	Difference
1976	.257	.338	.081***	.553	.583	.030***
1977	.257	.395	.138***	.509	.582	.073***
1978	.308	.317	.009	.497	.518	.021
1979	.235	.236	.001***	.422	.539	.117***
1980	.217	.289	.072	.532	.582	.050
1981	.216	.293	.077	.487	.557	.070
1982	.216	.309	.093*	.520	.584	.064*
1983	.151	.205	.054	.452	.493	.041
1984	.164	.142	−.022***	.461	.497	.036***
Average	.224	.280	.056***	.493	.549	.056***

[a] Predicted outcomes capture the simultaneous effects of offense seriousness and year of sentence, while holding constant at the mean the effects of the remaining variables. Less serious offenders are one standard deviation below mean seriousness, and more serious offenders are one standard deviation above the mean.
*$p \leq .05$; ***$p \leq .005$.

mean) or more serious than average (one standard deviation above the mean). The table indicates that differential treatment by race is quite noticeable at times and depends on the seriousness of the offense. Two major trends merit emphasis. First, blacks are almost always more likely than whites to be imprisoned, and this is the case for all but one year (1984), as well as for both more serious and less serious offenders.

Second, race differences are typically more pronounced for less serious offenders, and this was particularly evident in 1976, 1977, and 1982. For example, in 1977, less serious black offenders were 13.8% more likely than less serious white offenders to be incarcerated. Race differences were noticeably smaller among more serious offenders, where blacks were only 7.3% more likely than whites to be incarcerated.

In only two instances (1979, 1984) were race differences greater among more serious offenders. They were particularly noteworthy only in 1979, however, when the imprisonment risk serious black offenders faced was 11.7% greater than the risk faced by serious white offenders. In contrast, less serious black offenders experienced virtually the same treatment as less serious whites.

These exceptions aside, race differences in imprisonment risk are likely to be greater among less serious offenders. These findings corroborate the argument developed by Unnever and Hembroff (1986) that race becomes important in ambiguous situations, where legally relevant factors provide little guidance as to the appropriateness of a severe sanction. We must emphasize, however, that support for this argument is not unequivocal. Race differences among less serious offenders are not always significant or substantively greater than race differences experienced by serious offenders, and there are at least two instances where judges appear to single out more serious black offenders for particularly harsh treatment.

For offenders sentenced to some form of prison, we also examined the possibility that differential treatment could be due to race differences in a number of legally relevant factors (i.e., offense seriousness, conviction charges, and prior record). We found no evidence this is the case. Among offenders receiving split sentences, blacks were convicted of significantly more serious offenses than whites only in 1979, a year when they received more lenient split sentences. In 1984, we thought blacks would be more leniently treated than whites because they were convicted of significantly fewer offenses (1.4 vs. 1.6, $p = .04$). Instead, harshness toward blacks was particularly pronounced that year. In short, race differences in split sentences varied with time, but these changes bear virtually no resemblance to changes in legally relevant factors that could justify them.

The same is true for offenders receiving prison sentences. We found no evidence that the longer prison sentences imposed on blacks in 1976 occurred because they were significantly more serious than white offenders. Nor was the disproportionate lenience of 1979 and 1984 associated with the tendency for black offenders to be less serious than white offenders. Indeed, comparisons between black and white offenders produced an interesting anomaly. In 1979 and 1984, when blacks were more leniently treated, they were convicted of slightly (but not significantly) *more* serious offenses than whites.

One promising race difference merited closer scrutiny, but also bore no fruit. In 1980, when the prison sentences of blacks were significantly longer than those imposed on whites, blacks were also significantly more likely than whites to have been previously incarcerated in Georgia (.24 vs. .16, $p = .02$). A second-order interaction term controlled for this variation, was not significant, and produced no change in the findings. As was the case for split sentences, then, prison sentences vary by race, but this does not appear to be due to race differences in the obvious legally relevant factors.

In the following sections, we turn our attention to trends in the sentencing of specific types of offenders. We compare these trends with legislative activity, and find that its effect on sentencing behavior varies considerably. Not all legislation has an obvious effect on sentences, and obvious effects are not always sustained. The following sections also examine trends in the magnitude and direction of differential treatment. In general, we find that, even if sentences are consistently more (or less) severe than average, the magnitude of differences varies markedly. A few of these differences can be traced to fluctuations in the seriousness of offenders being sentenced, whereas others appear to be indirect effects of legislative activity. Some differences have no simple interpretation, and appear to require more contextually sensitive data (e.g., specific crime rates or newspaper coverage) than was available.

Trends in the Sentencing of Violent Offenders

During the period of this study, legislative concern with statutes governing common law violence was limited. There were no changes in laws against homicide or voluntary manslaughter. The only modification of rape statutes occurred in

1978 and removed the requirement for corroborative evidence (Georgia L., p. 3). This change undoubtedly had its largest impact on the conviction rate, but probably had few implications for judicial sentencing behavior.

Consequential changes were limited to three offenses: involuntary manslaughter, aggravated assault, and aggravated battery. In 1984, the legislature increased the maximum penalty for involuntary manslaughter from 5 to 10 years (Georgia L., p. 397). Pertinent changes in aggravated assault and battery laws were instituted in 1982, 1984, and 1985. In 1982, the legislature changed the maximum penalty for aggravated assault from 10 to 20 years (Georgia L., p. 1242). Two years later, it established minimum penalties for offenders convicted of assaulting persons 65 years or older (1984 Georgia L., p. 900). For aggravated assault the minimum was 3 years, and for aggravated battery it was 5 years. Most recently (1985), the legislature established minimums for assaults on correctional officers: 5 years for aggravated assault and 10 years for aggravated battery (Georgia L., p. 628).

On the basis of these legislative changes, we expected some increase in the severity of split sentences and the duration of prison sentences. Since legislation did not establish mandatory minimums, we expected the use of prison to increase, but only slightly. Table 5.5 presents predicted outcomes for common-law violent offenders during the period of this study. Note, first, the unanticipated tendency for the imprisonment risk to decline. The estimated probability that violent offenders would be incarcerated was .588 in 1977, and had declined to .355 by 1984. Also contrary to expectation, split sentences have not become more severe. Indeed since 1981, they have become slightly less severe.

Only for prison sentences do we find the expected increase, particularly since 1982. Additional analysis more clearly suggests that this increase might be due to recent legislative changes. We differentiated felonious assault from other violent crimes and reanalyzed the data (see Appendix Table E for complete results).[3] The prison sentences imposed on offenders convicted of assault increased quite dramatically, from 12.4 years in 1981 to 15 years in 1982, when legislation doubling the penalty was passed. Although sentences have declined slightly since 1982, they remain well above pre-1980 levels. Similar trends characterize split sentences, but they predate legislative activity. Split sentences tended to become more severe in 1980, and peaked the year the maximum penalty was doubled. As was the case for prison sentences, split sentences have become only slightly less severe since 1982 (in 1984, the mean was 46), suggesting continued concern with this offense. In short, then, an increase in legislative penalties for assault appears to have fostered a noticeable and relatively sustained increase in both the split sentences and the prison terms imposed on these offenders.

Table 5.5 also estimates the magnitude and direction of differential treatment over time. When compared with the average, offenders convicted of common-law violence are 5.8% more likely to be incarcerated. Their split sentences deviate little from average, but their prison sentences tend to be about 4.6 years longer than average. The magnitude and, to a lesser extent, the direction of these differ-

TABLE 5.5. Trends in predicted sentencing outcomes for violent offenders[a]

| | Type of offender | | |
| | Average | Common-law violent | Difference |
Year of sentence			
Type of sentence			
1976	.452	.451	−.001**
1977	.464	.588	.124***
1978	.459	.583	.124***
1979	.393	.425	.032
1980	.436	.495	.059
1981	.426	.479	.053
1982	.434	.465	.031
1983	.333	.394	.061
1984	.314	.355	.041
Average	.412	.470	.058***
Split sentence severity			
1976	51.210	51.661	.451
1977	48.515	48.122	−.393
1978	49.852	44.553	−5.299*
1979	49.724	51.293	1.569
1980	49.371	47.917	−1.454
1981	52.150	53.479	1.329
1982	49.504	48.526	−.978
1983	47.716	50.772	3.056*
1984	48.257	48.626	.369
Average	49.588	49.438	−.150
Prison sentence length			
1976	9.212	13.541	4.329
1977	9.607	14.611	5.004
1978	9.901	16.354	6.453***
1979	9.862	12.831	2.969***
1980	9.913	14.548	4.635
1981	11.144	15.962	4.818
1982	11.218	13.651	2.433***
1983	10.950	15.717	4.767
1984	12.139	18.409	6.270**
Average	10.438	15.069	4.631***

[a] Predicted sentences capture the effects of varying year of sentencing, while holding constant at the mean the effects of the remaining variables.
$*p \le .05; **p \le .01; ***p \le .005$.

ences in treatment vary over time, however. Some but by no means all of these changes could reflect judicial responses to legislative activity.

Contrary to expectation, for the initial decision to incarcerate, disproportionate harshness was most pronounced *prior* to legislative activity. In 1977 and 1978, the imprisonment risk for violent offenders was 12.4% greater than average, and since then differences in treatment have unevenly declined. Although violent offenders are still more likely than average to be incarcerated, the disproportionate harshness they receive is not nearly as pronounced as it was earlier.

The results presented in Table 5.5 also suggest slight and inconsistent differences in the split sentences imposed on violent offenders. Only two years diverge significantly from the overall mean. Violent offenders received less severe than average split sentences in 1978. Not surprisingly, in the year after legislative change in the maximum penalty for aggravated assault (1983), their split sentences were more severe than average.

Finally, violent offenders consistently receive longer than average prison sentences. This harshness was most pronounced in 1978 and 1984, when their sentences were over 6 years longer than average. Differential treatment was significantly less pronounced in 1979 and 1982, when prison sentences were less than 3 years longer than average. Since 1982, the gap between violent and other offenders has increased, and may reflect in part the stiffening of penalties for assaults. A closer look at assaults (see Appendix Table E) provides clearer evidence this is the case. Prison sentences for assault differed little from the average in 1979, but by 1984 had become over 3.5 years longer than average.

As was the case for race differences, we noted a tendency for the relative seriousness of violent crimes to vary with time. Figure 5.10 compares the seriousness of violent crimes with the average for the sample as a whole. Violent crimes are always significantly more serious than average, but the gap was particularly pronounced during the early years of the study. Recent declines in differential treatment for the initial imprisonment decision could merely reflect the tendency for violent crimes to become less serious over time.

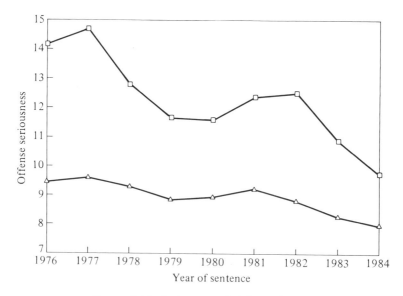

FIGURE 5.10. Seriousness of violent crimes.
□, Violent; △, average.

TABLE 5.6. Predicted imprisonment probabilities for violent offenders, by offense seriousness[a]

Year	Less serious offenders			More serious offenders		
	Average	Violent	Difference	Average	Violent	Difference
1976	.346	.354	.008	.638	.623	−.015
1977	.414	.498	.084	.558	.729	.171
1978	.403	.501	.098	.547	.711	.164
1979	.297	.339	.042	.553	.640	.087
1980	.416	.397	−.019***	.476	.690	.214***
1981	.323	.395	.072	.602	.659	.057
1982	.261	.378	.117***	.704	.663	−.041***
1983	.220	.297	.077	.556	.585	.029
1984	.155	.297	.142***	.636	.594	−.042***
Average	.315	.384	.069***	.585	.654	.069***

[a] Predicted outcomes capture the simultaneous effects of offense seriousness and year of sentence, while holding constant at the mean the effects of the remaining variables. Less serious offenders are one standard deviation below mean seriousness, and more serious offenders are one standard deviation above the mean.
*** $p \leq .005$.

To control for this tendency, we constructed a set of second-order interaction terms involving year of sentence, offense seriousness, and the vector representing violent offenses. The addition of these terms significantly increased the proportion explained by the interactive model, thus indicating that differences in treatment vary both by year of sentencing and by the seriousness of the conviction charge.[4] We therefore recomputed imprisonment probabilities for violent offenders whose crimes were one standard deviation below and one standard deviation above the mean. Table 5.6 presents these probabilities, and compares them with the average incarceration risk faced by less serious and more serious offenders.

Several features of these results merit attention. First, although harsher treatment of violent offenders continued to be particularly pronounced in 1977 and 1978, it was the more serious violent offender who bore the brunt of this harshness. In 1977, for example, serious violent offenders were 17% more likely than other serious offenders to be imprisoned, whereas their less serious counterparts were only 8.4% more likely than other minor offenders to be incarcerated.

The second noteworthy feature of these findings is the presence of isolated differences in treatment that occur at other points in time. To some extent, these differences coincide with the legislative changes we noted earlier. Prior to 1980, judges appeared to distinguish serious violent offenders from other serious offenders. In 1980, for example, they were 21.4% more likely to incarcerate serious violent offenders than other serious offenders. In contrast, judges did not appear to single out less serious offenders for disproportionately harsh treatment. Indeed, less serious violent offenders were 1.9% *less* likely than other less serious offenders to be incarcerated.

Since 1980, the situation has reversed, and judges appear to be drawing sharper distinctions among less serious offenders. In 1984, for example, serious violent offenders were 4.2% *less* likely to be incarcerated. In contrast, violent offenders convicted of less serious crimes were 14.2% *more* likely than other less serious offenders to be imprisoned.

Prior to 1981, then, differential treatment was likely to be greater for serious violent offenders than for less serious violent offenders. More recently, comparatively harsh treatment has been directed primarily at those convicted of less serious violent crimes, a pattern that coincides with recent concerns about the relatively less serious crimes of assault and involuntary manslaughter.

We also examined the possibility that the patterns of differential treatment reported for offenders sentenced to prison depend in part on variation over time in legally relevant factors. Apparently they do not. Recall that violent offenders received more lenient split sentences in 1978, but harsher split sentences in 1983. Neither trend would have been predicted on the basis of legally relevant differences. In 1978 (as in other years, e.g., 1976, 1977, 1980), violent offenders were convicted of significantly more serious crimes than other offenders (12.2 vs. 9.3, $p = .0001$), a fact that would lead us to expect harshness rather than the lenience we found. In contrast, we expected some lenience in 1983, because violent offenders had slightly fewer conviction charges and less serious prior records than other offenders. In actuality, sentences were harsher than average that year.

Similarly anomalies characterize the sample of offenders sentenced only to prison. In those years when the prison sentences imposed on violent offenders differed little from the average (1979 and 1982), their offenses tended to be much more serious than average. Conversely, when harsher treatment was most pronounced (1978 and 1984), differences in offense seriousness tended to be relatively small, and violent offenders had significantly *fewer* arrests than other offenders.

In sum, for the initial decision to incarcerate, the magnitude of differential treatment depends both on the year of sentence and the seriousness of the offenses. The patterns suggest a toughening attitude toward certain violent offenses (e.g., assaults), which has its counterpart in current legislative activity. Once the decision to incarcerate has been made, the differential treatment violent offenders experience depends primarily on the year of sentence, and does not appear to be linked with other legally relevant factors (e.g., offense seriousness). Again, however, many of these patterns of differential treatment coincide with legislative activity that has increased penalties for certain kinds of violent offenders.

Trends in the Sentencing of Robbery Offenders

Few legislative changes in robbery laws occurred between 1976 and 1985. Throughout the period of this study, armed robbery was punishable by death, life, or imprisonment of not less than 5 nor more than 20 years. A mandatory minimum of 10 years applied to offenders with a prior robbery conviction or those who inflicted serious bodily injury. Offenders convicted of armed robbery could not receive suspended sentences or probation.

A consequential change in robbery laws occurred in 1984, when the minimum sentence of 1 year was increased to 5 years for the robbery of persons 65 years and older (Georgia L., p. 900). In 1985, the legislature mandated a minimum of 10 years in prison for persons who in the course of an armed robbery steal controlled substances from a pharmacy (Georgia L., p. 1036). A mandatory minimum of 15 years was established if serious bodily injury occurred in the course of such a robbery.

Patterns in the sentences imposed on robbery offenders are presented in Table 5.7. Despite recent legislative changes, the predicted risk of imprisonment for robbery has declined with time and, although split sentences vary markedly from year to year, they too have become less severe in the past 2 years. Prison sentences, in contrast, have doubled over the course of the study, from 4.7 years in 1976 to 9.5 years in 1984. Particularly noticeable is the 2.3-year increase between 1983 and 1984 (which includes cases sentenced to May of 1985). This increase could well be a response to the legislative changes noted earlier. Thus, although judges have become increasingly reluctant to sentence robbery offenders to prison, they appear to have become increasingly punitive toward those selected for imprisonment.

Table 5.7 also compares the sentences imposed on robbery offenders with the average, and estimates the extent and nature of differential treatment. In comparison with other offenders, those convicted of robbery are consistently more likely to be incarcerated, receive more severe than average split sentences, and are given shorter than average prison sentences. The magnitude of these differences fluctuates, often dramatically, over time. The year 1982, noted primarily for drug legislation, was distinctive for judicial harshness toward robbery offenders. They were much more likely than average to be incarcerated (25.3%), and their split sentences were much more severe than average ($+11.4$). The comparative lenience they typically received in prison sentences was minimal: terms were only 1.5 years shorter than those imposed on other offenders.

Two other trends merit mention. First, differential treatment during the initial decision to incarcerate was particularly pronounced prior to 1982. In 1978, for example, robbery offenders were 29.3% more likely than average to be incarcerated, and an estimated three quarters of all robbery offenders received some form of incarceration. Since 1982, differences in the use of prison have declined, in large part because, as noted above, judges have become increasingly reluctant to incarcerate robbery offenders. Indeed, while the average imprisonment risk decreased by 12% between 1982 and 1984, the use of prison for robbery offenders declined much more precipitiously, by approximately 27%. As a result, by 1984, robbery offenders were only 10.4% more likely than average to be imprisoned. To some extent, these recent declines are anomalous, because they do not correspond to any tendency for robbery offenders to become less serious

TABLE 5.7. Trends in predicted sentencing outcomes for robbery offenders[a]

| | Type of offender | | |
Year of sentence	Average	Robbery	Difference
Type of sentence			
1976	.452	.706	.254
1977	.464	.690	.226
1978	.459	.752	.293***
1979	.393	.648	.255
1980	.436	.693	.257*
1981	.426	.691	.265**
1982	.434	.687	.253
1983	.333	.478	.145***
1984	.314	.418	.104***
Average	.412	.640	.228***
Split sentence severity			
1976	51.210	59.396	8.186
1977	48.515	50.138	1.623
1978	49.852	58.295	8.443
1979	49.724	51.566	1.842
1980	49.371	54.592	5.221
1981	52.150	57.126	4.976
1982	49.504	60.954	11.450***
1983	47.716	52.699	4.983
1984	48.257	51.933	3.676
Average	49.588	55.188	5.600***
Prison sentence length			
1976	9.212	4.721	−4.491
1977	9.607	7.103	−2.504
1978	9.901	6.631	−3.270
1979	9.862	7.005	−2.857
1980	9.913	5.377	−4.536*
1981	11.144	8.701	−2.443
1982	11.218	9.730	−1.488**
1983	10.950	7.150	−3.800
1984	12.139	9.475	−2.664
Average	10.438	7.321	−3.117***

[a] Predicted sentences capture the effects of varying year of sentence, while holding constant at the mean the effects of the remaining variables.
$*p \leq .05; **p \leq .01; ***p \leq .005$.

over time. Indeed, their offenses are always significantly more serious than those of other offenders, and this was especially the case in 1983 and 1984, years when differential treatment appears to have declined.

The second noticeable trend involves the prison sentences imposed on robbery offenders. In contrast to the first two sentencing outcomes, robbery offenders are at a comparative advantage for decisions about prison sentences. Furthermore, this lenience has remained fairly stable over time, with two exceptions. The first occurred in 1982 when, as noted earlier, robbery offenders received little lenience. Their prison sentences were only 1.5 years shorter than average. The second exception occurred 2 years earlier, when comparative lenience was quite pronounced: the prison sentences imposed on robbery offenders were approximately 4.5 years shorter than average. Neither of these patterns appear traceable to variation over time in legally relevant factors. The relative seriousness of robbery offenses has remained fairly constant over time, and robbery offenders did not differ significantly from other offenders in the number of conviction charges or in the extensiveness of their prior records.

In sum, judges have become increasingly less likely to imprison robbery offenders. Where split sentences were deemed appropriate, they have also become more lenient in recent years. In contrast and perhaps in response to recent legislation, judges have become increasingly harsh toward robbery offenders for whom a straight prison term was considered appropriate. A comparison with the average sentencing outcome puts these patterns in a broader perspective. In general, robbery offenders are more likely than average to be imprisoned. Their split sentences are also significantly more serious than average, whereas their prison sentences are shorter than average. The magnitude of these differences fluctuates with time, and for reasons that are not yet clear all trends were quite pronounced in 1982. Since then, the treatment of robbery offenders, at least for the initial decision to incarcerate and for split sentences, has begun to approximate the average. At this point, we cannot trace yearly fluctuations to changes in the legally relevant characteristics of robbery offenders. However, recent legislation, coupled with the ever-present spectre of prison overcrowding, appears to have prompted judges to be both more selective in the use of prison and harsher toward the relatively small group of offenders for whom prison is considered appropriate.

Trends in the Sentencing of Burglary Offenders

Although burglary statutes were revised several times during this study (e.g., in 1977, 1978, and 1980), most revisions were definitional (e.g., extending statutes to cover thefts from railroad cars). In 1978, however, the legislature required a minimum of 2 years in prison for offenders with one prior burglary conviction and 5 years for offenders with two prior burglary convictions. These minimums could not be suspended, probated, or deferred (Georgia L., p. 236).

The effect of this legislation is difficult to discern. As Table 5.8 indicates, there were no dramatic changes in sentencing patterns. Sanctions became more severe well after legislation was passed, and have not been sustained in recent years. The risk of being imprisoned declined between 1976 and 1979, and did not begin to increase until 1980, 2 years after legislation introducing mandatory minimums. The use of prison peaked in 1982 and since then has declined to its lowest level in 8 years. Split sentences responded more quickly to legislative changes, but also were not dramatic. They became more severe the year legislation was passed, and remained at elevated levels for 2 years. Since 1981, they too have begun to become less severe. Finally, prison sentences have become slightly longer over

TABLE 5.8. Trends in predicted sentencing outcomes for burglary offenders[a]

	Type of offender		
Year of sentence	Average	Burglary	Difference
Type of sentence			
1976	.452	.444	−.008
1977	.464	.445	−.019
1978	.459	.425	−.034
1979	.393	.342	−.051**
1980	.436	.367	−.069***
1981	.426	.412	−.014
1982	.434	.451	.017*
1983	.333	.340	.007
1984	.314	.316	.002
Average	.412	.393	−.019***
Split sentence severity			
1976	51.210	47.732	−3.478*
1977	48.515	48.026	−.489
1978	49.852	52.717	2.865*
1979	49.724	51.528	1.804
1980	49.371	52.060	2.689*
1981	52.150	50.140	−2.010*
1982	49.504	44.646	−4.858***
1983	47.716	48.199	.483
1984	48.257	48.118	−.139
Average	49.588	49.240	−.348
Prison sentence length			
1976	9.212	7.102	−2.110
1977	9.607	7.883	−1.724
1978	9.901	8.167	−1.734
1979	9.862	8.732	−1.130
1980	9.913	8.028	−1.885
1981	11.144	9.013	−2.131
1982	11.218	9.228	−1.990
1983	10.950	9.779	−1.171
1984	12.139	8.428	−3.711***
Average	10.438	8.484	−1.954***

[a] Predicted sentences capture the effects of varying year of sentence, while holding constant at the mean the effects of the remaining variables.
$*p \leq .05; **p \leq .01; ***p \leq .005.$

the course of this study, from 7.1 years in 1976 to 9.8 years in 1983, but there was no sharp increase in 1978 or the following year. Since 1983, the prison sentences imposed on burglary offenders conform to trends for the remaining outcomes, and have become slightly shorter. In sum, then, there were no sharp upswings in any sentencing outcome as a result of the 1978 legislation. Instead, this legislation appears to have had a more diffuse and delayed effect on sentencing.

To put the sentencing of burglary offenders in perspective, Table 5.8 compares their sentences with the average predicted outcome. One of the most noteworthy features of these comparisons is the relatively lenient treatment accorded burglary offenders. They are significantly, but slightly, less likely to be incarcerated. Their split sentences are also slightly (but not significantly) less severe than average, and their prison sentences are nearly 2 years shorter than average. An examination of year-specific differences indicates considerable variation in both the magnitude and direction of differential treatment, and a few of these variations could be indirect or delayed effects of mandatory minimums for burglary offenders with prior convictions.

The first trend was unanticipated. Although never strong, lenience in the initial imprisonment decision was particularly pronounced in the two years *following* legislative change (1979 and 1980). Since 1981, it has declined and burglary offenders tend to be treated little differently from the average offender.

Second, despite the absence of a significant overall difference, the split sentences imposed on burglary offenders were more severe than average in the years of legislative activity and shortly thereafter (1978–80). Before 1978 and after 1980, however, split sentences reverted to their comparative, although slight, lenience. Finally, comparative lenience in the imposition of prison sentences has always been slight, and it was apparently unaffected by legislative change. That is, lenient treatment was still evident in 1978 and thereafter. It was especially pronounced in 1984, well after legislative activity, when burglary offenders received sentences that were 3.7 years shorter than average.

As was the case for other types of offenders, we sought to estimate and remove the confounding influence of variation in legally relevant factors that could account for these fluctuations in differential treatment. First, we focused on the decline in differential treatment for the initial imprisonment decision. This trend could reflect the fact that, although burglary is always more serious than other offenses, the gap has widened in recent years. As Figure 5.11 indicates, this occurs because on the average offenses have become less serious, while the seriousness of burglary offenses has remained fairly constant. We controlled for this trend by adding a set of second-order interactions involving year of sentence, offense seriousness, and the vector for burglary offenses. The resulting increase in explained variance was significant, and we present reestimated imprisonment probabilities in the top half of Table 5.9.[5]

Of particular interest are comparisons in differential treatment that suggest judicial responses to the passage of legislation. In the years just following legislative change (1979–81), judges appeared to be drawing sharp distinctions between relatively minor burglars (e.g., attempts, possession of burglary tools) and those whose offenses were more serious. Offenders convicted of less serious burglaries were less likely than other minor offenders to be incarcerated. In contrast, judges were particularly severe toward serious burglary offenders, who were more likely than other serious offenders to be incarcerated. Differences in treatment were most pronounced in 1980, when less serious burglars were 26.6% *less* likely to be incarcerated, whereas serious burglary offenders were 21.9% *more* likely to be incarcerated. To a great extent, then, the disproportionate lenience reported in Table 5.8 is quite misleading, because it masks the very different treatment accorded burglary offenders on the basis of the seriousness of their offense.

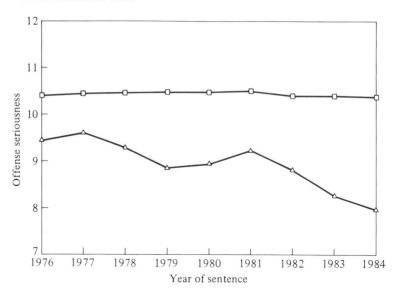

FIGURE 5.11. Seriousness of burglary offenses.
□, Burglary; △, average.

Since 1982, however, the situation has changed, and judges appear to be reverting to pre-1979 sentencing behavior. That is, in comparison with other serious offenders, judges treat those convicted of serious burglaries with comparative lenience. In 1984, for example, they were 15.9% *less* likely than other serious offenders to be incarcerated. Less serious burglary offenders, in contrast, were 11.1% *more* likely to be sentenced to prison. Once again, the results presented in Table 5.8, which do not distinguish offenders on the basis of offense seriousness, give a mistaken impression that the burglary offenders are treated much like the average offender. Clearly, this is not the case. The magnitude and direction of differential treatment depends on the seriousness of the offense as well as on the year the offender was sentenced. The legislative change in 1978 appears to have shifted judicial attention away from minor burglary offenders to those convicted of more serious offenses. This attention was relatively short-lived, however, and by 1982 serious burglary offenders were at the comparative advantage they enjoyed prior to 1978.

Our second investigation of the confounding influence of legally relevant factors focused on offenders receiving split sentences. On the surface, differential treatment over time corresponds roughly to variation in legally relevant factors. In 1976, when burglary offenders received greater than average lenience, they also had significantly fewer conviction charges and prior arrests, a pattern that occurred only that year. In 1978 and 1980, when burglary offenders experienced harsher than average treatment, they were likely to be much more serious than the average offender. We controlled for these trends by entering into the interactive model two sets of second-order product terms. The first set controlled for

TABLE 5.9. Predicted sentencing outcomes for burglary offenders, by offense seriousness[a]

Year	Less serious offenders			More serious offenders		
	Average	Burglary	Difference	Average	Burglary	Difference
Type of sentence						
1976	.361	.451	.090	.622	.485	−.137
1977	.375	.324	−.051	.589	.617	.028
1978	.397	.455	.058	.592	.425	−.167
1979	.256	.138	−.118	.579	.604	.025**
1980	.295	.029	−.266	.585	.804	.219***
1981	.318	.194	−.124	.580	.704	.124
1982	.333	.406	.073	.621	.559	−.062
1983	.236	.279	.043	.518	.467	−.051
1984	.221	.332	.111	.538	.379	−.159*
Average	.311	.290	−.021***	.581	.560	−.021***
Split sentence severity						
1976	44.842	47.124	2.282	57.912	42.985	−14.927
1977	41.967	47.916	5.949	54.551	47.968	−6.583
1978	41.573	40.225	−1.348	58.800	67.046	8.246
1979	37.374	60.279	22.905	70.856	42.767	−28.089***
1980	41.154	28.404	−12.750	56.618	80.390	23.772***
1981	46.132	44.395	−1.737	59.796	56.842	−2.954
1982	44.242	44.168	−.074	57.330	46.400	−10.930
1983	37.571	27.869	−9.702	59.821	69.703	9.882**
1984	33.157	20.449	−12.708	66.135	80.517	14.382*
Average	40.890	40.092	−.798	60.206	59.408	−.798

[a] Predicted outcomes capture the simultaneous effects of year of sentence and offense seriousness, while holding constant at the mean the effects of the remaining variables. Less serious offenders are one standard deviation below mean seriousness, and more serious offenders are one standard deviation above the mean.
$*p \leq .05; **p \leq .01; ***p \leq .005.$

temporal variation in the relative seriousness of offenses, and the second set controlled for the significant differences in prior arrests and conviction charges that occurred during 1976. Since the increase in explained variance was significant, we recomputed the estimated split sentences, and differentiated offenders by the seriousness of the conviction charge.[6] The bottom portion of Table 5.9 presents these results.

One of the interesting features of the findings is the dramatic fluctuations in differential treatment both over time and by seriousness of the conviction offense. Note that, as was the case for the use of prison, the disproportionate lenience accorded burglary offenders prior to 1978 was usually extended only to serious offenders. At that time, the split sentences imposed on less serious burglary offenders differed little from, or were more severe than, those imposed on other minor offenders. The situation changed dramatically in 1980, 2 years after legislative activity. Although delayed, the trend was the same as noted above for the initial decision to incarcerate, that is, a tendency for serious burglary offenders to be more harshly treated than other serious offenders. This pattern was particularly apparent in 1980, when serious burglary offenders received disproportionately more severe sentences (+23.8), whereas their less serious counterparts were treated more leniently than average (−12.7). Interestingly, however, disproportionate harshness was more sustained than during the initial imprisonment decision. Although 2 years of lenience followed the harshness of 1980, by 1983 serious burglary offenders were once again singled out for comparatively severe punishment. Their less serious counterparts received split sentences that were less severe than those imposed on other minor offenders.

Finally, we focused on differential treatment during the imposition of straight prison terms. As noted above, the greatest lenience toward burglary offenders sentenced to prison occurred in 1984, when their prison sentences were 3.7 years shorter than average. After comparing burglary with other offenses, we discovered several factors that could account for this difference. Although burglary is always more serious than the average offense, in 1984 that difference was quite small (10.4 vs. 9.6, $p = .004$). Moreover, burglary offenders had significantly fewer conviction charges (1.4 vs. 1.6, $p = .01$) and prior arrests (1.4 vs. 2.0, $p = .05$) than other offenders in 1984. The pronounced lenience we observed might simply reflect the fact that in 1984 judges were faced with less serious burglary offenders. To some extent, this is the case. We controlled for differences in legally relevant factors by adding second-order product terms to the original interactive model. Although still significant, the magnitude of lenience reported earlier declined. In 1984, the prison sentences of burglary offenders were only 1.8 rather than 3.7 years shorter than average.

Trends in the Sentencing of Property Offenders

Most revisions of property statutes were minor: a stiffening of penalties for passing bad checks, usually a misdemeanor; definitional changes in theft-by-taking statutes; and increases in the monetary threshold for classification as a felony (currently at $500). The most recent legislation (1984 Georgia L., p. 900) concerned theft by deception, and increased the minimum from 1 to 5 years in prison if the victim was 65 years or older. Of greater importance to this study was 1981 legislation that removed motor vehicle theft from the general category of theft, and replaced it with provisions specifying a maximum of 20, rather than 10, years in prison (Georgia L., p. 1576). Statutes also provided for a mandatory minimum of 3 years in prison for conviction of a second offense and 10 years for a third offense.

Given the prominence of vehicle theft legislation, we examine this category separately in the following section.[7] Here, we focus on the property theft and damage category as a whole. Table 5.10 presents the relevant sentencing outcomes. As was the case for robbery, the trends suggest that a growing reluctance to imprison property offenders is accompanied by stiffer prison terms imposed on offenders for whom prison was considered appropriate. The estimated imprisonment risk has declined slowly over time, from 33.6% in 1976 to 21.8% in 1984. In contrast, split sentences have fluctuated little with time. The most severe

TABLE 5.10. Trends in predicted sentencing outcomes for property theft and damage offenders[a]

| | Type of offender | | |
| | Average | Property theft and damage | Difference |
Year of sentence			
Type of sentence			
1976	.452	.336	−.116
1977	.464	.327	−.137
1978	.459	.323	−.136
1979	.393	.279	−.114
1980	.436	.301	−.135
1981	.426	.254	−.172**
1982	.434	.249	−.185***
1983	.333	.231	−.102**
1984	.314	.218	−.096***
Average	.412	.280	−.132***
Split sentence severity			
1976	51.210	48.077	−3.133
1977	48.515	43.473	−5.042
1978	49.852	44.428	−5.424
1979	49.724	48.642	−1.082
1980	49.371	48.143	−1.228
1981	52.150	46.989	−5.161
1982	49.504	44.771	−4.733
1983	47.716	45.038	−2.678
1984	48.257	47.736	−.521*
Average	49.588	46.365	−3.223***
Prison sentence length			
1976	9.212	9.694	.482
1977	9.607	9.621	.014
1978	9.901	9.682	−.219
1979	9.862	10.963	1.101
1980	9.913	10.455	.542
1981	11.144	11.013	−.131
1982	11.218	11.242	.024
1983	10.950	11.869	.919
1984	12.139	11.431	−.708
Average	10.438	10.663	.225

[a] Predicted sentences capture the effects of varying year of sentence, while holding constant at the mean the effects of the remaining variables.
$*p \leq .05; **p \leq .01; ***p \leq .005$.

sentences were imposed in 1976, 1979-80, and 1984, with less severe split sentences characterizing the intervening years. Finally, prison sentences have climbed gently but steadily upward, from 9.7 years in 1976 to 11.4 years in 1984.

Table 5.10 also compares predicted outcomes with the average, and presents estimates of differential treatment over time. When compared with the average, property offenders receive more lenient than average treatment in two of three sentencing outcomes. They are 13.2% less likely than average to be incarcerated, and their split sentences are slightly less severe than average (-3.2). In contrast, their prison sentences do not differ significantly from the average, nor is there significant variation over time in prison sentences.

The same cannot be said for decisions about imprisonment or split sentences, where the magnitude of differential treatment varies over time. For the initial decision to imprison, lenience was particularly pronounced in the early 1980s. In 1982, for example, property offenders were 18.5% less likely than average to be imprisoned. Since then, lenience has declined and by 1984, property theft and damage offenders were only 9.6% less likely than average to be incarcerated. These recent declines in lenience do not appear to be traceable to increases in the seriousness of property offenses. They are always less serious than other offenses, and their relative seriousness has remained fairly constant over time.

In recent years, lenience toward property offenders receiving split sentences has also declined. In 1984, differential treatment was significantly less pronounced than average. In addition, although property offenders sentenced in 1984 had significantly more prior arrests than other offenders, this was also the case in other years (e.g., 1976, 1983) where lenience was quite obvious. Hence, we found no evidence that legally relevant factors could account for the lack of lenience in 1984.

In sum, then, as was the case for robbery offenders, judges have become increasingly reluctant to imprison property offenders, but increasingly harsh toward those property offenders sentenced to prison. Split sentences, in contrast, have varied little with time, and there is no evidence of a consistent trend toward harshness (or lenience). When compared with the average offender, those convicted of property offenses are less likely to be incarcerated and their split sentences are significantly less severe. This preferential treatment has declined since the early 1980s, and property offenders have been receiving less lenience than has previously been the case.

The Sentencing of Vehicle Theft Offenders

Legislation appears to have had a noticeable impact on the sentencing of vehicle theft offenders. As Table 5.11 indicates, the risk of imprisonment increased sharply, from a 50% chance in 1981 to a 70.5% chance of incarceration a year later. Thereafter, the use of prison declined precipitously, suggesting that the effect of legislation was short-lived. In 1984, motor vehicle theft offenders had an estimated 32% chance of being sentenced to some form of prison.

Split sentences also became more severe, but these changes predated legislation. They began in 1977, and peaked the year following legislation. Since then, split sentences resemble trends for the use of prison, and have become less severe. Finally, changes in prison sentences, although relatively slight, also predated legislation, and increased between 1977 and 1980. As was the case with other sentencing outcomes, this increase was short-lived, and prison sentences have tended to become shorter since 1980. The one exception was 1983, a full 2

TABLE 5.11. Trends in predicted sentencing outcomes for vehicle theft offenders[a]

Year of sentence	Type of offender		Difference
	Average	Vehicle theft	
Type of sentence			
1976	.361	.401	.040
1977	.430	.407	− .023*
1978	.413	.480	.067
1979	.354	.478	.124
1980	.395	.491	.096
1981	.399	.500	.101
1982	.418	.705	.287***
1983	.286	.311	.025
1984	.296	.320	.024
Average	.377	.460	.083***
Split sentence severity			
1976	51.674	68.948	17.274*
1977	46.943	49.946	3.003
1978	47.234	45.136	−2.098
1979	48.929	50.382	1.453
1980	48.924	57.268	8.344
1981	50.524	61.695	11.171
1982	48.085	52.900	4.815
1983	47.174	54.376	7.202
1984	47.750	42.867	−4.883*
Average	48.582	53.725	5.143***
Prison sentence length			
1976	9.638	12.568	2.930
1977	9.997	11.024	1.027
1978	10.061	11.811	1.750
1979	10.229	12.184	1.955
1980	9.981	12.268	2.287
1981	11.036	10.694	− .342
1982	11.800	10.255	−1.545
1983	11.704	15.858	4.154
1984	11.565	10.453	−1.112
Average	10.668	12.434	1.766***

[a] Predicted sentences capture the effects of varying year of sentence, while holding constant at the mean the effects of the remaining variables.
*$p \leq .05$; **$p \leq .01$; ***$p \leq .005$.

years after legislation, when prison sentences increased by over 5 years from the previous average of 10.2 years. This increase is particularly surprising because, as is always the case, vehicle thefts are much less serious than the average offense. Furthermore, vehicle theft offenders sentenced in 1983 did not differ significantly from other offenders in the number of conviction charges or in the severity of their prior records.

Table 5.11 also compares the predicted outcomes imposed on vehicle theft offenders with average outcomes, and estimates the amount of differential treatment they receive. Unlike property offenders in general, who tend to be more leniently treated, those convicted of vehicle theft are usually treated more harshly than the average offender. They are significantly more likely to be incarcerated, and both their split and prison sentences are more severe than average. These trends remain fairly constant over time, with two major exceptions. Not surprisingly, harshness was significantly more pronounced in 1982, the year following legislation, when vehicle theft offenders were 28.7% more likely than average to be incarcerated. This is in stark contrast to the comparatively lenient treatment that occurred 5 years earlier (1977), when they were 2.3% *less* likely to be incarcerated. Also, disproportionately harsh split sentences were imposed on vehicle theft offenders in 1976, whereas lenience characterized the split sentences imposed in 1984.

Again, we explored the possibility that these trends are spurious, and traceable to changes in the relative seriousness of vehicle theft offenses over time. Apparently, they are not. In 1977 and 1982, when differences in imprisonment risk were so pronounced, vehicle theft offenders were still significantly less serious than other offenders. The disproportionately more severe split sentences of 1976 also cannot be explained by temporal variation in legally relevant factors. As was usually the case, vehicle theft offenders were significantly less serious (5.0 vs. 10.3, $p = .0001$), and for that year only they had significantly *fewer* prior arrests (1.5 vs. 3.0, $p = .01$). Hence, we would expect lenience, rather than the harshness that actually occurred. Similarly, the lenience of 1984 does not reflect legally relevant differences because, with the exception of offense seriousness, vehicle theft offenders did not differ significantly from other offenders in either prior record or number of conviction charges.

In sum, legislative change had a noticeable effect on the use of prison. For other outcomes, severe sanctions predated legislative change. Recent years have witnessed a decline in the seriousness of all sanctions, suggesting that the impact of legislation might have been short-lived. Unlike other property offenders, those convicted of vehicle theft are treated more severely than average, and these differences in treatment vary little with time. After the legislation of 1981, differences in imprisonment risk were quite pronounced, but they too have since declined. Differential treatment of those receiving split and prison sentences has also remained fairly constant over time, and fluctuations cannot directly be linked either with legislative activity or with changes in the legally relevant characteristics of offenders convicted of motor vehicle theft.

Trends in the Sentencing of Drug Offenders

The most sustained and intense legislative activity focused on statutes governing the possession and sale of dangerous and controlled substances. Many changes were relatively minor or tangential to our interests. Pharmacy regulations were added or clarified; drugs were classified as dangerous or as controlled substances; and controlled substances were reclassified. For example, in 1978 phencyclidine (PCP) was upgraded from a Schedule III drug, and added to Schedule II as a depressant (Georgia L., p. 1668). The next year, it was reclassified as a hallucinogen, and placed in Schedule I (1979 Georgia L., p. 859). Within 2 years, then, the maximum penalties for possessing phencyclidine increased from 10 to 15 years, with the possibility of a 5- to 30-year sentence upon a second conviction.

Major drug legislation involved the passage of laws prohibiting trafficking. In 1980, trafficking in cocaine, illegal drugs (e.g., Schedule I drugs such as heroin), and marijuana was outlawed (Georgia L., p. 432). Provisions defining and criminalizing trafficking in methaqualone were instituted in 1982, and subsequently revised in 1983 to lower the quantity of drugs needed to prove trafficking (1982 Georgia L., p. 2215; 1983 Georgia L., p. 620). With the exception of accomplices providing evidence to the state, penalties for trafficking could not be suspended, probated, or deferred until the mandatory minimum was served. The length of mandatory imprisonment depends on the quantity of the drug in possession. For cocaine, marijuana, and methaqualone, it ranges from 5 to 15 years. For other illegal drugs (e.g., heroin), mandatory minimums range between 5 and 25 years. Since 1983, accomplices who assist the district attorney in arresting or convicting traffickers could be exempted from mandatory minimums, upon a motion to the judge from the district attorney.

Given the small percentage of offenders prosecuted for trafficking, we did not expect to see dramatic changes in sentencing outcomes. Nevertheless, Table 5.12 indicates that the legislative activity of 1980, 1982, and 1985 was accompanied by a tendency for both the risk of imprisonment and the length of prison sentences to increase slightly from the previous year. Split sentences, in contrast, tended to decline or remain the same.

Table 5.12 also compares drug offenders with other offenders, and notes changes in the direction and magnitude of differential treatment over time. Overall, drug offenders are less likely than average to be incarcerated, their split sentences are slightly less severe than average, and their prison sentences do not differ significantly from the average prison sentence. Lenience was particularly pronounced prior to legislative activity concerned with trafficking. In 1978, for example, drug offenders were 24.7% less likely than average to be incarcerated. In contrast, they have received comparatively little lenience since then. By 1984, drug offenders were only 4.9% less likely to be incarcerated.

Lenience in split sentences also declined after the legislation of 1980. By 1983, however, it was at pre-1980 levels. Finally, the prison sentences imposed during legislative activity (i.e., in 1980, 1982, and 1985) were longer than average, but not significantly so. They contrast, however, with the comparatively lenient treatment drug offenders received during years without such activity (i.e., 1979, 1981). Although not absent, then, disproportionate harshness toward drug offenders sentenced to prison appears to be a slight and short-lived response to legislative changes.

As before, we sought to estimate and remove the confounding influence of temporal variation in legally relevant factors. For the sample as a whole, we noted a tendency for differential treatment to decline as drug offenders approximate

TABLE 5.12. Trends in predicted sentencing outcomes for drug offenders[a]

Year of sentence	Type of offender		Difference
	Average	Drug	
Type of sentence			
1976	.452	.322	−.130
1977	.464	.270	−.194
1978	.459	.212	−.247***
1979	.393	.273	−.120
1980	.436	.322	−.114
1981	.426	.291	−.135
1982	.434	.318	−.116
1983	.333	.221	−.112
1984	.314	.265	−.049***
Average	.412	.277	−.135***
Split sentence severity			
1976	51.210	49.189	−2.021
1977	48.515	52.817	4.302***
1978	49.852	49.268	−.584
1979	49.724	45.592	−4.132
1980	49.371	44.145	−5.226*
1981	52.150	53.017	.867
1982	49.504	48.628	−.876
1983	47.716	41.872	−5.844*
1984	48.257	44.873	−3.384
Average	49.588	47.713	−1.875**
Prison sentence length			
1976	9.212	11.002	1.790**
1977	9.607	8.816	−.791
1978	9.901	8.672	−1.229*
1979	9.862	9.781	−.081
1980	9.913	11.158	1.245
1981	11.144	11.030	−.114
1982	11.218	12.240	1.022
1983	10.950	10.236	−.714
1984	12.139	12.951	.812
Average	10.438	10.654	.216

[a] Predicted sentences capture the effects of varying year of sentence, while holding constant at the mean the effects of the remaining variables.
*$p \leq .05$; **$p \leq .01$; ***$p \leq .005$.

other offenders in seriousness. As Figure 5.12 indicates, the relative seriousness of drug offenses has declined with time, largely because offenses for the sample as a whole have become less serious. Similar trends characterize offenses resulting in split sentences or prison terms. In addition, the pronounced lenience of 1980 could be an outcome of the fact that drug offenders receiving split sentences that year had significantly fewer charges than other offenders that year (1.2 vs. 1.5, $p = .005$).

For each sentencing outcome, then, variation over time in legally relevant factors might account for variation in differential treatment. We controlled for these

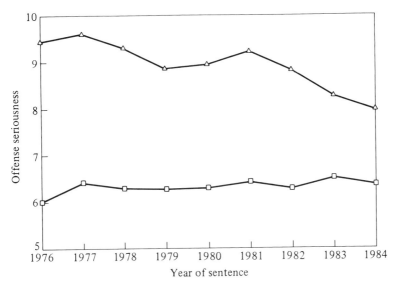

FIGURE 5.12. Seriousness of drug offenses.
□, Drug; △, average.

variations by constructing second-order product terms, entering them into interactive models, and reanalyzing the data. With the exception of prison sentence length, the increases in explained variance were statistically significant, thus indicating that differential treatment is a complicated function of offense seriousness and the year during which the offender was convicted.[8]

Table 5.13 presents reestimated outcomes for type of sentence and split sentence severity. The most noteworthy feature of these results concerns shifts in the treatment of less serious and more serious drug offenders. Until 1980, more serious drug offenders received proportionately more lenience than did their counterparts convicted of less serious drug offenses. For example, in 1980, more serious drug offenders were 35.9% less likely than other serious offenders to be incarcerated, whereas less serious drug offenders were only 12.4% less likely to be incarcerated.

The situation changed in 1981, the year following legislative activity. Comparative lenience toward serious drug offenders declined sharply or was replaced with harsher than average treatment. In 1982, for example, less serious drug offenders were still 12.9% less likely that other minor offenders to be incarcerated, whereas more serious drug offenders were slightly *more* likely than other serious offenders to be incarcerated. Thus the comparative lenience reported in Table 5.12 applies primarily to less serious drug offenders.

The second half of Table 5.13 compares the reestimated split sentences imposed on more serious drug offenders and their less serious counterparts. Again, we find that the differential treatment noted earlier is confined to certain subgroups of drug offenders. In general, more serious drug offenders experience greater differences in treatment than do less serious drug offenders. Unlike the

TABLE 5.13. Predicted sentencing outcomes for drug offenders, by offense seriousness[a]

	Less serious offenders			More serious offenders		
Year	Average	Drug	Difference	Average	Drug	Difference
Type of sentence						
1976	.345	.214	−.131	.630	.523	−.107
1977	.414	.225	−.189	.558	.282	−.276
1978	.403	.156	−.247	.547	.233	−.314
1979	.297	.181	−.116	.553	.394	−.159
1980	.416	.292	−.124***	.476	.117	−.359***
1981	.323	.183	−.140	.602	.475	−.127
1982	.260	.131	−.129***	.704	.733	.029***
1983	.220	.090	−.130	.556	.475	−.081
1984	.155	.060	−.095***	.636	.725	.089***
Average	.315	.170	−.145***	.585	.440	−.145***
Split sentence severity						
1976	41.442	37.195	−4.247*	60.952	68.108	7.156*
1977	38.972	37.758	−1.214*	59.636	73.687	14.051*
1978	43.577	44.366	.789	56.447	52.862	−3.585
1979	33.860	27.183	−6.677	70.400	75.675	5.275
1980	46.012	44.439	−1.573*	52.654	38.859	−13.795*
1981	47.491	49.912	2.421	57.607	53.734	−3.873
1982	42.540	36.997	−5.543***	59.838	66.049	6.211***
1983	40.475	40.349	−.126*	58.079	45.659	−12.420*
1984	37.939	39.923	1.984***	62.743	48.941	−13.802***
Average	41.546	40.197	−1.349	59.636	58.287	−1.349

[a] Predicted outcomes capture the simultaneous effects of offense seriousness and year of sentence, while holding constant at the mean the effects of the remaining variables. Less serious offenders are one standard deviation below mean seriousness; more serious offenders are one standard deviation above mean seriousness.
$*p \leq .05; ***p \leq .005$.

initial decision to incarcerate, these differences usually involve pronounced *lenience*. That is, the split sentences imposed on more serious drug offenders tended to be much less severe than those imposed on other serious offenders. In contrast, the split sentences imposed on less serious drug offenders differed little from the split sentences imposed on less serious offenders as a whole.

In the years after legislation, then, judges appeared to toughen their stance toward more serious drug offenders in an important respect: they were more likely to incarcerate them or to offer them less lenience than was previously the case. In another respect, however, judges were disproportionately lenient toward serious drug offenders for whom imprisonment was considered appropriate: they imposed less severe than average split sentences on these offenders.

Summary

The context of time, like other contexts, has two quite different implications for sentencing. To a very limited extent, it affects the severity of sanctions and, more importantly, it conditions the magnitude and direction of differential treatment based on race and offense. We begin this summary with a discussion of general patterns in sentencing behavior, then consider race and offense differences in sentencing outcomes.

An examination of sentencing outcomes over time revealed two general patterns in sentencing behavior over the course of this study. The first trend was the increase in the severity of all sanctions in the early 1980s, and the second was the dramatic downturn that followed these increases. The use of prison declined and split sentences became less severe after 1982. Prison sentences declined quite precipitously but much more recently, in the early months of 1985. To account for these trends, we examined changes in both the seriousness and type of offenders judges sentenced during the period of the study. We were fairly successful in tracing trends in the use of prison to changes in these legally relevant factors. The increase in the use of prison that occurred between 1980 and 1982 coincided with increases in the seriousness of offenses and in the proportion of offenders convicted of burglary. The decline since 1982 lagged a year behind declines in offense seriousness, but roughly coincided with increases in the proportion of offenders convicted of relatively minor property offenses and drug possession, and corresponding decreases in burglary.

In contrast, trends in split sentences bore little resemblance to changes in legally relevant factors. Although the decline since 1982 might be due to decreases in the proportion of violent offenders receiving split sentences, it is inconsistent with the corresponding growth in the proportion of drug offenders convicted of trafficking and other serious drug offenses. Instead, declines in the severity of split sentences could well be an outcome of growing concerns with, and litigation over, prison overcrowding. We were also somewhat less successful in tracing changes in prison sentences to fluctuations in legally relevant factors. The increase in prison terms that occurred between 1976 and 1980 had its counterpart in an increase in the seriousness of offenses. That prison sentences remained at elevated levels thereafter, despite subsequent declines in offense seriousness, might reflect sustained intolerance toward certain kinds of violent crime (e.g., assaults) and drug offenders (e.g., traffickers), both of whom constituted a growing proportion of offenders sentenced to prison in the 1980s. Although tentative because it is based on data for only part of the year, the sharp decline in 1985 coincides with sharp declines in offense seriousness, traceable in part to drastic reductions in the proportion of offenders convicted of violent crimes and sentenced to prison.

Once the legally relevant attributes of offense seriousness and type, as well as county and court variables, were held constant, sentencing outcomes varied little with time, and the trends presented earlier in the chapter were not nearly as pronounced. The risk of imprisonment continued to decline significantly after 1983, and was coupled with a tendency for prison sentences to be longer than average. Taken together, these trends suggest greater selectivity in the use of prison and greater punitiveness toward the small group selected for incarceration. This sentencing strategy may well be an attempt to cope simultaneously with administrative injunctions not to exacerbate prison overcrowding and with public demands for harsher punishment.

As was the case for other contexts, the element of time was more influential as a conditioner of differential treatment during sentencing. The first purpose of the analysis was to determine whether, in the face of litigation, race differences have declined with time. Apparently, they have not. Differences, often slight, occurred throughout the time period of the study, and they varied not only with time, but also by sentencing outcome and by the seriousness of the offense. Blacks were usually more likely than whites to be incarcerated, and differential treatment was significantly more pronounced in 1981 and less pronounced in 1979 and 1984. Until 1982, black offenders usually received longer prison sentences than whites, and harshness was particularly apparent in 1976 and 1980. Since 1982 the situation has reversed, and it is the prison sentences imposed on whites that are longer. The most recent data suggested virtually no difference in imprisonment risk, lenience toward blacks sentenced only to prison, and harshness toward blacks receiving a combination of prison and probation. To some extent, the slight race differences in the initial decision to incarcerate were misleading, because additional analysis indicated that, during several years, differences were likely to be pronounced only among less serious offenders. These results support the argument developed by Unnever and Hembroff (1986) that race will figure prominently in ambiguous situations, where legally relevant factors provide little strong guidance about the appropriate sanction.

The second purpose of the analysis was to trace the impact on sentencing behavior of legislative changes that occurred during the time period of the study. With the exception of drug offenses, most legislative change was relatively minor and typically involved an increase in maximum penalties and/or the imposition of minimum prison terms for certain types of offenders. Legislative concern with statutes governing common-law violence was confined to the comparatively less serious crimes of involuntary manslaughter, aggravated assault, and aggravated battery. Maximum penalties for these offenses were doubled, and the legislature established minimum penalties when assaults involved persons over 65 years of age or correctional officers. These changes appear to have produced noticeable and relatively sustained upswings primarily in the length of prison sentences. The use of prison for violent offenders in general has declined since 1981, and split sentences have become less severe. However, a closer examination of the sentences imposed on assault offenders indicated fairly sharp and sustained increases in differential treatment. Also, after differentiating less serious violent offenders from their more serious counterparts, we discovered that since 1980 differential treatment involving comparative harshness toward less serious violent offenders has increased, and they are much more likely than other relatively minor offenders to be incarcerated.

The only consequential changes in robbery laws were quite recently instituted (1984, 1985). They entailed legislated minimums for offenders who rob persons 65 years and older, and mandatory minimums for robberies involving the theft of controlled substances from a pharmacy. Given the recency of these changes, we had expected little perceptible impact in this sample. However, the 2.3-year increase in average prison sentences that occurred between 1983 and 1984 (which included 1985 data) could well be a response to legislative change.

Revisions of burglary statutes were primarily definitional, but in 1978 the legislature instituted mandatory minimums for offenders with prior burglary convictions. The impact of this legislation was difficult to gauge and appears to have been delayed or confined only to certain subgroups of offenders (e.g., more serious burglary offenders). No dramatic changes in sentencing patterns occurred after 1978, and the risk of incarceration did not begin to increase until 2 years after legislation was passed. Prison sentences became only slightly longer throughout the period of the study. Just after legislation (1979–81), however, judges appeared to single out more serious burglary offenders for particularly harsh treatment, while reserving lenience for less serious burglary offenders. This harshness, where burglary offenders were more likely than other serious offenders to be incarcerated, was short-lived, and by 1982 serious burglary offenders were once again treated more leniently than other serious offenders. A delayed, but longer lived, pattern characterized the treatment of serious burglary offenders who received a combination of prison and probation.

Among other property crimes, the only substantial change involved a doubling of the maximum penalty for motor vehicle theft in 1981 and the institution of mandatory minimums for convictions of a second or third offense. This legislation appears to have produced a noticeable upswing in the risk of imprisonment, but it was short-lived and followed by precipitous declines. In contrast, increases in both the severity of split sentences and the length of prison terms predated legislation, beginning in 1977 and 1978, respectively.

The most intense legislative activity focused on drug offenses, where controlled and dangerous substances were continually added or reclassified. Major drug legislation occurred in the early 1980s and involved the passage of laws that prohibited and set stiff mandatory minimums (up to 25 years) for trafficking in cocaine, illegal drugs (e.g., heroin), marijuana, and methaqualone. This legislation appears to have resulted in more modest and short-lived increases in incarceration risk and prison sentences. For example, during legislative activity (1980, 1982, 1985), the prison terms imposed on drug offenders became longer than average, but not significantly so. More noticeable changes became apparent after comparing the treatment accorded less serious and more serious drug offenders. In 1981, the year following the passage of trafficking legislation, comparative lenience toward serious drug offenders declined sharply or was replaced with harsher than average treatment. In 1982, for example, less serious drug offenders were still less likely than other minor offenders to be incarcerated. In a departure from the lenience they usually received, more serious drug offenders were more likely than other serious offenders to be incarcerated. The situation differed for serious drug offenders receiving a split sentence, however, and they tended to be treated much less severely than other serious offenders. In comparison with the sentences imposed on other serious offenders, then, judges combined a willingness to imprison serious drug offenders with a reluctance to impose severe split sentences.

Legislative changes aside, sentences varied over time for reasons that must remain largely speculative. For example, judges evinced a growing reluctance to incarcerate robbery and property offenders, but a willingness to impose stiff prison terms on those offenders selected for imprisonment. As noted earlier, whether conscious or not, this sentencing strategy is one way of demonstrating sensitivity to overcrowding problems and to public charges that judges are too lenient.

To the extent the data allowed, we could eliminate one possible explanation for variation in sentencing behavior, namely, year-specific variation in the legally relevant attributes of specific types of offenders. Temporal variation in legally relevant factors was common, and often underscored the anomalous nature of some results. For example, blacks who received split sentences in 1979 were convicted of significantly more serious crimes than whites, but during that year their split sentences were *less* severe than those imposed on whites. Harshness toward violent offenders sentenced to prison was particularly pronounced in 1978 and 1984, when violent offenders differed little from the average in offense seriousness *and* had significantly fewer arrests than other offenders. For robbery offenders, 1982 was a difficult year, because they were much more likely to be incarcerated, their split sentences were more severe than average, and the leniency they typically received in prison sentences was minimal. Yet we found no evidence that robbery offenders were particularly serious that year. Similarly, for reasons that are not clear the prison sentences imposed on vehicle theft offenders increased in 1983 by 5 years over the previous average of 10.2 years. What makes this finding anomalous was that, as always, vehicle theft offenders are convicted of less serious than average offenses. Moreover, those sentenced in 1983 did not differ from other offenders in either the number of conviction charges or the severity of their prior record.

In several instances, we thought that variation in legally relevant factors could account for differential treatment and reanalyzed the data after constructing a product term to control for the relevant interaction. At times, this strategy had no effect on the original pattern. In 1980, for example, the prison sentences of blacks were longer than those imposed on whites, and this trend persisted after controlling for the fact that the blacks sentenced that year were slightly more likely than whites to have been previously incarcerated in Georgia. Only rarely did the introduction of higher-order interactions radically alter the findings. Most notably, interactions attenuated the lenience we found toward burglary offenders in 1984, when their prison terms were 3.7 years shorter than the average term. Differences in treatment declined after we controlled for the fact that burglary offenders sentenced in 1984 approximated the average offender in seriousness and had significantly fewer conviction charges and prior arrests. Controlling for offense- and year-specific differences reduced the amount of lenience, and the estimated prison sentences imposed on burglary offenders were only 1.8 years longer than average.

More commonly, the second-order interactions were significant, and indicated that year-specific trends in differential treatment depended on legally relevant factors such as offense seriousness. As noted above, over the course of the study, the differential treatment of blacks was sometimes quite pronounced, but was limited to less serious offenders. An examination of higher-order product terms also enabled us to pinpoint more accurately the kinds of offenders most likely to experience disproportionate harshness. In many instances, the targets for comparative harshness such as serious burglary and drug offenders, as well as relatively minor violent offenders, tended to be precisely those offenders who had evoked considerable concern in the legislature.

Conclusion

Sentences in Georgia varied considerably over time, and this variation was both general and offense-specific. Some variations are interpretable as judicial responses to legislative concern with specific crimes, responses that differed in magnitude and duration for each offense. Dramatic changes (such as those for motor vehicle theft) were often, but not always, short-lived, whereas other changes were delayed or limited to certain types of offenders within a general category (e.g., serious drug and burglary offenders). Variations in sentences also reflect changes in the legally relevant characteristics of offenders, and these changes are both year- and offense-specific. Finally, other variations such as the tendency to combine a growing reluctance to incarcerate robbery and property offenders with harsher terms for those sentenced to prison have no clear origin, and we can only speculate that they reflect more general concerns with prison overcrowding and public demands for punitiveness.

Notes

1. As a precaution, we estimated prison sentences using metric coefficients from the expanded interactive model. They were virtually identical to those based on the original interactive model.
2. The increase in explained variance was .08 ($F = 3.52$, $8/27,523$ df, $p \leq .0001$).
3. In differentiating aggravated assaults from other violent offenses, we added eight more product terms and a vector in which assaults were coded 1, drug offenses were designated the excluded category (-1), and the remaining offenders were coded 0. The addition of these terms significantly increased the proportion of explained variance in each sentencing outcome. For type of sentence, the increase was .87 with an F ratio of 38.7 ($8/27,522$ df, $p \leq .0001$); for split sentence severity, the increase was .86 with an F ratio of 5.9 ($8/4,175$ df, $p \leq .0001$); and for prison sentence length, the increase was .59 with an F ratio of 11.6 ($8/4,926$ df, $p \leq .0001$).
4. The proportion of explained variance increased by .72, producing an F ratio of 31.9 ($8/27,523$ df, $p \leq .0001$).
5. The increase in explained variance was .3, producing an F ratio of 13.2 ($8/27,523$ df, $p \leq .0001$).
6. The increase in explained variance was 1.97 ($F = 9.98$, $11/4,173$ df, $p \leq .0001$).
7. For interested readers, the results for larceny, white-collar theft, and other property crimes are presented in Appendix Tables F, G, and H, respectively.
8. For type of sentence, the increase in explained variance was .72 ($F = 31.9$, $8/27,523$ df, $p \leq .0001$). For split sentence severity, the proportion of explained variance increased by .92 ($F = 6.3$, $8/4,176$ df, $p \leq .0001$). For prison sentences, the increase (.006) failed to reach statistical significance ($F = 1.16$, $8/4,935$ df, $p > .25$).

6
Summary and Conclusions

The preceding analyses of felony sentencing demonstrate that criminal sentencing is a complex and multifaceted process. In summarizing the results of these analyses and commenting on their significance, it is helpful to draw an analogy with the theater.[1] Anyone who has ever attended a play, musical, or ballet is aware of the importance of spotlights. To highlight an individual or group of performers, theater technicians use a variety of lights. When focusing on an individual or scene, all beams are concentrated in what appears to be a single light so as to direct the audience's attention. It is neither possible nor desirable to rely on a single spotlight for this effect because the resulting illumination would obviously fall far short of the effect of several beams combined as one.

In similar fashion we used different lights to highlight the sentencing process. These consist of the contexts of county, court, and time. When focused together in summary, if not in actual analysis, these three spotlights help us to understand sentencing more comprehensively than if we had relied on a single context. In this chapter, we summarize this total illumination and focus on three questions. First, what did we learn about sentencing in our three independent analyses? Second, what are the theoretical ramifications of this research? Finally, what is the practical significance of our general findings?

Summary

General

Three general and important conclusions can be drawn from our separate studies of felony sentencing in the contexts of county, court, and time. These include the absence of evidence of system-wide bias or discrimination, variation in the power of legally relevant variables, and perhaps most importantly, the contextually based nature of sentencing processes. Here we will briefly consider each.

The analyses reported in previous chapters indicate that there is little system-wide discrimination against blacks in criminal sentencing. This is an important finding, because general charges of discrimination are common not only in some interpretations of conflict theory, but also in some sectors of the popular and academic press. To be sure, the absence of evidence of system-wide discrimination does not mean that all courts and judges are blind in the administration of criminal law. Interactive analysis revealed context-specific patterns of discrimination. Importantly, however, there were many instances in which blacks receive disproportionately lenient punishment. Although this pattern may suggest a paternalism that is just as discriminating as disproportionate punitiveness, it nevertheless indicates that courts in Georgia do not have a heavy hand with black defendants in the general systemic sense or in every context where differential treatment is observed.

A second striking feature of both the additive and interactive analyses is the power of legally relevant variables, especially the seriousness of the offense. As outlined in the first chapter, we would expect judges with a more cautious or restrained judicial posture to focus on legally relevant criteria in sentencing. The fact that this variable features most prominently in the analysis of sentence length, however, tells us that the three sentencing decisions under scrutiny lend themselves with varying degrees of precision to this traditional conception of judicial power. When faced with determining prison sentence length, judges appear to rely heavily on the seriousness of the offense, suggesting that this last phase of the sentencing decision is the most clearly conceptualized. As we shall see later, the other two sentencing decisions (the initial probation/prison distinction and the split term) better lend themselves to varying justifications and interpretations. This is evident in the fact that the seriousness of the offense, although substantial and significant, did not carry as much weight in those processes as with the determination of prison sentence length. It is also evident in the related tendency for models to account for a modest portion of the variance in those outcomes, again in contrast to the more substantial variance explained in the study of prison length.

As we have stressed repeatedly in this book, the results of additive analyses can be misleading, because they mask important contextual effects. Although the predictive capability of interactive models varied in virtually every instance, interactive effects added significantly to the explained variance. In general, then, the results indicated quite graphically that aspects of the county, court, and time condition the direction and intensity of the influence exerted by the attributes of central interest: race and offense.

This general conclusion is important because race and offense are critical indicators of contrasting expectations about sentencing. The first suggests that sentencing is a rational decision in which penalties correspond to the seriousness of the offense. The second suggests that sentencing is largely shaped by extralegal concerns, with race the most obvious and constitutionally suspect. If the role of race and offense is affected by a variety of contexts, then we can assume that other variables, whether legally relevant or not, are similarly conditioned. This general conclusion can be substantiated by summarizing the results of the three analyses reported in Chapters 3 through 5.

The County Context

In Chapter 3 we examined the direct and indirect effects that the county context exerted on felony sentencing. With the exception of split sentences, direct effects were quite limited in scope and modest in magnitude. Nevertheless, they suggest that we cannot safely extrapolate the effects of county variables from one sentencing outcome to another. Most notably, judges in urban areas counterbalance a willingness to use prison with a reluctance to impose long prison terms on those incarcerated.

As emphasized earlier, the indirect impact of the surrounding county was more pronounced and important, and it clearly conditioned the relevance of race and offense during sentencing. Its influence, however, varied by decision, and not all outcomes were equally sensitive to the indirect effects of county attributes. County characteristics exerted their strongest conditioning influence during the initial decision to imprison or probate, and were less important for offenders who had received some form of incarceration.

As explained in Chapter 3, interactive analyses of the relationship between felony sentencing and county characteristics helped us to address five important questions. In the process, we gained deeper insight into the relationship between judicial processes and the broader social context in which courts function. These questions focused on five propositions: (1) the degree to which urbanization conditioned race differences in sentencing; (2) the tendency of courts in economically unequal counties or those with large subordinate populations to punish property offenders more severely; (3) the tendency of these same counties to punish black offenders more punitively than whites; (4) the relationship between economic conditions and the sentencing of violent offenders; (5) and the degree to which high crime rates foster punitiveness in criminal sentencing.

In summary, we found that urbanization did not condition race differences in treatment, a result that contrasts with the pattern noted in earlier research. Additionally, we found limited support for concluding that property offenders receive more punitive sanctions in counties with economic problems or a large subordinate population. For many property offenders and sentencing decisions, there was little evidence of harsher than average treatment and an unexpected amount of lenience. We also found little reason to extend the inequality argument to black offenders. Neither of the two measures of inequality affected race differences in punishment, and the size of the subordinate population had extremely limited or unanticipated implications for the criminal penalties imposed on black offenders. Contextual analysis indicated that economic conditions have substantial, if unexpected and variable, implications for the punishment of violent offenders. In contexts where racial inequities were pronounced and black populations were large, violent offenders were at the comparative advantage we expected. In contrast, the presence of pronounced *within-group* income inequality and a large population of unemployed persons appeared to lower the tolerance level for violence and foster punitiveness. Finally, high crime rates were consistent and powerful determinants of race and offense differences in sentencing. Violent offenders were at a particular disadvantage if sentenced in counties with high violent crime rates. The same was true for drug offenders sentenced in counties faced with serious property crime problems. In contrast, the punishment imposed on property offenders was not invariably harsher where property crime rates were high. Indeed, the opposite was more often the case.

The Court Context

In Chapter 4 we examined the direct and indirect impact of two kinds of court variables: characteristics of the judge and the organizational character of the court itself. The initial additive analyses indicated that judge and court characteristics were relatively unimportant predictors of sentence outcomes, and were overshadowed by variables commonly regarded as legally relevant. The absence of some direct effects was surprising. For example, conservative judges, judges with strong ties to the local community, and judges who were electorally vulnerable did not exhibit any pronounced punitiveness in sentencing.

Judge and court characteristics, however, were impressive conditioners of race and offense effects on all three sentencing outcomes: imprisonment probability, split sentencing, and straight prison terms. In many of these instances, interactive models yielded evidence that contrasted with additive results. For example, in additive models that included legal and extralegal attributes as well as court and judge characteristics, the results indicated that blacks were slightly more likely than whites to be incarcerated and to receive longer prison terms. However, interactive analyses demonstrated that there were many situations where blacks received more lenient treatment than whites. Similarly, the importance of the offense varied according to the court context.

As explained in Chapter 4, research on appellate court processes prompted several propositions about the conditioning influence of judge characteristics. Some of these propositions centered on the specific background attributes of sex, age, religion, prosecutorial experience, involvement in the community, and electoral vulnerability. In each instance, these attributes shaped the role of race and offense, often in an unexpected manner. Whereas older and presumably more conservative judges were more likely to imprison and impose severe split sentences on black offenders, the same cannot be said of judges whose attributes have also been linked with conservatism or community involvement. Baptist judges were *less* likely to imprison black offenders than non-Baptists, and former prosecutors were indeed tougher, but toward white offenders! Rather than lenience, female judges appeared to be more severe than their male colleagues, particularly toward white offenders sentenced to prison. In short, presumably conservative judges seldom singled out black offenders for disproportionate harshness, nor did their more liberal counterparts extend them lenience.

Similarly complex patterns obtained when we examined the relationship between judge characteristics and the type of offense. The results provided somewhat greater support for the contention that judges who are conservative politically or socially involved in the community, or electorally vulnerable will be especially punitive toward offenders who appear dangerous to the community. For example, former prosecutors did sentence some offenders (e.g., violent, burglars, robbers, drug) more severely than judges without prosecutor experience. However, older and Baptist judges, as well as the electorally vulnerable, were selectively punitive, and sentenced several types of offenders more *leniently* than their counterparts. Older judges were more lenient than their young counterparts with burglary and violent offenders, but more punitive with some property and drug offenders. Perhaps the most unexpected findings are the tentative patterns of punitiveness we found on the part of courts where female judges preside. Not only did they tend to sentence rape offenders more severely than their male colleagues, but they also evinced greater intolerance in general and toward white and property offenders in particular. Also unexpected was the harshness displayed by male judges toward female offenders.

When analyzing the direct and indirect effects of judge characteristics, we assumed that these background attributes corresponded to ideological orientation, an assumption derived from previous research. In examining the importance of court characteristics, we focused on indicators of bureaucratization. Here we posed two central questions. Does bureaucratization, independently of urbanization, affect differential treatment? If so, does it reduce or intensify race and offense differences in treatment? Here we relied on two key indicators of bureaucratization: caseload pressure and specialization. Caseload pressure did not condition race differences in treatment. Instead, differential treatment depended on the degree to which courts specialized in felony cases. Specialization reduced but did not eliminate race differences, suggesting that bureaucratization does not foster the uniform evenhandedness that Weberian theory would lead one to expect. Instead, bureaucratization put black offenders at a disadvantage in two senses: by increasing their risk of being imprisoned and by fostering significantly less lenience toward blacks sentenced to prison than toward their white counterparts.

Bureaucratization also affected differences in treatment based on offense. The most important general finding centered on evidence that the legally relevant variable of offense was not highlighted in bureaucratized courts, an expectation of rationalist Weberian theory. Although differences among offenses declined somewhat with the degree of bureaucratization, there were pointed contrasts. In comparison with judges presiding in less crowded or specialized courts, those in highly bureaucratized courts sentenced violent offenders more leniently and were more severe toward property and drug offenders.

Whether defined in terms of court bureaucratization or the background attributes of the judge, the court context emerged as an important conditioner of race and offense differences in sentencing. More importantly, this conditioning influence did not always conform to expectations generated from previous research or orthodox organizational theory.

The Temporal Context

In Chapter 5 we considered the relationship between felony sentencing and the context of time. In that analysis we examined change in the aggregate sentencing patterns over time, the net effect of time on sentencing severity, and the interactive impact of that context.

Aggregate sentence patterns over the time period of this research generally corresponded to trends noted in the literature. Specifically, the use of imprisonment declined sharply, a similar but weaker pattern held for split sentences, and the length of prison increased, albeit not consistently. In general, these results suggest that sentencing in Georgia's felony courts is somewhat more lenient today than approximately 10 years ago.

To account for these temporal patterns, we examined the degree to which sentencing patterns coincided with changes in the offender population. After discovering that the characteristics of convicted offenders did change over time and contributed to aggregate patterns, we held constant all potentially explanatory variables (case, county, and court) and estimated the net effect of time. Interestingly, we found that time exerts a very small effect on sentencing. In virtually every instance, the case, county, and court variables continued to have the same effects as reported in earlier chapters. To put the matter differently but more emphatically, the year offenders are sentenced has a very small direct effect on sentencing. In this regard, the temporal context is virtually identical to that of the county and court. Simply put, no context is a powerful *direct* determinant of sentence severity.

In examining the interactive effect of time, we asked two questions. Has the effect of race declined in significance over time, and has the treatment of offenders within specific crime categories fluctuated? As with other contexts, the interactive results reported in Chapter 5 were complex. Throughout the time period, blacks, particularly those convicted of less serious offenses, were slightly more likely than whites to be imprisoned. Once we moved beyond the initial decision to imprison, however, there were no clear trends in differential treatment. Instead, race differences fluctuated by year and by sentencing outcome. For example, from 1977 to 1982, blacks received more lenient split sentences than whites. On the other hand, until 1982 and especially in 1976 and 1980, they often received longer prison terms. In the most recent time period (1984–85), there were virtually no differences in imprisonment risk, harsher penalties for blacks sentenced to split terms, and shorter prison sentences for those receiving only incarceration.

When examining the degree to which time indirectly affected the import of offense, we explicitly looked for patterns that might correspond to changes in the state's penal code or to year- and offense-specific changes in the composition of the offender population. Dramatic, although not necessarily long-lived, increases in severity accompanied legislation involving violence and motor vehicle theft. In contrast, the impact of revisions in robbery, burglary, and drug statutes was often less noticeable, delayed, and/or limited to a subset of offenders (e.g., more serious burglary offenders). Temporal variation in the legally relevant attributes of specific offender types was common, but only rarely did it account for the differences in treatment we observed. Instead, an examination of the extent and consequences of this variation proved useful in two senses: it allowed us to pinpoint more accurately the specific types of offenders that received disproportionate harshness and, relatedly, to trace more clearly the impact of specific legislative changes.

Theoretical Significance

As indicated earlier, we did not set out to test a particularly theory about the relationship between courts and society, or the functions served by criminal law. We did, however, find patterns that spoke to some theoretical currents, albeit not consistently. As summarized, there was evidence supporting both conflict as well as consensual interpretations. Likewise, we found that courts were affected by urbanization, although not in the direction suggested in the literature. Finally, sentencing did not always conform to the rationalist perspective outlined in Weberian theory where the more bureaucratized the organization, the more formalized the decision-making process.

In considering this inconsistent evidence, it is important to note that observed patterns did not always explain large portions of the variance in outcome. In fact, only one of the three sentence outcomes, the length of imprisonment, lent itself to comprehensive statistical explanation. How do we account for this?

The failure to account for substantial portions of the variance in sentencing is not unusual in social science research (Wilbanks, 1987). Equally typical are two possible explanations: methodological shortcomings and theoretical oversimplification. We will deal with both and then comment on the related ramifications of the research in question.

Every scientific enterprise suffers from some methodological shortcomings, and ours is no exception. Of central importance were the unavailability of potentially critical variables and the questionable validity of others. Recent studies of capital sentencing (e.g., Baldus et al., 1983) suggest that the race of the victim is an important predictor of sentencing punitiveness. Wilbanks (1987) underscored this point in his recent book on the myth of racism in criminal justice. The data sets used in this analysis did not contain any information on victim race.[2] Furthermore, there were no indicators of evidentiary strength, another potentially important factor, and one emphasized in site visits to selected courts. One probation officer, for example, explained that "the district attorney will probably have a weak case and there is the danger he couldn't prove it before a jury and they will agree to a certain sentence and then won't try him." Similarly, several judges referred to "junk cases," where the state was not sure about the victim's willingness to testify, and even less confident about the eventual substance of the testimony.

Another potentially serious omission was the absence of information on or perceptions about prison overcrowding. Although the prison system was consistently crowded during the time period of this study, judicial awareness and consideration of that fact may have varied. Site visits hinted at the potential importance of judicial perceptions. Virtually every court official acknowledged the state prison crisis and stressed that overcrowding limited their reliance on imprisonment. One judge even referred to formal communications from the Department of Corrections in which judges were encouraged to use alternatives to incarceration and, if they did incarcerate, to impose less severe terms. Although it is difficult to know how perceptions of prison overcrowding affected decision making, it was obvious that judges were troubled by the problem. Many shared the sentiment of one judge who lamented that "it cost so darn much money to house prisoners."

Complicating the methodological deficiencies created by the absence of critical information was the questionable validity of a key legally relevant variable: prior record. Early statistical tests yielded counterintuitive findings on the impact of prior convictions. For example, in preliminary analysis, the length of imprisonment declined as the number of prior convictions increased! Communications with the Department of Corrections, our primary data source, confirmed our suspicion that there had been considerable coding error, leading to the virtual absence of reliability.

Although we did have and used alternative measures of prior record (e.g., prior arrest and prior incarceration), their validity is open to question, forcing us to qualify any conclusions on the effect of that legally relevant variable. This qualification is appropriate if we recognize the powerful effect criminal history has displayed in other research (e.g., Farrell and Swigert, 1978; Petersilia, 1985), the consistent power of legally relevant variables in sentencing research (Wilbanks, 1987), and the importance of different measures of criminal history (Welch et al., 1984).

Complicating methodological problems are questions of theoretical relevance. In short, residual variation may simply reflect theoretical shortcomings, most notably an undue reliance on a single theoretical framework or an unrealistically formal model of decision making. Ignatieff (1983) spoke to the first in his review of the social histories of criminal punishment. Detailing the limited relevance of both conflict and consensual models, he suggested that criminal punishment cannot be adequately explained if we insist on explaining social behavior with one intellectual tradition. Ignatieff (1983:100) suggested that we broaden the scope of our inquiry, recognize the complexity inherent in criminal punishment, and try to identify the ways in which criminal punishment relates to other civil sanctioning and dispute resolution systems.

The second theoretical explanation for the residual variation in this and virtually every other sentencing study rests on the distinction between formal and pragmatic models of decision making (Carter, 1986). In jurisprudence, schools of thought focus on the degree to which judicial decision making can or cannot be regulated. Formalist approaches assume that judicial decisions are the simple applications of well-defined doctrines, principles, and rules. Pragmatic conceptions "downplay the importance of the linkage between rules and choices" (Carter, 1986:1), and focus on the experiential and more intangible dimensions of decision. In constitutionalism, these positions pit strict constructionists against more critical legal scholars where debate rages on the degree to which the constitution lends itself to one or several interpretations.

Admittedly, these models of formalism and pragmatism have been largely applied to appellate court processes. There is, however, an application and theoretical point to be made to the study of trial courts. Let us assume that social theories (e.g., conflict or consensual) represent a formal model for trial court decision making, sentencing in particular. Limited success in the application of one or more of these theories could speak to the potential importance of more pragmatic or idiosyncratic dimensions of decision making.

Although we did not set out to test comprehensively the vitality of any social theory of court decision making, we did find evidence that spoke to contradictory frameworks and we were left with some substantial residual variation. How viable, then, is a more pragmatic explanation?

The only way we can even begin to address this issue is to return to the insights gleaned from site visits to selected circuits. To be sure, during these visits many respondents spoke in conflict or consensual terms. Others, however, emphasized the idiosyncratic element more germane to pragmatic interpretations. For example, in several interviews respondents referred to quirks of personality or temperament that might intervene in sentencing. Some judges emphasized the need to "do right," and others suggested that the defendant's penitence or remorse played a part during sentencing. The most cynical expression of this position was the probation officer who argued that "sentencing variation can be traced to judicial personality and to the emotional disposition of the judge on any given day." Less cynical was the comment of one judge that sentencing was "not really instinct, but . . . a developed judgment based on experience."

How do our research results speak to the competing dimensions of formal and pragmatic decision models? First, the mixture of resulting evidence suggests that the available formal models are not adequate and need to be refined, a point that Ignatieff (1983) detailed. Second, the difference between additive and interactive models noted in the previous chapters suggests a need to consider the possibility of more pragmatic interpretations. These two conclusions pose substantial theoretical challenge for contemporary social science, challenges that fall on conceptual and methodological grounds.

If sentencing and any judicial behavior is a function of what judges want to do, what they should do, and what they are able to do (Gibson, 1983), then we need to develop decision theories that integrate attitudinal with role and social theories. As summarized earlier in this chapter, our research demonstrates that additive models of sentencing are inadequate, and the simple addition of role or situational variables to models with case level attributes will not yield substantially better explanations. Rather, our research illustrates how the impact of case attributes is sharply conditioned by the social, organizational, and temporal contexts in which courts function. This conditioning must be recognized in abstract conceptualizations of decision making if we are to have any hope of successfully analyzing sentencing and other judicial behavior.

Of course, it stands to reason that integrative theories cannot be tested without valid and reliable indicators of key concepts. These include the standard legally relevant variables of offense and criminal history, but also the organizational pressures reflected in evidentiary case strength and prison capacity. More importantly, perhaps, formal theory testing must be accompanied by efforts to identify the degree to which sentencing disparities are locally and/or personally conditioned. Our research demonstrates that formal theories are not totally irrelevant. However, it also hints at the potential explanatory power of less quantifiable factors.

Formal and pragmatic approaches, however, are difficult to reconcile in a single study. A major theoretical task, then, centers on the integration of contrasting research strategies. Although the development of ethnographic approaches in the study of criminal and civil courts (e.g., Mather, 1979) speaks to pragmatic concerns, there are virtually no models for the integration of quantitative and qualitative evidence. If such integration is not possible, then our research suggests an alternative approach. Let us take the question of racism and criminal law as an example. If one were concerned about the degree to which criminal law unfairly discriminated against a class of defendants, the first step would center on the identification of systemic bias. If such a study indicated, as ours did, that there was no evidence of systemic bias but a suggestion of localized discriminating then intensive study of jurisdictions at both ends of the discrimination spectrum, so to speak, would be necessary. To argue that intensive investigations of single jurisdictions is the only way to study trial courts is, in our judgment, unfounded. There is much to be learned from such studies, particularly as they help us understand decision making in more pragmatic terms, but the systemic inquiries are just as necessary if we are to gain a broad picture of the character of justice. The most serious challenge our study carries, then, is the challenge to integrate attitudinal, role, and social theories in decision-making models and to synthesize the results if not the actual applications of both formal and pragmatic models of decision making.

Practical Significance

Though not designed to test a particular policy proposal or reform, the results of this study do carry some practical implications. In this section, we consider these ramifications and focus on the legislative and judicial processes related to criminal sentencing. In closing, we offer general comments on the relationship between law and science.

Sentencing policy frequently focuses on disparity, and although disparity is used interchangeably with discrimination in the popular and even academic press, the two are not synonymous. As the National Academy of Science emphasized, disparity reflects differential treatment, whereas discrimination falls on objectionable distinctions.

Discrimination exists when some case attribute that is objectionable – typically on moral or legal grounds – can be shown to be associated with sentence outcomes after all other relevant variables are adequately controlled . . .

Disparity exists when "like cases" with respect to case attributes – regardless of their legitimacy – are sentenced differently. . . . Disparity refers to the influence in sentence outcomes of factors in the decision-making process. (Blumstein et al., 1983:8)

As Blumstein and his colleagues pointed out, discrimination does not require disparity. For example, if all sentencing judges in Georgia were prejudiced against black offenders and expressed their prejudice in punitive penalties, there would be considerable discrimination but no disparity. There can also be disparity without discrimination because differentiating factors such as prior record can be legitimate considerations during sentencing.

Many legislatures have changed their sentencing laws – totally or partially – on a variety of empirical assumptions. These include the existence of disparities, the effect that such disparities have on the deterrent or incapacitative effectiveness of law, and the discriminatory character of some penalties. Recent research (e.g., Goodstein and Hepburn, 1985; Shane-Dubow et al., 1985) suggests that most of these changes have not lived up to expectations.

The research in this book does not speak directly to this failure. Nor were we interested in systematically evaluating the consequences of the incremental changes in sentencing adopted by the Georgia General Assembly in the last 9 years. Our scientific assessment of sentencing, however, carries some policy ramifications for the political process in general and legislative and judicial functions in particular.

Our results suggest that considerable progress has occurred in the state's criminal justice system. If we recall that we found no evidence of systematic racial discrimination in Georgia and if we note that social science and historical research has documented such discrimination in this region in the past, that finding is not unimportant. Of course, qualifications are in order because of the methodological shortcomings previously noted. Even with these qualifications, however, one needs to recognize that this finding conforms to most current sentencing research (Wilbanks, 1987).

Moving beyond the systemic evidence, however, let us consider the ramifications of our interactive findings. As summarized earlier, we found that both the legally relevant variable of offense and the extralegal attribute of race were conditioned by the county, court, and temporal contexts in sentencing. In some instances, this conditioning was rather marked. This suggests several interpretations, one of which is the possibility that there are excessively harsh and excessively lenient judges whose decision patterns, in effect, cancel out in the general system. Certainly, there was evidence of this in the analyses of the impact of race because the contextually-specific treatment of blacks involved both disproportionate punitiveness and leniency.

If the legislature is concerned with equity in the criminal process, and one would assume it should be, this evidence may require as much consideration as the systemic variety. In fact, it suggests that the legislature should reconsider the range of penalties it allows for major crimes. If it is impossible to eliminate differential treatment entirely, and it most assuredly is, then some restriction in range might help to reduce the most extreme instances of differential treatment.

In addition to this rejoinder, there is another important, if less obvious, policy implication for legislative bodies. This falls on the degree to which we were not equally successful in accounting for all three sentence outcomes under scrutiny. As considered earlier, there are a variety of factors that might account for the residual variation in the outcomes of imprisonment probability and split sentencing. In considering our success in explaining length of imprisonment, however, one interpretation may suffice. Simply put, there may be considerable consensus of opinion – in and out of the legislature – on the purposes served by incarceration. These consist of the desire to punish a severe wrong and/or to protect society from an individual who has committed a severe wrong. In both instances, legally relevant variables would serve as important decision indicators, as, indeed, they did in our analysis.

If this is the case, what are the implications for legislative responsibility? Basically, this suggests that the legislature needs to clarify the purposes served by criminal law in general and alternatives to incarceration in particular. Site visits suggested that judges approach probation as an alternative to incarceration or in combination with a limited prison term in a variety of ways. Some regarded it as a means of facing prison overcrowding, whereas others seemed committed to the rehabilitative ideal. If the legislature is concerned with the fact that legally relevant variables account for small portions of the variance in these two sentence outcomes, they might consider clarifying the purpose ascribed for criminal law and the immediate objectives they hope will be realized by alternatives to incarceration.

In addition to the aforementioned obvious and more subtle ramifications of our research for legislative process, our study sheds some light on the failure of current sentencing reform schemes to live up to expectations. Several shortcomings could account for this failure, among them the failure to address the empirical assumptions underlying the changes, to balance competing political objectives in the reform process, and to adequately support the implementation process. Our research suggests that the first shortcoming may be more consequential than assumed. As demonstrated in earlier chapters, sentencing is far more complex than we had assumed. The contextual effects of the county, court, and time suggest that at least one criticism of previous sentencing research is on target. In his review of the impact of race in criminal justice, Wilbanks (1987) pointed out that most sentencing studies to date have not considered the interaction between race and other independent variables. Potentially successful reform requires adequate data. Our research, however limited, suggests that adequate data will have to consist of something more than simple additive analysis of sentencing outcomes. Although these analyses are important for identifying the degree of systemic deficiencies, they can only provide a general and potentially misleading picture of the process at hand.

In many respects, our results speak most directly to appellate review of criminal sentences. In these instances, most of which center on capital penalties, statistical evidence is frequently introduced to document a discrimination claim. Typically, evidence is drawn from additive analyses, where sentencing is studied against a broad range of variables with no attention to interactive effect. Our results indicate that such evidence is not and will not be very useful. Systemic evidence of no discrimination may mask very real and serious contextual discrimination. Similarly, systemic evidence of discrimination may not adequately characterize every context in a jurisdiction.

Whether speaking to legislative or judicial decision makers, it is obvious that lessons learned from this research suggest that the process of obtaining good information for legislators or judges is time consuming and costly. Furthermore, it suggests that even comprehensive attempts such as this one fall short on selected dimensions.

The more general obstacle to an easy transference of this study to the policymaking process, however, centers on the tensions inherent in the law and science relationship. In setting criminal penalties or ruling on the merits of a specific criminal appeal, legislators and judges have to make some empirical assessments. Legislators have to address the assumptions underlying the changes they want to make—assumptions about the need for reform, the chances that reform will be successful, and the cost that such changes will entail. In ruling on the specific claims of an individual defendant, judges have to decide if the evidence, that is, the facts of the case, substantiate the broader claim or charge. In each instance, science has a role to play.

However, it will be difficult to apply social science in both forums not only because of the political and normative judgments that must be considered, but also because of the inevitable tensions in trying to apply cumulative, probabilistic findings to decisions that are couched in more rigid, inflexible terms. This tension exacerbates the more obvious problems associated with the standards guiding research evaluation, and the ability of social scientists and lawyers to converse in each other's language.

In this study of the social contexts of criminal sentencing, we have been concerned with science. Specifically, we have tried to answer two questions about sentencing: how is it affected by the county, court, and the element of time, and do these contexts condition the impact of race and offense? Our answers to these questions challenge pertinent social theories on the relationship between law and society, provide direction to future scientific analyses of criminal court processes, and carry a number of important implications for policies designed to foster more equitable punishment.

Notes

1. This metaphor was adopted from Fowlkes (1983).
2. One of the conditions of the NIJ grant that supported earlier research on this project was the use of preexisting data sets. This condition posed some methodological problems because we did not have the opportunity to collect all the information we wanted and we were unable to take every step to ensure data reliability.

Appendix A
The Consequences of Aggregating Judicial Information

As noted in Chapter 2, most judge information was based on aggregated data, obtained from all judges presiding in the circuit the year the offender was sentenced. This procedure introduced an unavoidable amount of imprecision into measures of judicial characteristics. In this section, we explore the possibility that imprecision may account, in part, for the weak effects judicial characteristics have on sentencing outcomes. As will become apparent below, judge characteristics have a weak influence on sentencing, regardless of whether judicial information is exact or aggregated.

To examine this issue, we constructed a set of interaction terms between each judge characteristic and a variable that measured the way judge information was obtained. Cases for which sentencing judge information was known were assigned a value of 1, and cases whose judge information was based on aggregated data were assigned a score of 0. We added these interaction terms to the additive model, and tested for the significance of the increase in proportion of explained variation. Table A.1 presents these results.

For two sentencing outcomes, type of sentence and split sentence severity, the increase in explained variance was statistically significant ($p \leq .005$). This finding suggests that the effects of judicial characteristics depend on whether information about these characteristics is exact or aggregated. To explore interactions in more detail, we differentiated common effects from those that were specific to the type of judicial information we obtained. Common effects refer to regression coefficients that are virtually identical for both types of cases, that is, those where judge information is exact and those where it was aggregated. We present common effects for judge characteristics whose product term with the variable, type of judge information, was not statistically significant ($p > .05$). Data-specific effects, in contrast, are parameter estimates that differ significantly depending on the type of judge information. We report these effects for variables whose product term with type of judge information was significant ($p \leq .05$).

Table A.1 indicates that significant interactions are relatively common for the initial decision to imprison. In contrast, only two interactions are significant for split sentence severity (i.e., religion and election history). For neither outcome,

TABLE A.1. Standardized regression coefficients for judge characteristics, by type of judge information[a]

Variable	Type of sentence Common effects	Sentencing judge data Exact	Sentencing judge data Aggregated	Split sentence severity Common effects	Sentencing judge data Exact	Sentencing judge data Aggregated
Sex	.078***			.045**		
Age	.001***			−.017		
Religion		.028***	.060***		.041*	−.054
Years as prosecutor		.007***	.002**	.085***		
Circuit of origin	.017**			−.037		
Membership in community organizations	.009***			.091***		
Years in local government		−.003***	−.001	.033		
Opponents in primary		−.084***	−.006	−.061**		
Election history	.047***				−.040*	.134***
R^2 additive model		.204			.203	
R^2 interactive model		.207			.209	
F (df)		13.04 8/27,577			4.01 8/4,230	
$p \leq$		.0001			.0001	

[a] Regression coefficients represent the effect of judge characteristics on sentencing outcomes while controlling for the effects of case characteristics, court bureaucratization, and county variables.

however, did aggregation consistently weaken the effects of judicial characteristics. Instead, the effects of aggregation are more complex. In some instances, judicial characteristics have weaker effects among cases with aggregated information. In others, their effects are stronger or opposite in sign.

First, in three instances, judicial characteristics have slightly weaker effects among those cases, where sentencing judge information was aggregated. These involve previous experience as prosecutor, years in local government, and opposition in primaries. Where judge data were aggregated, these variables have no significant effect on the initial decision to imprison. In contrast, where judge data are exact, these variables have a significant effect. Yet even among these cases, the three court factors have a slight influence on outcomes ($\beta \leq .09$).

Second, we found one instance where a judicial characteristic, religion, has a slightly stronger effect among cases where judge information was aggregated. Yet even among those cases its influence is slight ($\beta = .06$).

Finally, for split sentence severity, aggregation appears to affect both the direction and magnitude of the influence exerted by judge characteristics. Both religion and election history have quite different effects, depending on the source of judicial information. In cases where the sentencing judge was known, the results support our expectation that Baptists and electorally vulnerable judges will impose more severe split sentences. Among aggregated cases, however, the results disconfirm expectations. Religion has a slight, but insignificant, negative effect, suggesting leniency on the part of Baptist judges. The same is true for judges who are less established. The split sentences they impose are slightly less severe than those imposed by judges who have been elected three or more times. Particularly for religion and election history, then, the nonsignificant additive effects presented in Table A.1 are misleading, because they fail to capture the very different effects these factors have on the sentences imposed by the two types of courts.

This exception aside, none of the results alter our general conclusion that judicial characteristics have a quite small direct influence on sentencing behavior. Moreover, the aggregation procedure does not appear to weaken or otherwise alter the influence that most judicial characteristics exert on sentencing outcomes.

Appendix Tables

TABLE A. Zero-order correlations among court and county variables

Variable	2	3	4	5	6	7	8	9
1. Urbanization	.539*	.532*	−.110*	.035*	.101*	.211*	.170*	−.031*
2. Income standard deviation		.637*	−.184*	.108*	.143*	.186*	.198*	−.016
3. Racial income inequality			−.142*	.261*	.182*	.182*	.207*	−.100*
4. Lagged unemployment rate				.122*	−.076*	−.036*	−.282*	.075*
5. Percent black					−.111*	.209*	.163*	−.032
6. Lagged crime rate						.120*	−.031*	−.037*
7. Caseload pressure							.030*	.003
8. Court specialization								−.008
9. Judge sex								
10. Judge age								
11. Judge religion								
12. Years as prosecutor								
13. Circuit of origin								
14. Membership in community organizations								
15. Years in local government								
16. Opponents in primary								
17. Election history								

TABLE A. (*Continued*)

Variable	10	11	12	13	14	15	16	17
1. Urbanization	.100*	−.156*	−.126*	−.211*	.014	−.078*	.080*	.013
2. Income standard deviation	.132*	−.113*	−.056*	.018*	.006	.028*	.095*	.027*
3. Racial income inequality	.255*	−.089*	−.070*	.044*	.046*	−.009	.103*	−.023*
4. Lagged unemployment rate	.034*	.023*	.050*	.029*	.028*	−.034*	−.043*	−.082*
5. Percent black	.165*	−.029*	.024*	.218*	.125*	.029*	−.129*	−.014
6. Lagged crime rate	.020*	−.103*	−.039*	.031*	.068*	−.007	.040*	.041*
7. Caseload pressure	.082*	−.055*	.018*	.154*	.173*	.064*	−.094*	.013
8. Court specialization	.027*	.031*	.024*	−.094*	.029*	−.044*	−.024*	.106*
9. Judge sex	−.068*	−.039*	.090*	.041*	−.046*	.053*	.023*	−.009
10. Judge age		.137*	.084*	.206*	.177*	.070*	−.046*	.233*
11. Judge religion			.054*	.029*	.164*	−.016	.007	.090*
12. Years as prosecutor				−.078*	.060*	−.180*	−.193*	−.063*
13. Circuit of origin					.034*	.107*	.134*	.028*
14. Membership in community organizations						.069*	.015	.164*
15. Years in local government							.217*	−.014
16. Opponents in primary								−.244*
17. Election history								

*$p \leq .005$.

TABLE B. Seriousness of selected offenders, by level of county urbanization

Type of offender	Measure of seriousness	Urbanization[a]			
		Lowest quartile		Highest quartile	
Type of sentence					
Burglary	Offense seriousness	10.48	(2089)	10.33	(1436)***
Property theft/ damage	Offense seriousness	6.51	(2247)	6.24	(2273)***
Split sentence severity					
Common-law violent	Offense seriousness	8.23	(187)	13.88	(220)***
	Number of conviction charges	1.25	(187)	1.81	(220)***
	Prior arrests	1.25	(185)	2.81	(216)***
	Prior incarceration	.11	(187)	.16	(220)
Robbery	Offense seriousness	17.31	(89)	16.49	(149)
	Number of conviction charges	1.49	(89)	2.06	(149)***
	Prior arrests	2.00	(88)	2.32	(145)
	Prior incarceration	.18	(89)	.17	(149)
Burglary	Offense seriousness	10.54	(424)	10.37	(273)**
	Number of conviction charges	1.40	(424)	1.94	(273)***
	Prior arrests	1.62	(407)	3.29	(259)***
	Prior incarceration	.16	(424)	.30	(273)***
Prison sentence length					
Common-law violent	Offense seriousness	20.44	(333)	20.26	(360)
	Number of conviction charges	1.30	(333)	1.96	(360)***
	Prior arrests	1.62	(331)	2.97	(354)***
	Prior incarceration	.16	(333)	.25	(360)***
Robbery	Offense seriousness	18.84	(145)	19.02	(166)
	Number of conviction charges	1.43	(145)	2.37	(166)***
	Prior arrests	2.21	(145)	3.29	(160)*
	Prior incarceration	.21	(145)	.26	(166)
Burglary	Offense seriousness	10.53	(461)	10.43	(314)
	Number of conviction charges	1.39	(461)	2.23	(314)***
	Prior arrests	1.95	(435)	3.58	(296)***
	Prior incarceration	.21	(461)	.31	(314)***

[a] Number of offenders in parentheses.
*T-test significant at $p \leq .05$; **T-test significant at $p \leq .01$; ***T-test significant at $p \leq .005$.

TABLE C. Seriousness of offenders sentenced to prison, by race of offender and sex composition of bench

	Percent male			
Measure of seriousness	50–75%		100%	
Black offenders				
Offense seriousness	13.53	(123)	13.17	(2735)[a]
Number of conviction charges	1.50	(123)	1.62	(2735)
Prior arrests	2.17	(118)	2.56	(2635)
Prior incarceration	.16	(123)	.24	(2735)[b]
White offenders				
Offense seriousness	11.13	(67)	12.61	(2361)
Number of conviction charges	1.66	(67)	1.61	(2361)
Prior arrests	3.20	(65)	2.75	(2279)[c]
Prior incarceration	.23	(67)	.19	(2361)

[a] Difference with white offenders also sentenced by male judges is significant at $p = .05$. Male judges tend to sentence black offenders who have been convicted of more serious crime than white offenders.

[b] Difference with white offenders sentenced by male judges is significant at $p = .005$. Difference with black offenders sentenced in courts with female judges is significant at $p = .05$. Male judges sentence black offenders who are more likely to have been incarcerated in Georgia than both blacks sentenced by female judges and whites sentenced by male judges.

[c] Difference with white offenders sentenced in courts with female judges is significant at $p = .005$. Male courts sentence whites who have fewer arrests than whites sentenced in courts where female judges preside.

TABLE D. Distribution of offender and offense characteristics over time

Characteristic	Year of sentence									
	1976	1977	1978	1979	1980	1981	1982	1983	1984	1985
Legally relevant factors										
Mean offense seriousness	9.45	9.62	9.31	8.86	8.95	9.24	8.83	8.28	8.09	7.64
Percent convicted of:										
Common-law violent	15.7	16.9	16.4	15.0	14.1	15.2	13.3	12.8	13.4	10.9
Robbery	6.7	5.3	5.5	4.3	5.1	5.3	5.2	3.8	3.8	3.1
Burglary	27.4	29.6	29.5	28.4	29.2	30.2	26.5	25.2	23.1	23.8
Property theft/damage	34.6	33.7	33.1	35.3	33.3	30.9	31.6	35.4	34.6	34.1
Drug	15.5	14.5	15.6	17.0	18.3	18.3	23.4	22.8	25.1	28.0
Mean prior arrests	3.04	2.60	2.30	2.39	2.33	2.45	2.11	3.12	2.57	.36
Mean prior incarceration	.27	.23	.23	.21	.18	.17	.14	.24	.19	.02
Social background (means)										
Sex	.91	.90	.91	.89	.89	.90	.89	.85	.85	.84
Race	.55	.57	.56	.70	.60	.59	.57	.56	.57	.55
Age	26.12	26.49	26.70	26.64	26.06	26.02	26.64	26.95	27.20	26.92
Marital status	.28	.29	.32	.33	.24	.25	.26	.33	.33	.22
Employment status	.74	.72	.74	.76	.78	.79	.75	.43	.38	.63

TABLE E. Trends in predicted sentencing outcomes for assault and other violent offenses[a]

Year	Predicted outcome			Deviation from average outcome	
	Average	Assault	Other violent	Assault	Other violent
Type of sentence					
1976	.429	.273	.640	−.156*	.211
1977	.451	.430	.749	−.021	.298
1978	.435	.379	.864	−.056	.429***
1979	.400	.429	.571	.029*	.171*
1980	.409	.321	.666	−.088	.257
1981	.425	.384	.733	−.041	.308
1982	.423	.348	.738	−.075	.315
1983	.325	.284	.589	−.041	.264
1984	.296	.286	.437	−.010	.141***
Average	.399	.348	.665	−.051***	.266***
Split sentence severity					
1976	50.858	53.156	50.220	2.298	−.638
1977	47.095	43.634	52.597	−3.461	5.502
1978	49.938	47.473	39.951	−2.465	−9.987***
1979	48.325	47.101	56.375	−1.224	8.050
1980	46.201	35.369	54.165	−10.832*	7.964
1981	49.969	45.013	57.927	−4.956	7.958
1982	49.346	50.488	45.015	1.142	−4.331***
1983	47.014	48.062	58.704	1.048	11.690*
1984	47.589	45.933	54.106	−1.656	6.517
Average	48.480	46.246	52.116	−2.234*	3.636***
Prison sentence length					
1976	7.561	9.530	16.128	1.969	8.567
1977	8.063	10.624	15.714	2.561	7.651
1978	7.961	10.592	18.451	2.631	10.490***
1979	8.240	9.057	14.138	.817*	5.898
1980	8.879	13.467	14.536	4.588	5.657
1981	9.608	12.396	16.290	2.788	6.682
1982	10.935	14.982	11.779	4.047	.844***
1983	10.142	14.579	13.841	4.437	3.699*
1984	10.542	14.214	19.550	3.672	9.008*
Average	9.102	12.159	15.601	3.057***	6.499***

[a] Predicted outcomes capture the effect of varying year of sentence, while holding constant at the mean the effects of the remaining variables.
*$p \le .05$; ***$p \le .005$.

TABLE F. Trends in predicted sentencing outcomes for larceny offenders[a]

| Year of sentence | Type of offender | | Difference |
	Average	Larceny	
Type of sentence			
1976	.361	.266	−.095
1977	.430	.336	−.094
1978	.413	.202	−.211***
1979	.354	.195	−.159
1980	.395	.201	−.194***
1981	.399	.306	−.093
1982	.418	.285	−.133
1983	.286	.169	−.117
1984	.295	.213	−.082***
Average	.377	.246	−.131***
Split sentence severity			
1976	51.674	43.045	−8.629***
1977	46.943	40.821	−6.122
1978	47.234	54.087	6.853**
1979	48.929	50.954	2.025
1980	48.924	46.348	−2.576
1981	50.524	42.896	−7.628*
1982	48.085	41.240	−6.845
1983	47.174	45.430	−1.744
1984	47.750	51.887	4.137
Average	48.582	46.301	−2.281*
Prison sentence length			
1976	9.638	7.615	−2.023
1977	9.997	8.003	−1.994
1978	10.061	8.249	−1.812
1979	10.229	8.283	−1.946
1980	9.981	8.413	−1.568
1981	11.036	10.024	−1.012
1982	11.800	10.255	−1.545
1983	11.704	14.993	3.289***
1984	11.565	10.257	−1.308
Average	10.668	9.566	−1.102***

[a] Predicted sentences capture the effect of varying year of sentence, while holding constant at the mean the effects of the remaining variables.
*$p \leq .05$; **$p \leq .01$; ***$p \leq .005$.

TABLE G. Trends in predicted sentencing outcomes for white-collar offenders[a]

| Year of sentence | Type of offender | | Difference |
	Average	White-collar[b]	
Type of sentence			
1976	.361	.329	−.032**
1977	.430	.366	−.064
1978	.413	.209	−.204***
1979	.354	.257	−.097
1980	.395	.308	−.087
1981	.399	.251	−.148*
1982	.418	.201	−.217***
1983	.286	.232	−.054***
1984	.295	.234	−.061***
Average	.377	.270	−.107***
Split sentence severity			
1976	51.674	50.953	−.721*
1977	46.943	44.108	−2.835
1978	47.234	38.029	−9.205
1979	48.929	44.815	−4.114
1980	48.924	49.008	.084*
1981	50.524	39.171	−11.353
1982	48.085	37.871	−10.214
1983	47.174	41.191	−5.983
1984	47.750	42.812	−4.938
Average	48.582	43.107	−5.475***
Prison sentence length			
1976	9.638	11.555	1.917*
1977	9.997	11.285	1.288
1978	10.061	10.581	.520
1979	10.229	11.498	1.269
1980	9.981	10.868	.887
1981	11.036	11.312	.276
1982	11.800	9.845	−1.955*
1983	11.704	11.123	−.581
1984	11.565	12.399	.834
Average	10.688	11.163	.475

[a] Predicted sentences capture the effect of varying year of sentence, while holding constant at the mean the effects of the remaining variables.

[b] This category includes offenders convicted of forgery, fraud, and embezzlement.

$*p \leq .05; **p \leq .01; ***p \leq .005.$

TABLE H. Trends in predicted sentencing outcomes for other property offenders[a]

Year of sentence	Average	Other property[b]	Difference
Type of sentence			
1976	.361	.173	−.188**
1977	.430	.322	−.108
1978	.413	.442	.029***
1979	.354	.236	−.118
1980	.395	.284	−.111
1981	.399	.229	−.170**
1982	.418	.243	−.175***
1983	.286	.194	−.092
1984	.295	.254	−.041***
Average	.377	.269	−.108***
Split sentence severity			
1976	51.674	45.392	−6.282
1977	46.943	42.848	−4.095
1978	47.234	36.072	−11.162
1979	48.929	46.001	−2.928
1980	48.924	41.261	−7.663
1981	50.524	47.767	−2.757
1982	48.085	51.046	2.961*
1983	47.174	43.924	−3.250
1984	47.750	51.766	4.016***
Average	48.582	45.120	−3.462**
Prison sentence length			
1976	9.638	8.629	−1.009
1977	9.997	11.307	1.310
1978	10.061	9.969	−.092
1979	10.229	10.921	.692
1980	9.981	8.497	−1.484
1981	11.036	11.075	.038
1982	11.800	14.365	2.565
1983	11.704	10.091	−1.613
1984	11.565	10.276	−1.289
Average	10.668	10.570	−.098

[a] Predicted sentences capture the effect of varying year of sentence, while holding constant at the mean the effects of the remaining variables.

[b] This category includes offenders convicted of damaging property or possessing stolen goods.

*$p \leq .05$; **$p \leq .01$; ***$p \leq .005$.

References and Court Cases

Adamson, Christopher
  1983   "Punishment after slavery: southern penal systems, 1865–1890." Social
          Problems 30:555–69.
  1984   "Toward a Marxian penology: captive criminal populations as economic
          threats and resources." Social Problems 31:435–58.
Allison, Paul D.
  1977   "Testing for interaction in multiple regression." American Journal of Sociology
          83:144–53.
Alpert, Lenore, Burton M. Atkins and Robert C. Ziller
  1979   "Becoming a judge: the transition from advocate to arbiter." Judicature
          62:325–35.
Austin, Thomas L.
  1981   "The influence of court location on type of criminal sentence: the rural-urban
          factor." Journal of Criminal Justice 9:305–16.
Ayers, Edward L.
  1984   Vengeance and Justice: Crime and Punishment in the 19th-Century American
          South. New York: Oxford University Press.
Bailey, William C.
  1981   "Inequality in the legal order: some further analysis and commentary." Social
          Problems 29:51–60.
  1984   "Poverty, inequality, and city homicide rates: some not so unexpected find-
          ings." Criminology 22:531–50.
Baldus, David C., Charles Pulaski and George Woodworth
  1983   "Comparative review of death sentences: an empirical study of the Georgia
          experience." Journal of Criminal Law and Criminology 74:661–753.
Baldus, David C., George Woodworth and Charles Pulaski
  1983   Discrimination and Arbitrariness in Georgia's Capital Charging and Sentenc-
          ing System: A Preliminary Report. Iowa City: University of Iowa Law School.
          Unpublished manuscript.
Balkwell, James W.
  1983   "Metropolitan structure and violent crime: A further examination of the Blau
          and Blau relative deprivation thesis." Revised version of a paper presented at
          the annual meetings of the American Society of Criminology, Denver.

Bartley, Numan V.
1983   The Creation of Modern Georgia. Athens, GA: University of Georgia Press.
Bedau, Hugo A.
1964   "Death sentences in New Jersey." Rutgers Law Review 19:1-64.
1965   "Capital punishment in Oregon, 1903-64." Oregon Law Review 45:1-39.
Belsley, David A., Edwin Kuh and Roy E. Welsch
1980   Regression Diagnostics: Identifying Influential Data and Sources of Col-
        linearity. New York: John Wiley & Sons.
Berk, Richard A.
1983   "An introduction to sample selection bias in sociological data." American
        Sociological Review 48:386-98.
Berk, Richard A., Kenneth J. Lenihan and Peter H. Rossi
1980   "Crime and poverty: some experimental evidence from ex-offenders." Ameri-
        can Sociological Review 45:766-86.
Berk, Richard A. and Subhash C. Ray
1982   "Selection biases in sociological data." Social Science Research 11:352-98.
Bernstein, Ilene N., William R. Kelly and Patricia A. Doyle
1977   "Societal reactions to deviants: the case of criminal defendants." American
        Sociological Review 42 (October):743-55.
Black, Donald
1976   The Behavior of Law. New York: Academic Press.
Blalock, Hubert
1967   Toward a Theory of Minority-Group Relations. New York: John Wiley & Sons.
Blau, Peter M.
1974   On the Nature of Organizations. New York: John Wiley & Sons.
Blau, Judith R. and Peter M. Blau
1982   "The cost of inequality: metropolitan structure and violent crime." American
        Sociological Review 47:114-29.
Blau, Peter M. and Reid M. Golden
1986   "Metropolitan structure and criminal violence." The Sociological Quarterly
        24:15-26.
Blumstein, Alfred
1982   "On the racial disproportionality of United States prison populations." Journal
        of Criminal Law and Criminology 73:1259-81.
Blumstein, Alfred, Jacqueline Cohen, Susan E. Martin and Michael H. Tonry (eds.)
1983   Research on Sentencing: The Search for Reform. Volume I. Washington, D.C.:
        National Academy Press.
Box, Steven and Chris Hale
1982   "Economic crisis and the rising prisoner population in England and Wales."
        Crime and Social Justice 17:20-35.
1985   "Unemployment, imprisonment, and prison overcrowding." Contemporary
        Crises 9:209-28.
1986   "Unemployment, crime, and imprisonment, and the enduring problem of
        prison overcrowding." Pp. 72-96 in Roger Matthews and Jock Young (eds.),
        Confronting Crime. London: Sage Publications, Ltd.
Braithwaite, John
1979   Inequality, Crime, and Public Policy. London: Routledge and Kegan Paul.
Bridges, George S. and Robert D. Crutchfield
1985   "On law, social structure and racial inequality in imprisonment." Revised ver-

sion of a paper presented at the annual meetings of the American Sociological Association, Washington, D.C.

Bryan, Thomas Conn
1953   Confederate Georgia. Athens, GA: University of Georgia Press.

Bureau of Justice Statistics
1986   Criminal Victimization in the United States, 1984. A National Crime Survey Report. Washington, D.C.: U.S. Department of Justice.

Cantor, David and Kenneth C. Land
1985   "Unemployment and crime rates in the post-World War II United States: a theoretical and empirical analysis." American Sociological Review 50:317–32.

Carroll, Leo and Mary Beth Doubet
1983   "U.S. social structure and imprisonment." Criminology 21:449–56.

Carroll, Leo and Pamela Irving Jackson
1982   "Minority composition, inequality and the growth of municipal police forces, 1960–71." Sociological Focus 15:327–46.

Carter, Lief H.
1985   Contemporary Constitutional Lawmaking: The Supreme Court and the Art of Politics. New York: Pergamon Press.
1986   "How trial judges talk: speculations about formalism and pragmatism in legal culture." Paper presented at the annual meetings of the American Political Science Association, Washington, D.C.

Chambliss, William J. and Robert B. Seidman
1971   Law, Order and Power. Reading, MA: Addison-Wesley.

Chapin, Bradley
1983   Criminal Justice in Colonial America, 1606–1660. Athens, GA: University of Georgia Press.

Chilton, Bradley Stewart
1986   "A chronology of Guthrie v. Evans." Paper presented at the annual meetings of the Law and Society Association, Chicago.

Chiricos, Theodore G.
1987   "Rates of crime and unemployment: a review of aggregate research evidence." Social Problems 34(3):in press.

Chiricos, Theodore G. and Gordon P. Waldo
1975   "Socioeconomic status and criminal sentencing: an empirical analysis of a conflict proposition." American Sociological Review 40:753–72.

Choper, Jesse H.
1980   Judicial Review and the National Political Process: A Functional Reconsideration of the Role of the Supreme Court. Chicago: University of Chicago Press.

Clayton, Obie, Jr.
1983   "A reconsideration of the effects of race in criminal sentencing." Criminal Justice Review 8:15–20.

Coleman, Kenneth, Numan V. Bartley, William F. Holmes, F. N. Boney, Phinizy Spalding and Charles E. Wynes
1977   A History of Georgia. Athens, GA: University of Georgia Press.

Cook, Beverly B.
1973   "Sentencing behavior of federal judges: draft cases – 1972." University of Cincinnati Law Review 42:597–633.
1977   "Public opinion and federal judicial policy." American Journal of Political Science 21:567–600.

Cooper, Philip
  1987   Hard Judicial Choices. New York: Oxford University Press.
Coulter, E. Merton
  1947   Georgia, A Short History. Chapel Hill, NC: University of North Carolina Press.
Daly, Kathleen
  1986   "Gender in the adjudication process: are judges really paternalistic toward women?" Revised version of a paper presented at the 1985 annual meetings of the American Society of Criminology, San Diego.
  1987   "Structure and practice of familial-based justice in a criminal court." Law and Society Review 21:in press.
Danziger, Sheldon and David Wheeler
  1975   "The economics of crime: punishment or income redistribution." Review of Social Economy 33:113–31.
Dixon, Robert G., Jr.
  1972   Democratic Representation: Reapportionment in Law and Politics. New York: Oxford University Press.
Durkheim, Emile
  1933   The Division of Labor in Society. New York: The Free Press.
  1973   "Two laws of penal evolution." Economy and Society 2:285–308.
Eisenstein, James and Herbert Jacob
  1977   Felony Justice: An Organizational Analysis of Criminal Courts. Boston: Little Brown.
Ely, John Hart
  1980   Democracy and Distrust: A Theory of Judicial Review. Cambridge, MA: Harvard University Press.
Engle, Charles D.
  1971   Criminal Justice in the City. A Study of Sentence Severity and Variation in the Philadelphia Criminal Court System. Unpublished Ph.D. Dissertation, Temple University.
Farnworth, Margaret and Patrick M. Horan
  1980   "Separate justice: an analysis of race differences in court processes." Social Science Research 9:131–9.
Farrell, Ronald A. and Victoria Lynn Swigert
  1978   "Prior offense as a self-fulfilling prophecy." Law and Society Review 12:437–54.
Federal Bureau of Investigation
  1985   Crime in the United States, 1984. Washington, D.C.: Government Printing Office.
Flynn, Charles L., Jr.
  1983   White Land, Black Labor: Caste and Class in Late Nineteenth-Century Georgia. Baton Rouge: Louisiana State University Press.
Forslund, Morris A.
  1969   "Age, occupation, and conviction rates of white and negro males: a case study." Rocky Mountain Social Science Journal 6:141–6.
Foucault, Michel
  1977   Discipline and Punish: The Birth of the Prison. New York: Pantheon Books.
Fowlkes, Diane L.
  1983   How Feminist Theory Reconstructs American Government and Politics. Washington, D.C.: American Political Science Association.

Frank, Jerome
  1949   Courts on Trial: Myth and Reality in American Justice. New York: Athenuem.
Frazier, Charles E. and E. Wilbur Bock
  1982   "Effects of court officials on sentence severity: do judges make a difference?"
          Criminology 20:257–72.
Galanter, Marc, Frank S. Palen and John M. Thomas
  1979   "The crusading judge: judicial activism in trial courts." Southern California
          Law Review 52:699–741.
Galster, George C. and Laurie A. Scaturo
  1985   "The U.S. criminal justice system: unemployment and the severity of punish-
          ment." Journal of Research in Crime and Delinquency 22:163–89.
Georges-Abeyie, Daniel (ed.)
  1984   The Criminal Justice System and Blacks. New York: Clark Boardman.
Gibson, James L.
  1978a   "Judges' role orientations, attitudes, and decisions: an interactive model."
          American Political Science Review 72:911–24.
  1978b   "Race as a determinant of criminal sentences: a methodological critique and
          a case study." Law and Society Review 12:455–78.
  1979   "A role theoretical model of criminal court decision-making." Pp. 83–99 in
          Peter Nardulli (ed.), The Study of Criminal Courts: Political Perspectives.
          Cambridge, MA: Ballinger.
  1980   "Environmental constraints on the behavior of judges: a representational
          model of judicial decision making." Law and Society Review 14:343–70.
  1983   "From simplicity to complexity: the development of theory in the study of
          judicial behavior." Political Behavior 5:7–50.
  1986   "The social science of judicial politics." Pp. 141–166 in Herbert F. Weis-
          berg (ed.), Political Science: The Science of Politics. New York: Agathon
          Press.
Golden, Reid M. and Steven F. Messner
  1986   "Dimensions of racial inequality and rates of violent crime." Paper presented
          at the annual meetings of the American Society of Criminology, Atlanta.
Goldman, Sheldon
  1975   "Voting behavior on the U.S. courts of appeals revisited." American Political
          Science Review 69:491–506.
Goodstein, Lynne and John Hepburn
  1985   Determinate Sentencing and Imprisonment: A Failure of Reform. Cincinnati,
          OH: Anderson Publishing.
Green, Edward
  1961   Judicial Attitudes in Sentencing. London: Macmillan and Company
  1964   "Inter- and intra-racial crime relative to sentencing." Journal of Criminal Law,
          Criminology, and Police Science 55:348–58.
Greenberg, David F.
  1977   "The dynamics of oscillatory punishment processes." Journal of Criminal Law
          and Criminology 68:643–51.
Gruhl, John, Cassia Spohn and Susan Welch
  1981   "Women as policymakers: the case of trial judges." American Journal of Politi-
          cal Science 25:308–22.
Hagan, John
  1974   "Extra-legal attributes and criminal sentencing: an assessment of a sociologi-
          cal viewpoint." Law and Society Review 8:357–84.

Hagan, John
1975   "Parameters of criminal prosecution: an application of path analysis to a problem of criminal justice." Journal of Criminal Law, Criminology, and Police Science 65:536–44.
1977   "Criminal justice in rural and urban communities: a study of the bureaucratization of justice." Social Forces 55:597–612.
Hagan, John and Kristin Bumiller
1983   "Making sense of sentencing: a review and critique of sentencing research." Pp. 1–54 in Alfred Blumstein, Jacqueline Cohen, Susan E. Martin and Michael H. Tonry (eds.), Research on Sentencing: The Search for Reform. Volume II. Washington, D.C.: National Academy Press.
Hagan, John and Patricia Parker
1985   "White collar crime and punishment: the class structure and legal sanctioning of securities violations." American Sociological Review 50:302–16.
Hagan, John, John H. Simpson and A. R. Gillis
1979   "The sexual stratification of social control: a gender-based perspective on crime and delinquency." British Journal of Sociology 3:25–38.
Halpern, Stephen and Charles Lamb (eds.)
1982   Supreme Court Activism and Restraint. Lexington, MA: D. C. Heath.
Hanushek, Eric A. and John A. Jackson
1977   Statistical Methods for Social Scientists. New York: Academic Press.
Hardy, Kenneth A.
1983   "Equity in court dispositions." Pp. 183–207 in Gordon P. Whitaker and Charles David Phillips (eds.), Evaluating Performance of Criminal Justice Agencies. Beverly Hills, CA: Sage Publications.
Harries, Keith D.
1974   The Geography of Crime and Justice. New York: McGraw-Hill.
Hindelang, Michael
1965   "Equality under the law." Journal of Criminal Law, Criminology, and Police Science 60:306–13.
Hindus, Michael Stephen
1980   Prison and Plantation: Crime, Justice, and Authority in Massachusetts and South Carolina, 1767–1878. Chapel Hill, NC: The University of North Carolina Press.
Hogarth, John
1971   Sentencing as a Human Process. Toronto: University of Toronto Press.
Holmes, Oliver Wendell
1963   The Common Law. Boston: Little Brown.
Horan, Patrick M., Martha A. Myers and Margaret Farnworth
1982   "Prior record and court processes: the role of latent theory in criminological research." Sociology and Social Research 67:40–58.
Horowitz, Donald L.
1977   The Courts and Social Policy. Washington, D.C.: The Brookings Institution.
Huff, C. Ronald and John M. Stahura
1980   "Police employment and suburban crime." Criminology 17:461–70.
Hughes, Melvin Clyde
1944   County Government in Georgia. Athens, GA: University of Georgia Press.
Ignatieff, Michael
1983   "State, civil society, and total institutions: a critique of recent social histories

of punishment." Pp. 75–105 in Stanley Cohen and Andrew Scull (eds.), Social Control and the State. New York: St. Martin's Press.

Jackson, Pamela Irving and Leo Carroll
1981   "Race and the war on crime: the sociopolitical determinants of municipal police expenditures in 90 non-southern U.S. cities." American Sociological Review 46:290–305.

Jacobs, David
1978   "Inequality and the legal order: an ecological test of the conflict model." Social Problems 25:515–30.

1979   "Inequality and police strength: conflict theory and coercive control in metropolitan areas." American Sociological Review 44:913–25.

1981a   "On theory and measurement: a reply to McGranahan." American Sociological Review 46:241–5.

1981b   "Inequality and economic crime." Sociology and Social Research 66:12–28.

Jacobs, David and David Britt
1979   "Inequality and police use of deadly force: an empirical assessment of a conflict hypothesis." Social Problems 26:403–12.

Jankovic, Ivan
1977   "Labor market and imprisonment." Crime and Social Justice 8:17–31.

Johnson, Elmer H.
1957   "Selective factors in capital punishment." Social Forces 36:165–9.

Johnston, Richard E.
1976   "Supreme Court voting behavior: a comparison of the Warren and Burger courts." Pp. 71–110 in Robert L. Peabody (ed.), Cases in American Politics. New York: Praeger.

Joubert, Paul E., J. Steven Picou and W. Alex McIntosh
1981   "U.S. social structure, crime, and imprisonment." Criminology 19:344–59.

Kempf, Kimberly L. and Roy L. Austin
1986   "Older and more recent evidence on racial discrimination in sentencing." Journal of Quantitative Criminology 2:29–48.

Kleck, Gary
1981   "Racial discrimination in criminal sentencing: a critical evaluation of the evidence with additional evidence on the death penalty." American Sociological Review 46:783–805.

Koppel, Herbert
1984   Sentencing Practices in 13 States. Washington, D.C.: Bureau of Justice Statistics.

Krahn, Harvey, Timothy F. Hartnagel and John W. Gartrell
1986   "Income inequality and homicide rates: cross-national data and criminological theories." Criminology 24:269–94.

Kritzer, Herbert M.
1978   "Political correlates of the behavior of federal district judges: a 'best case' analysis." Journal of Politics 40:25–58.

1979   "Political cultures, trial courts, and criminal cases." Pp. 131–169 in Peter F. Nardulli (ed.), The Study of Criminal Courts: Political Perspectives. Cambridge, MA: Ballinger.

Kritzer, Herbert M. and Thomas M. Uhlman
1977   "Sisterhood in the courtroom: sex of judge and defendant in criminal case disposition." Social Science Journal 14:77–88.

Krohn, Marvin D.
  1978   "A Durkheimian analysis of international crime rates." Social Forces 57:654–70.
Kruttschnitt, Candace
  1984   "Sex and criminal court dispositions: the unresolved controversy." Journal of Research in Crime and Delinquency 21:213–32.
  1985   "Legal outcomes and legal agents: adding another dimension to the sex-sentencing controversy." Law and Human Behavior 9:287–303.
Kruttschnitt, Candace and Donald E. Green
  1984   "The sex-sanctioning issue: is it history?" American Sociological Review 49:541–51.
Kuklinski, James H. and John E. Stanga
  1979   "Political participation and government responsiveness: the behavior of California Superior Courts." American Political Science Review 73:1090–9.
Lemert, Edwin M. and Judy Rosberg
  1948   "The administration of justice to minority groups in Los Angeles County." University of California Publications in Culture and Society 2:1–28.
Levin, Martin A.
  1977   Urban Politics and Criminal Court. Chicago: The University of Chicago Press.
Lieberman, Joel B., S. A. Schatter and J. M. Martin
  1972   The Bronx Sentencing Project of the Vera Institute of Justice. Washington, D.C.: U.S. Government Printing Office.
Liska, Allen E. and Mitchell B. Chamlin
  1984   "Social structure and crime control among macrosocial units." American Journal of Sociology 90:383–95.
Liska, Allen E., Joseph J. Lawrence and Michael Benson
  1981   "Perspectives on the legal order: the capacity for social control." American Journal of Sociology 87:413–26.
Lizotte, Alan J.
  1978   "Extra-legal factors in Chicago's criminal courts: testing the conflict model of criminal justice." Social Problems 25:564–80.
Lizotte, Alan J. and David J. Bordua
  1980   "Firearms ownership for sport and protection." American Sociological Review 45:229–43.
Lizotte, Alan J., James Mercy, and Eric Monkkonen
  1982   "Crime and police strength in an urban setting: Chicago, 1947–1970." Pp. 129–48 in John Hagan (ed.), Quantitative Criminology: Innovations and Applications. Beverly Hills, CA: Sage Publications.
Loftin, Colin and Robert Nash Parker
  1985   "An errors-in-variable model of the effect of poverty on urban homicide rates." Criminology 23:269–87.
Long, Sharon K. and Ann D. Witte
  1981   "Current economic trends: implications for crime and criminal justice." Pp. 69–143 in Kevin N. Wright (ed.), Crime and Criminal Justice in a Declining Economy. Cambridge, MA: Oelgeschlager, Gunn and Hain.
Marenin, Otwin, Alexander W. Pisciotta and Tom J. Juliani
  1983   "Economic conditions and social control: an empirical assessment of the rela-

tionship between unemployment and incarceration in the U.S.A., 1958–1978."
Criminal Justice Review 8:43–53.

Martin, Roscoe
1934   "The defendant and criminal justice." The University of Texas Bulletin No.
3437. Austin, TX: Bureau of Research in the Social Sciences.

Mather, Lynn
1979   Plea Bargaining or Trial? Lexington, MA: Lexington Books.

McDowell, Gary
1982   Equity and the Constitution. Chicago: University of Chicago Press.

Melossi, Dario and Massimo Pavarini
1981   The Prison and the Factory: Origins of the Penitentiary System. New York:
Barnes and Noble.

Messner, Steven F.
1980   "Income inequality and murder rates: some cross-national findings." Comparative Social Research 3:185–98.

1982   "Poverty, inequality, and the urban homicide rate: some unexpected findings."
Criminology 20:103–14.

1983   "Regional and racial effects on the urban homicide rate: the subculture of violence revisited." American Journal of Sociology 88:997–1007.

Messner, Steven F. and Scott J. South
1986   "Economic deprivation, opportunity structure, and robbery victimization:
intra- and interracial patterns." Social Forces 64:975–91.

Messner, Steven F. and Kenneth Tardiff
1986   "Economic inequality and levels of homicide: an analysis of urban neighbor-
hoods." Criminology 24:297–317.

Miethe, Terance D. and Charles A. Moore
1986   "Racial differences in criminal processing: the consequences of model selection on conclusions about differential treatment." The Sociological Quarterly
27(2):217–37.

Miller, Arthur Selwyn
1982   Toward Increased Judicial Activism: The Political Role of the Supreme Court.
Westport, CT: Greenwood Press.

Moulds, Elizabeth F.
1980   "Chivalry and paternalism: disparities of treatment in the criminal justice system." Pp. 277–99 in Susan Datesman and Frank Scarpitti (eds.), Women,
Crime and Justice. New York: Oxford Press.

Myers, Martha A.
1979   "Offended parties and official reactions: victims and the sentencing of criminal defendants." Sociological Quarterly 20:529–40.

1987   "Economic inequality and discrimination in sentencing." Social Forces
65:746–66.

Myers, Martha A. and Susette M. Talarico
1986a   "Urban justice, rural injustice? Urbanization and its effect on sentencing."
Criminology 24:367–91.

1986b   "The social contexts of racial discrimination in sentencing." Social Problems
33:236–51.

Myrdal, Gunnar
[1944]   An America Dilemma. New York: McGraw-Hill.
1964

Nagel, Ilene H. and John Hagan
  1983   "Gender and crime: offense patterns and criminal court sanctions." Pp. 91–144 in Michael Tonry and Norval Morris (eds.), Crime and Justice: An Annual Review of Research. Volume 4. Chicago: The University of Chicago Press.
Nagel, Stuart S.
  1961   "Political party affiliation and judges' decisions." American Political Science Review 55:843–50.
  1969   The Legal Process from a Behavioral Perspective. Homewood, IL: The Dorsey Press.
Nardulli, Peter F., Roy B. Flemming and James Eisenstein
  1984   "Unraveling the complexities of decision-making in face-to-face groups: a contextual analysis of plea-bargained sentences." American Political Science Review 78:918–28.
Neubauer, David W.
  1979   America's Courts and the Criminal Justice System. North Scituate, MA: Duxbury.
Parker, Robert Nash and Allan V. Horwitz
  1986   "Unemployment, crime and imprisonment: a panel approach." Criminology 24:751–73.
Partridge, Anthony and William B. Eldridge
  1974   2nd Circuit Sentencing Study: A Report to the Judges of the 2nd Circuit. Washington, D.C.: Federal Judicial Center.
Pedhazur, Elazar J.
  1982   Multiple Regression in Behavioral Research. Second edition. New York: Holt, Rinehart and Winston.
Perry, Michael J.
  1982   The Constitution, the Courts, and Human Rights. New Haven, CT: Yale University Press.
Petersilia, Joan
  1983   Racial Disparities in the Criminal Justice System. Santa Monica, CA: RAND Corporation.
  1985   "Racial disparities in the criminal justice system: a summary." Crime and Delinquency 31:15–34.
Peterson, Ruth D. and John Hagan
  1984   "Changing conceptions of race: towards an account of anomalous findings of sentencing research." American Sociological Review 49:56–70.
Phillips, Charles David
  1986   "Social structure and social control: modeling the discriminatory execution of blacks in Georgia and North Carolina, 1925–1935." Social Forces 65:458–75.
Pope, Carl E.
  1976   "The influence of social and legal factors on sentencing dispositions: a preliminary analysis of offender based transaction statistics." Journal of Criminal Justice 4:203–21.
Pruitt, Charles R. and James Q. Wilson
  1983   "A longitudinal study of the effect of race on sentencing." Law and Society Review 17:613–35.
Quinney, Richard
  1974   Critique of Legal Order: Crime Control in Capitalist Society. Boston: Little Brown.
  1977   Class, State and Crime: On the Theory and Practice of Criminal Justice. New

York: David McKay Company, Inc.

Radelet, Michael L.
1981   "Racial characteristics and the imposition of the death penalty." American Sociological Review 46:918–27.

Ragona, Anthony J. and John Paul Ryan
1983   Beyond the Courtroom: A Comparative Analysis of Misdemeanor Sentencing. Executive Summary. Chicago: American Judicature Society.

Rothman, David J.
1971   The Discovery of the Asylum: Social Order and Disorder in the New Republic. Boston: Little Brown.
1980   Conscience and Convenience: The Asylum and its Alternatives in Progressive America. Boston: Little Brown.

Rusche, Georg and Otto Kirchheimer
1939   Punishment and Social Structure. New York: Columbia University Press.

Ryan, John Paul
1980   "Adjudication and sentencing in a misdemeanor court: the outcome is the punishment." Law and Society Review 15:79–108.

Sampson, Robert J.
1985a   "Race and criminal violence: a demographically disaggregated analysis of urban homicide." Crime and Delinquency 31:47–82.
1985b   "Structural sources of variation in race-age-specific rates of offending across major U.S. cities." Criminology 23:647–73.

Saye, Albert B.
1950   "Georgia's county unit system of elections." Journal of Politics 12:93–106.

Schur, Edwin M.
1984   Labeling Women Deviant: Gender, Stigma, and Social Control. New York: Random House.

Sellin, Thorsten
1928   "The negro criminal: a statistical note." The Annals of the American Academy of Political and Social Science 140:52–64.

Shane-DuBow, Sandra, Alice P. Brown and Erik Olsen
1985   Sentencing Reform in the United States: History, Content, and Effect. Washington, D.C.: U.S. Department of Justice, National Institute of Justice.

Shelley, Louise I.
1981   Crime and Modernization. Carbondale, IL: Southern Illinois University Press.

Simon, Rita J.
1975   Women and Crime. Lexington, MA: D.C. Heath.

Spitzer, Steven
1975   "Toward a Marxian theory of deviance." Social Problems 22:638–51.

Spohn, Cassia, John Gruhl and Susan Welch
1981-82 "The effect of race on sentencing: a reexamination of an unsettled question." Law and Society Review 16:71–88.

Steffensmeier, Darrell J.
1977   "The effects of judge's and defendant's sex on the sentencing of offenders." Psychology: A Journal of Human Behavior 14:3–9.

Steffensmeier, Darrell and John H. Kramer
1982   "Sex-based differences in the sentencing of adult criminal defendants: an empirical test and theoretical overview." Sociology and Social Research 66(3):289–304.

Sutton, L. Paul
 1978   Variations in Federal Criminal Sentences: A Statistical Assessment at the National Level. Albany, NY: Criminal Justice Research Center.
Swigert, Victoria Lynn and Ronald A. Farrell
 1976   Murder, Inequality and the Law: Differential Treatment in the Legal Processes. Lexington, MA: D.C. Heath.
Talarico, Susette M.
 1979a   "What do we expect of criminal justice? Critical questions of sanction policy, sentencing purpose and the politics of reform." Criminal Justice Review 4:55–72.
 1979b   "Judicial decisions and sanction patterns in criminal justice." Journal of Criminal Law and Criminology 70:110–24.
Tate, C. Neal
 1981   "Personal attribute models of the voting behavior of U.S. Supreme Court justices: liberalism in civil liberties and economic decisions, 1946–1978." American Political Science Review 75:355–67.
Tepperman, Lorne
 1973   "The effects of court size on organization and procedure." Canadian Review of Sociology and Anthropology 10:346–65.
Thomas, D. A.
 1979   Principles of Sentencing. London: Heineman.
Thomson, Randall J. and Matthew T. Zingraff
 1981   "Detecting sentencing disparity: some problems and evidence." American Journal of Sociology 86:869–80.
Tiffany, Lawrence P., Yakov Avichai and Geoffrey W. Peters
 1975   "A statistical analysis of sentencing in federal courts: defendants convicted after trial, 1967–1968." Journal of Legal Studies 4:369–90.
Toner, Robin and Jim Galloway
 1985   "Pride thwarts county mergers." Atlanta Journal and Constitution, April 28:1A.
Turk, Austin T.
 1969   Criminality and Legal Order. Chicago: Rand McNally.
Uhlman, Thomas M.
 1977   "The impact of defendant race in trial-court sanctioning decisions." Pp. 19–51 in John A. Gardiner (ed.), Public Law and Public Policy. New York: Praeger.
 1978   "Black elite decision making: the case of trial judges." American Journal of Political Science 22:884–95.
Uhlman, Thomas M. and N. Darlene Walker
 1979   "A plea is no bargain: the impact of case disposition on sentencing." Social Science Quarterly 60:218–34.
Ulmer, S. Sidney
 1973   "Social background as an indicator to the votes of Supreme Court justices in criminal cases: 1947–1956 terms." American Journal of Political Science 17:622–30.
Unnever, James D.
 1982   "Direct and organizational discrimination in the sentencing of drug offenders." Social Problems 30:212–25.

Unnever, James D., Charles E. Frazier and John C. Henretta
1980   "Race differences in criminal sentencing." The Sociological Quarterly 21:197–205.

Unnever, James D. and Larry A. Hembroff
1986   "When judges discriminate." Revised version of a paper presented at the 1985 annual meetings of the American Society of Criminology, San Diego.

Vines, Kenneth N.
1964   "Federal district judges and race relations in the South." Journal of Politics 26:337–57.

Wallace, Don
1981   "The political economy of incarceration trends in late U.S. capitalism: 1971–1977." The Insurgent Sociologist 10:59–67.

Weber, Max
1954   On Law in Economy and Society. Max Rheinstein (ed.). New York: Simon and Schuster.

Welch, Susan, John Gruhl and Cassia Spohn
1984   "Sentencing: the influence of alternative measures of prior record." Criminology 22:215–27.

Wheeler, Stanton, David Weisburd and Nancy Bode
1982   "Sentencing the white-collar offender: rhetoric and reality." American Sociological Review 47:641–59.

Wilbanks, William
1987   The Myth of a Racist Criminal Justice System. Monterey, CA: Brooks/Cole.

Williams, Kirk R.
1984   "Economic sources of homicide: reestimating the effects of poverty and inequality." American Sociological Review 49:283–9.

Williams, Kirk R. and Susan Drake
1980   "Social structure, crime and criminalization: an empirical examination of the conflict perspective." The Sociological Quarterly 21:563–75.

Williams, Kirk R. and Michael Timberlake
1984   "Structured inequality, conflict, and control: a cross-national test of the threat hypothesis." Social Forces 63:414–32.

Williams, Oliver and Richard J. Richardson
1976   "The impact of criminal justice policy on blacks in trial courts of a southern state." In R. Cole (ed.), Readings in Criminal Justice. Belmont, CA: Duxbury Press.

Wolfgang, Marvin E., Arlene Kelly and Hans C. Nolde
1962   "Comparison of executed and convicted among admissions to death row." Journal of Criminal Law, Criminology, and Police Science 53:301–11.

Yeager, Matthew G.
1979   "Unemployment and imprisonment." Journal of Criminal Law and Criminology 70:586–8.

Zatz, Marjorie S.
1984   "Race, ethnicity, and determinate sentencing: a new dimension to an old controversy." Criminology 22:147–71.
1987   "The changing forms of racial/ethnic biases in sentencing." Journal of Research in Crime and Delinquency 24(1):69–92.

Court Cases

Arthur S. Guthrie v. David C. Evans (originally filed as Guthrie, et al. v. Caldwell, et al.) (U.S. Dist. Crt. for Northern District of GA., Atlanta; Civ. Action No. 17318).
Warren McCleskey v. Walter D. Zant, 580 F. Supp. 338 (1984).
Warren McCleskey v. Ralph Kemp, 753 F. 2d 877 (1985).

Author Index

Subject Index